The Fasting Diaries
A Weight Loss Journey

Callie M. Stephens

This edition first published August 2015 by

Peathraichean Publishing
Los Angeles, CA

www.peathraicheanpublishing.com

Copyright © 2015 Callie M. Stephens

All rights reserved. No part of this publication may be reproduced, stored or transmitted in any form without the express written permission of the publisher.

ISBN13: 978-0-9966930-0-4
ISBN10: 0-99669-300-9

Library of Congress Control Number: 2015949953

Some names and identifying details have been changed to protect the privacy of individuals.

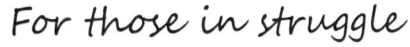

INTRODUCTION

When I decided to go to college I worried about being able to keep up, academically. I'd been a lazy high school student and after three years away from an educational institution I wasn't sure if I'd fit in. And I didn't. Physically. At 319 pounds I struggled to climb stairs, quickly became winded when walking across campus and had to awkwardly angle my hips when attempting to slide into or out of the adult-sized desks. I was fat, miserable, hopelessly desperate and jealous. My best friend was losing weight, seemingly without effort. When anyone asked her how she was doing it she'd simply answer, "I don't eat." After inquiring further she would explain that she usually fasted a few days a week, but once went ten days without eating. I thought, well, if she could do it then so could I, right? Was it really that easy, I wondered. And then I remembered a time when I was eight or nine and my Mother and I kick-started our 'annual summer diet' with a three day fast. I fasted before, I can do it again, I told myself. So I challenged myself to fast for a week: Monday to Monday before December finals. It was easier and more effective than I expected and motivated me to start fasting as a means for weight loss. A few weeks later I started recording my progress and thoughts.

JANUARY

January 2, Monday
294 ½
Fast
Had to buy Pepsi. Target was out of Diet. It's beside the point. Managed not to eat. Bought a shit load of puzzles. Started New Year's resolution of no chocolate. I did it before, I can do it again. Need to get Dad to exercise. He's really puffed out. Planned to go with Mom on a visitation to Oakland, up and back the same day. Need to write a note to Mr. Judge to see if I can get into his class and call Karen to see if we can match up any of our classes. Then call Eric, then Jackie. Depressed. Came across some papers. I weighed in at 307 about four years ago, lost 20 lbs. two years later, then this November I bounced up to 319. Right now I'm 294 ½ - a cow. I don't deserve to eat for a long time.

January 3, Tuesday
Fast
Had to work today. 8:30-12:30. We had to reset the store but I left early to take Maria to the doctor. She had unusual bleeding. Didn't accomplish much else. Mom asked if I had any plans for lunch – NO. If I had any hopes or desires – NO. Had I already had lunch – NO. I never even looked up from my puzzle. I think she was holding money. It was kinda hard, but I'm a fat cow and don't deserve hopes and desires in food. In fact, that's a pretty sick concept – isn't it? Hopes and desires regarding food? It's like she lives to eat. Not me. It's a pleasure I don't deserve. Made it through another day without

eating. Mom and Larissa both ate sandwiches, at different times. The bread smelled so good. Mom brought out some of her pumpkin cookies. Larissa and she kept popping them. Neither offered me one, not that I would have one, but they didn't even offer.

January 4, Wednesday
Fast
Larissa woke me up about 11:30. She wanted to thank me. She weighed in at 270, which apparently was a new low. I need to get The Cranberries – No Need To Argue. I called her a bitch and then said your welcome. Yesterday she ended up skipping dinner because of me. I can't weigh in until Monday. 5 days. I was so tempted. My urine was unreal – almost orange. Oh, no BM yesterday. KROQ will announce at 7:15 tomorrow something about REM coming to LA. Should be good. Larissa wants me to eat Rice-A-Roni with her. Made it through day three. Larissa put corn and meat in the rice. It smelled so good, but I had not one bite. I think she ended up finishing it off. Mom/Dad offered Jack in the Box. Larissa was going. Got nothing, stayed in my room and watched TV. Asked Larissa later what she got – Jr. Ultimate cheeseburger and egg rolls. I guess she already broke her only resolution (only red meat once a week – sausage pizza on the first.) I guess she's also not doing the chocolate thing. I hope she gains 5 lbs. Mom and Dad eating ice cream at 12:30. Dad took a walk yesterday – he should do that more often. 12:40 – all the Pepsi is gone. Now it's Diet and water. Yeah!

January 5, Thursday
Fast
Woke up feeling light headed. I've gone a week before without that. I hope it passes. The lightheadedness did pass, although stepping up on the chair in my room was pretty scary. More neon pee. That's my trophy. Made it through another day. Rachel offered to buy me something but I was good. Larissa tells me Mom bought fixings for a boiled dinner. That's gonna hurt. Made it through day 4 – yeah!!! Only 66 more to go – I can taste success. It's all I can taste. Need to exercise. REM coming May 9 (Forum), 12 (Pond), 14 (B word – on

Blockbuster Pavilion. Left LA today for Australia 7 p.m. MTV – damn, I wish we had cable.

January 6, Friday
Fast
Yeah! Made it another day. Felt a little lightheaded when I first woke up, but it passed. I'm getting the frontal/forehead headache. It's really annoying. I wonder how long it will last. Don't remember hearing my stomach growl. Had a BM – it was nothing. Clumpy – sort of like diarrhea. Barely felt it. Mom told Larissa today that she only provides breakfast and if we want to eat anything else we fend for ourselves. Excuse me! Since when? This wasn't a part of my agreement when I went back to school. Does it mean I get my $2500 back??!! No. She hasn't actually told me. I'm glad I'm prepared. I realize I'm not eating right now, but that's not even the point. George's stopping by next Friday. REM tickets go on sale Saturday, January 21. Wonder what I'll do. Got my Socio grade – an A. That only pisses me off more that the History bitch gave me a B. I worked my ass off for that class. Study group every other day and staying until 4 a.m. at Solange's for a B!

January 7, Saturday
No energy. Feeling woozy. Felt lousy. Larissa got Wok Express and so did I. Blew it on day 6. 2 egg rolls. Barely got much more down. BM right after – diarrhea. 2nd BM for the day. Then another around nine – diarrhea. Have to work tomorrow. Had a few of Larissa's Nutter Butter Bites. That was really dumb. Broke 2 resolutions today and haven't been exercising. Reading Fit or Fat. Got to the Fasting chapter. It depressed me. I don't want to get sick. I want to be thin and healthy.

January 8, Sunday
282
Worked a full shift today. Got really hungry. Cleaning the back tables I came across a Halloween popcorn tin – still ½ full. I had about 20 kernels of the cheese. That was really stupid. Had a swallow of flat Pepsi too. That was even more stupid than the popcorn. Mom offered to have my car serviced at Jiffy Lube. About time she did something for me.

January 9, Monday
284 ½
Fast
One week, one meal. Down 10 ¼ lbs. What a gyp. Today 284 ½ - yesterday 282. Started period (1 a.m.) this morning. I hope a few pounds are due to water retention. Pearl Jam had a show on KROQ last night started at 7:30. Tuned in at 8. Suppose to end at 10 – went until 12 p.m. Sounded like college radio. They played, which was good. Talked, which for the most part wasn't. A lot of mumbling inside jokes. Into vinyl. Talked about MS. Magazine and abortion. Said it was a freedom we voted on and so should protect. When did we vote? I'm pro-choice, but if he's trying to educate he shouldn't confuse. He left a # to call him. I didn't take it. Should have, that point is still bothering me. I agree with him, but don't want the facts screwed up. I'm pissed I only dropped 10 lbs. Comparing measurements from almost two years ago - up 1 inch in thigh, hip and bust. Neck, waist and arm are the same. Chest down 1 ½. Strange. Slept from 4-7 p.m. No energy. Hard time falling asleep.

January 10, Tuesday
Fast
Another rainy day. I like sleeping in on rainy days. I wonder how I would do in Seattle. Inventory tonight. Yesterday Rachel offered to buy me something to eat twice (8:30-2) – breakfast, lunch, snack. I was good. Made it another day. Felicia had to put clothes out and didn't know what to do, so I helped when asked. Rachel figured it out when Felicia was telling her what she did. These co-managers just don't got it. Last Thursday Allison called and told Rachel she had her on the rookie list for inventory. Rachel explained that she had done several, but it wasn't until she told her I was working it with her that Allison said, oh in that case I can take you off the rookie list. Damn I'm good! I kind of miss it, the good stuff. Especially the paycheck. I hope I know what I'm doing.

  I feel kind of weak. Picked up a glass and it felt so heavy. Must be a combination of not eating and my period. This is day 2, which tends to be heavy. I've noticed I haven't gotten the farts like usual. Maybe it's a good thing not to eat during the cycle. Also, now that I think about it I drank a lot

Sunday but not much came out. Must be water retention. Made it another day. That's #8 this month. Mom offered pizza, then took back the offer – what a BITCH. Rachel's brother-in-law hung himself in his garage. Hadn't had a job in 5 years. Into drugs. Bought a gram of coke, but didn't finish it. Alice put her apron on display. Rachel almost called me out to dinner, but then didn't. Alice was paying – Acapulco. Sounds so good right now but it's better this way – I guess.

January 11, Wednesday
280 ½
School starts in one week. I have a serious problem. I'm not getting up early. I need to snap out of it. Weighed in even though I shouldn't have. 280 ½, down 1 ½ from Sunday. Didn't eat the last three days though so it kinda sucks. I deserve to weigh less than Larissa. This weekend is the Oakland thing – how am I going to make it? And we might be leaving Saturday and spending the night!? That's if we go at all – all depends on Mom and the weather. Haven't had a BM since Saturday night. Mom asked if I need anything at Sav-On. I'm impressed. Didn't need anything though. Then she told me that there was pancake batter available. It sounds so good. When Mom came home she had a pizza – black olive and mushroom. I'm glad I had skipped the pancakes. I had 3 slices, too much. Went diarrhea three times. The last two really hurt. Never realized how much water flushes out when you have diarrhea. First round looked kinda blackish. I hope this doesn't happen on the road to Oakland, or maybe I'll be lucky and we won't go. Shouldn't have had the pizza – it was just too tempting. Then had ½ of Larissa's killer pancake and a slice of Monterey Jack cheese. What was I thinking? Larissa gave me a talk. She's worried, thinks I should eat even if it's a little a day. Yeah, well I'm still a fat cow. Even she weighs less than I do. I have to lose weight – NOW!

January 12, Thursday
280 – kinda depressing
Fourth day of period. Went to school. Requested UCLA transcript. Bought most, but not all books. $290. Talked to Jackie from PoliSci. Mom paid for Jiffy Lube. They left a blue thing on my front plate. Went to Blockbuster Music. Wanted

KROQ calendar. They were out. Usually they have tons of leftovers, but this year they included a CD so totally sold out. I still don't have a wall calendar. It's annoying. Went to Lucky to buy some chips. Had nachos with Larissa. Figure I better eat something even if it's not much every day or else I'll have a diarrhea fit on the way to or from Oakland. That would be scary and nasty. Spent like $225 at Blockbuster. What was I doing? I need an at home type job. Bought four REM CD's, one of which I already had – sort of. They're imports – more songs on them. Now I have three copies of Life's Rich Pageant! They don't even consider it one of their best albums. What was I thinking??? I wasn't.

January 13, Friday
The REM concert tour kicked off in Australia today. Boy, do I wish I was there and not here. Had to open at work. Stayed on an extra two hours…to do freight. Rachel and I kinda fooled around. She's lost 38 lbs. and now she's ready to gain. WHAT?!?! Wore my cranberry velour t-neck that used to be snug. It's loose now. Cool! Need money. Rachel bought me El Polo Loco. Only ate 1 piece (large) and 1 tortilla. She noticed my pants have gotten looser… they are a lot looser than when I wore them in November. Mom and Dad haven't even noticed anything. Mom bought doughnuts and offered. We're leaving tomorrow morning instead of Sunday. Larissa wants nachos tonight. Haven't shit since Wednesday and I ate Thursday (?) Had a buttermilk bar. That was really stupid. Then Mom offered a grocery run for the trip and nachos for everyone. Had nachos with hamburger. Larissa ate red meat again. I can't believe I had meat twice in one day. Didn't think George was coming. Showed up at 8:37 p.m. By then I had changed – no bra, V-neck sweater, non-matching shorts. Apparently this was about the time he was to be expected? At least according to him. It was nice to see him again, sort of. Felt awkward, forced. Tomorrow's a long day – need gas.

January 14, Saturday
283
Weighed in at 283. Bummed, yet surprised it isn't more considering how much I ate yesterday and I haven't had a BM

in three days. Do I really want to do this? Drove up to Oakland. Ate at a diner, tuna melt and cheese sticks.

January 15, Sunday
Oakland
Grand Slam with bacon and sausage, steak sandwich

January 16, Monday
286 ½
About the weekend… Stopped at the Buttonwillow Truck Stop. Had tuna sandwich, fries and mozzarella (3) sticks with blue cheese. Played cards at the hotel. Ate some Cheetos and Vegetable Thins. Larissa and Mom had Whoppers. We all had very large chocolate shakes. Sunday we went to Denny's for breakfast. That took forever. Grand slam, 2 bacon, 2 eggs, 2 sausage, 2 pancakes. The Visitation was OK. Talked to Megan for a long time. Everyone's having kids, or has them already. Francine, Denise, Melissa, Bella, Shannon, Nicole and they're getting married. Lord, have mercy. Talked to my girlies. They're total geeks. Talked to Ms. Wilson (Grace's Mom). That was really nice. Grace's been promoted at the hospital and she recommends Northwestern for Film Studies. Megan was there. Ate at Applebee's afterward. They took forever. Had a Philly Cheese Steak sandwich. Took six hours driving time up and five hours, fifteen minutes on the way back. Put about 800 miles on my car, and 6 ½ lbs. on my butt. Yes, that's right I'm back to 286 ½ - gotta get it off. School starts Wednesday – oh no. Last Wednesday I had that shit attack, then I didn't go. Saturday I started to become concerned because I didn't want to be in Oakland and have a problem. So at the visitation right before escort I had to go. I could feel it. Fortunately I was okay waiting until after. Small clumps. Went again at the restaurant. Mushy – had to wipe three times. Went two more times today. Asked Larissa to go to El Rey Taco after Mom left for Fullerton. Surprised she actually went. Sort of wish she didn't. Had two green quesadillas, rice and beans. She also went to McDonald's for herself. Mom has a Page this year and apparently another girl's mother is upset about it. Poor Maddie, and now she's part of Diamond Bar. Mom was on the phone at least 40 minutes – 'til 11:35 and barely said anything. Larissa and I figured out our schedules. I'm taking

English in the morning instead – that is if I can petition. Sophia called Saturday wanted to change schedules – did with Isabella. Called Amanda. Talked for about a half hour. That was cool. Tried Robbie. Got four wrong numbers – two no answers and one message.

January 17, Tuesday
287
School starts tomorrow!!! Have to work tonight – yuck! Went up another ½ lb. What was I doing having El Rey Taco? I'm a 287 lb. cow! At least I didn't eat meat. I've had 8 meals so far. Five had meat. Three red meats. I still have leftover Wok Express in the fridge. Oh well. It can stay there a while. I've lost 30 lbs., but more needs to go. Finally, back on track. In 'N' Out smelled soooo good when I was leaving work too. Had two Diet Pepsi's and 17 oz. of water. Tomorrow will be a challenge. All day at school! Yuck. Wonder if I'll make it all day. Need to go to Robinson's-May.

January 18 - Wednesday
First day of school – Yuck! Have Joe in Comp. Biology. Got into Geography. Larissa came home from her inventory early and with pizza. We shared. I shouldn't have. It prompted me to also finish my Wok Express. Eating at 11:30 is just plain stupid. So close to making it another day and I blew it. I don't deserve to live. Started writing a song in the cafeteria.

January 19, Thursday
Showed up at Bowling. Left before 8. Came back home to waffles. Dumb. Went back to petition English. Didn't get in. Had gut problems twice and boy was it nasty. Film/polisci lady in Bio Lab. Hope she's my partner. Erica's cousin also in there. Tried to get away from her as fast as possible. I wonder if that's what she thinks. I don't want her as a partner. No way! Went to grocery with Larissa. Chips to finish nachos. Why did I get a croissant? What was I thinking getting sherbet? That was really STUPID. Called Karen. She totally wants me to take English with her. I don't really want night classes T-W-Th, but it does make sense and at this point it may be my only choice. Typed Larissa's essay late. I'm definitely writing from my perspective.

January 20, Friday
So close to getting caught. Had to show registration page to English teacher and handed her the wrong one. By acting confused I passed it by her and got her to sign Larissa's. Damn I'm good. Talked to Joe about Poli 3. Wish I could take it. Mr. Magoo saw me, I think. Wonder what he was thinking. Came home and had a croissant and a very long nap. Don't know what to do about REM tickets. Want good seats, but don't want to pay up the kazoo. Tickets officially go on sale at 9 a.m. tomorrow. Gotta make a decision. I guess I'm gonna pay and go through an agency. I'm such a pig. I don't deserve to eat anything for a long time. Turned in first essay. We had to write about ourselves. Ugh. Ate El Rey Taco.

January 22, Sunday
Worked a full shift.

January 23, Monday
290
Registration + archery and English

January 24, Tuesday
English class

January 25, Wednesday
Geography US/Canada quiz
Mailed university application, cinema stuff

January 26, Thursday
English class

January 28, Saturday
Sausage pizza during 6 ½ hour shift at work.

January 29, Sunday
Fast
Worked a full shift. Super Bowl Sunday. There was pizza, but not for me.

January 30, Monday
288 ½

Fast

January 31, Tuesday
Fast
English rough draft due.

FEBRUARY

February 1, Wednesday
Fast
Larissa ordered a class ring.

February 3, Friday
Fast
Worked 6 hour shift.

February 5, Sunday
277
Fast
Worked 5 ½ hours.

February 6, Monday
Fast
Had ATD test.

February 7, Tuesday
Fast
English peer response.

February 8, Wednesday
Fast
Geography test.

February 9, Thursday
Fast
Essay 1 due

February 10, Friday
Fast
13 days now ☺
LBUSD Aide test
Really grouchy, acid mouth, missed Biology.
Closing shift.

February 11, Saturday
Bra inventory, late shift.
Larissa enticed me to go to the grocery store with her. Everything was tempting. I want to break my fast, but I want to keep losing weight. She tells me to eat something, anything even if it's only a slice of bread.

February 12, Sunday
273

February 13, Monday
Worked 5:30-9:30

February 14, Tuesday
El Rey Taco
Pecan pie
Skip archery
+ Bowling

February 15, Wednesday
Skipped all three classes

February 16, Thursday
No archery due to rain

February 18, Saturday
Worked at the bakery all day.
Delivery at Beverly Hills Regency
Olive Garden for dinner afterwards with everyone. Pizza

February 19, Sunday
Morning meeting with the district at Cerritos.
Lunch at the Hut after with the gang after. I was so stupid hungry that I starting eating Julie's tortillas, not even realizing

that they couldn't possibly be mine. Hello, I did not order tortillas. So embarrassing.

February 20, Monday
Work. Went in late 5:50-9:50

February 21, Tuesday
Skipped English
Bad bowling day
3 missed Archery

February 22, Wednesday
Person essay due

February 23, Thursday
English rough draft due
Flu
Archery
Bio Lab

February 24, Friday
LATE
Skipped English
Bio test
Work 6-9:30; Bakery 9:45-3 a.m.

February 25, Saturday
Work 2:30-7:30

February 26, Sunday
Markdowns 9:30-12:30

February 27, Monday
282 ¼ with blue robe
Cereal, toast, slice of cheese
Bio 41 – 75% C ☹
Engl 1/3 ☺

February 28, Tuesday
English peer response
Amanda came to archery range

MARCH

March 1, Wednesday
282
Fast
Geography quiz postponed, Professor forgot the quiz at home. Had diarrhea three times. Skipped PoliSci. Felt nauseated during Biology. In English my essay was read to the class. For the first time in forever I had to excuse myself during a class session to go to the bathroom. For another round of diarrhea. Ended the day with a total of seven rounds and a very sore ass.

March 2, Thursday
278 ¼
Yesterday's colon flush rewarded on the scales. YES!
Essay 2 due (in class)
Toast with butter, Rice-A-Roni
No archery today because of the RAIN.
One Bowel Movement

March 3, Friday
Skipped English
Denny's grill cheese sandwich, mozzarella sticks, onion rings
Worked at the Bakery 9:45-11
Made icing roses. Brought home leftover cake samples, ate one thin slice.
Three rounds of diarrhea.

March 4, Saturday
278
Work 12-3 p.m.
Finished the Rice-A-Roni I made the other day. Also had toast and eggs. Then cake.
Played cards for three hours.

March 5, Sunday
Work 10:30-6:30
Casa DeEscabar for lunch at work: nachos
Worked on place essay
CUT HAIR. Just really felt like I needed a change. Dramatic change. Whacked it off but good.

March 6, Monday
280 ¼
Fast
Hunter gave me an essay contest application and said she wanted a photocopy of it after I filled it out. Yikes! Bought my dress, the one I've had my eye on, the one I wasn't going to buy until I could buy it in a size smaller and now I can so I did. Allison was visiting the store and hounded me about my weight loss. She asked me 'How much have you lost?' so many times I lost count. As if it's any of her business. She just wants to know 'cause she's a gossip. Received a letter stating I'm ineligible for a Pell Grant. That blows.

March 7, Tuesday
Amanda's spice cake, green quesadilla, bean and cheese burrito
Bowling/Archery, above average every time

March 8, Wednesday
Political Science exam
Geography quiz
Journal due (not collected!!!)
Green quesadilla, rice and noodle Roni box, garlic

March 9, Thursday
Archery high 30, Lab exam
No English class - Conte was sick
Three eggs and three slices of toast.

March 10, Friday
English placed in reading groups
Played cards
Ice Skating (World's)
El Rey Taco nachos, green quesadilla; Foster's sundae with fries; two slices of toast.

March 11, Saturday
Work 3:30-7:30 (scheduled for)
Ice skating
Party at work
Three fourths of the lights went out at work. Had to stay until 8:45 for electrician to finish.
Green quesadilla, rice, bean/cheese burrito; three eggs, chips, salsa, two slices of cheese

March 12, Sunday
278, then a shit, 277 ½
Fast
Ice Skating, Worked on Place Essay

March 13, Monday
273 ¼
Fast
Rough drafts due
PoliSci first exam
Pepsi 16 oz., water 16.7, 1 lt. + 1/3 of 2 lt. of Orange Slice

March 14, Tuesday
272? I think
Fast
Bowling - two 101's
Archery comp. this week
Total score 95
FEVER
Skipped English

March 15, Wednesday
Fast
Geography Unit 2 test
Skip English

PoliSci – couldn't answer
Geography, big headache KILLER
Still fighting fever, 98.2

March 16, Thursday
268 ¼ - Whoop! Slipped on past the 50 pound mark.
Fast
Bio Lab midterm – know I missed two for sure
Archery
English assignments were given
Dr. Slice (20 oz.)

March 17, Friday
268
Fast
Final draft due
5 hour shift
Pepsi at bakery. Wrapped and shaved white chocolate.
Offered pizza at bakery and chicken at home, but still made it.
Alice has enlarged heart and serious arthritis

March 18, Saturday
267 ½
2 deliveries (5 tiers)
Haven't had a shit all week. Ate KFC buttermilk biscuits to push it out. In one hour, BM. Gave in and ate two pieces of chicken, original. Damn it! Drumstick and breast (gave part of it to Larissa.) Small scoop of potatoes and gravy. One spoon Cherry Vanilla ice cream. Pretzels. Five hours after chicken, two rounds of diarrhea.

March 19, Sunday
268
Work 1:30-6:30
Mom's party = BAD GIRL PIG OUT
2 slices of meatloaf, scalloped potatoes, broccoli and cheese sauce, bunt cake, olives, shrimp, crab
BLOATED

March 20, Monday
PoliSci unit II exam

Take novel to English
No Bio today
270 ¾
BAD GIRL ate 24 Shrimp ☹
Chips/salsa, roll with butter, potatoes
5 miles on bike, approx. 22 minutes + weights + stretch

March 21, Tuesday
270 ¼
BAD GIRL
Thought today I'd make it, but no.
Bowled every game above average.
Archery – raining
English – research and quotes
Shrimp, meatloaf, Cheez Its, two rolls with butter
30 minute bike, 7 minute stretch

March 22, Wednesday
270 ½?
No English – sign in sheet not posted!
Copied bio notes
PoliSci – professor thanked us for showing up. We're serious students to attend the day after a test is given.
30 minutes bike, 7.25 miles
Stretch, 10 sit ups
3 grapes

March 23, Thursday
Rough draft of 3rd English essay due
Bowel Movement – the first in five days; Heavy Flow day
3 grapes
30 minutes on bike, 7.4 miles

March 24, Friday
268 ¾
Start computer class!!!
Sartre essay in class, Bio exam – think I did good
30 minutes, 7.25 miles
2 BM (1D)
At work - not given .25 raise because I'm already overpaid for the store and Allison's being a little bitch. My numbers are

there, my performance is there, even if the store's overall numbers aren't. Allison MADE Rachel redo my review taking away the raise I was due. What. A. Bitch. But I was offered to be temp manager for six weeks with no additional funds offered. Ummmm… let me think about this for not even a half-second - NO WAY. You can't afford to give me the raise I earned and give me a bullshit performance rating to justify not doling out the raise I deserve and yet you want me to work more hours and tack on greater responsibilities? If you wanted that maybe you should have let my original review with the raise stand, Alli-fucking-son?!
Hang at Bakery and not shopping as planned
2 quesadillas, beans, chips, salsa, Pepsi

March 25, Saturday
268 ¾
Big Cake Day – 10 a.m.
Work 4:30 – 7:30
33 minutes, 8 miles on the bike
Deli roast beef sandwich, potato wedges
3 piece chicken meal (2 drumsticks, 1 breast)
Work at the bakery

March 26, Sunday
272 ½
Joint birthday gathering at Wizard's ($30) at Universal City Walk with the gang. Ava kept looking at me like I was a foreigner or something. Couldn't believe how much thinner I am. Unfortunately I still have a long way to go.
Angela - $25 Rob-May certificate, Mom – ab isolator, Dad – phone cord, Larissa – cow earrings, Rachel – shoes, earrings, Alice – earrings, wallet, dinner, cake
Beef, sherbet, cake, 2 drinks
BM
30 minutes, 7.5 miles on the bike

March 27, Monday
272 ½
English – lots to do
Bio – no results yet
PoliSci – 1 point

Sausage pepperoni pizza
Chicken taco, cake
Bike 30 minutes, 7.6 miles
Left message on Vivian's machine
1 BM

March 28, Tuesday
Essay due
Bowled a high of 114
Archery
Dropped off essay
Ice Skating
Sausage pepperoni pizza – 4 slices
Bike 30 minutes, 7.75 miles

March 29, Wednesday
273 ¼
Fast
Geography world map quiz, missed Sweden
Read Riddle & Exis.
PoliSci – earned 5 bean bags
Hiked it through the parking lots at the Forum in the dark, alone, to finally get to my seat at 9:50, just to end up being the only one to show. People suck.
Hell Night

March 30, Thursday
269 ½
Fast
Found out the hard way that my archery partner this whole time, Holly, is Hunter's granddaughter. Someone was asking about English teachers, who's good, easy, that sort of thing. I was like, whatever you do, don't take Hunter. She's old and forgets assignments and I said it all in front of Holly who rather sheepishly said, that's my grandma. I could not apologize enough. I mean, how do you come back from that? A couple of the guys were like, you better watch out, she's armed ya know. But really, it was just a quiet, awkward class session. The poor, sweet girl wouldn't even make eye contact with me. I felt horrible. Just horrible.
NEED MASK, GLOVES, GOGGLES for Bio

Perfect 10 on respiration quiz
Eng – knees sore
Bike 30 minutes, 7.35 miles
Weight lifting (few reps), stretch, 3+ abs

March 31, Friday
268 ½, after 3 BM, 267 ¾
Fast
Six bowel movements before school, five more at school
265 at 4:10
Work 5:30-9:30
NEED DISKS
Bike 30 minutes, 7.45 mile

APRIL

April 1, Saturday
264
Worked 1:30 – 8:30, 7 hours straight, no break
Wore a dress that was made for me when I was fourteen.
30-35 cheez ball puffs, 2 slices of garlic bread
34 minutes, 8 miles on the bike, 10 sit ups
3 BM

April 2, Sunday
263
Fast
R/O Oral presentation
Read Geography/PoliSci & type notes, English paper
Treadmill 35 minutes, 39.4 calories?, 1.6 miles
2 ½ BM

April 3, Monday
262
First draft of philosophy paper
Skipped English, didn't tell Larissa
Whole box of Noodle Roni, broccoli au gratin
Bike 30 minutes, 7.6 miles; Weights
2 ½ BM

April 4, Tuesday
263
Oral Presentation, second up

Bowling 130 – new high
Wok Express – chow mien noodles, chicken teriyaki
Told Rachel mgmt???
Biked 33 minutes, 8.3 miles

April 5, Wednesday
Geography test 3
PoliSci test
Think I did well on both tests
Salad with blue cheese dressing
3 slices of pizza (2 with black olives)
Biked 30 minutes, 7.31 miles
Weights and abs

April 6, Thursday
Wake up to major gut pain
Oral presentations
Rice, 2 slices of sausage pizza, apple pie
Biked 30 minutes, 7.5 miles
Weights, abs
2 BM

April 7, Friday
Work 5:30-9:30
Nachos, Cran-grape juice
PoliSci notebook due
English paper due
Mid term
Nodding off in Biology
Biked 30 minutes, 7.6 miles
Abs, weights
4 BM

April 8, Saturday
State convention starts; driving up tomorrow
Went through closet trying to find something to wear
2 slices of toast
¼ cup mac and cheese
Frosted Flakes with milk
KFC 2 piece – drumstick and thigh
Biked 30 minutes, 7.75 miles

April 9, Sunday
Spring Break is ON
Drive up with Amanda
Both my newly appointed girls are from the north
Taco Bell – tostada, bean burrito; Soup and salad, chicken tenders, onion rings

April 10, Monday
Breakfast in the convention banquet hall
Eggs, Sausage, hash browns, muffin, OJ, 1 bacon strip, fruit, Pepsi
Drive home with Amanda
Sweet Tarts, Cool Ranch Doritos
Chicken tostada, taco, beans, green quesadilla
Larissa and Dad arrive home around 11 PM
Walk around the block

April 11, Tuesday
Hamburger, chili
269 ¾
Called Grandma and wished her a happy birthday
Fosters – bacon/cheeseburger, chili cheese fries, butterscotch sundae
Toast (1)
Biked 30 minutes, 7.9 miles
Ab, weights

April 12, Wednesday
269 ½
BBQ – top sirloin, spare rib dinner
5 Pringle chips
2 BM
Bike 45 minutes, 11 miles; Ab, weights

April 13, Thursday
269 ¼
9:30-6 work
Worked all day with Rachel
Nachos with shredded beef
Jumbo coke
45 minutes bike, 11.15 miles

April 14, Friday
268 ½
Work 3:30-9:30
Toast, 2 lt. of Coke, 20 oz. Pepsi, KFC 2 pieces, Subway footlong Tuna sandwich, chicken tostada, green quesadilla, ½ rice and beans
Bike 30 minutes, 7.5 miles
Weights, ab 35

April 15, Saturday
Work 12-7:30
Finish rice/beans
Cheese and chips, Jumbo Coke
Angel food cake 1/3
15 shrimp
1/3 Dad's Foster's hamburger
Bunny cookie
Olive Garden salad & 2 breadsticks
30 minutes bike, 7.75 miles
Weights, ab 35

April 16, Sunday
271 ¾
Scalloped potatoes, cereal, green beans, cottage cheese, chips, salsa, toast, sherbet
Worked on flash cards
Bike 30 minutes, 7.8 miles

April 17, Monday
PoliSci Unit III test = A
Wok Express – rice, noodle, teriyaki chicken, BBQ pork
Coke
Starting to get sick
Bike 30 minutes, 7.9 miles
35 ab, weights

April 18, Tuesday
Essay 4 due – peer revision
SICK
Leftover Wok Express, cheese, egg, toast, Coke
Raining – no archery

April 19, Wednesday
English paper back
A minus midterm
Skipped Bio
86% on Geography test ☹
SICK
4 crackers, Coke, OJ

April 20, Thursday
Tide Pools due in Bio
SICK
Cottage cheese, 4 crackers, Coke, OJ
Essay due, Rat dissection
Skip Archery
15 minute bike, 3.75 miles

April 21, Friday
265 ¼
Work 5-10:30
Whopper with cheese, raised glazed donut, buttermilk bar, Starburst, cottage cheese, cran-grape juice

April 22, Saturday
265 ½
Work scheduled for 12:30-9 ouch!
Left closer to 8:30
Mashed potatoes with gravy, corn cob, 2 KFC pieces
Nachos with guacamole, jumbo Coke, medium Coke

April 23, Sunday
267 ¼
Work 9:30-4:30
1 lt. Pepsi
Philosophy paper
20 minute bike, 5.25 miles

April 24, Monday
264 ¼
Randi is an IDIOT!!!
Work on def. paper
HOT DAY!

Cranberry juice cocktail
60 minutes bike, 14.4 miles
Weights, 40 ab

April 25, Tuesday
263
In Archery I was singled out for a demonstration because of my "perfect form." Awesome!
2 Pepsi's
30 minutes bike, 7.6 miles
Weights, ab 35

April 26, Wednesday
261
Geography map quiz, PoliSci test
Definition paper
Pretzels/bite of gingerbread, OJ & Pepsi

April 27, Thursday
260 ¼
Fast
Archery, Bio lab, Eng – logic
Doing paper late
20 minute bike, 5.1 miles

April 28, Friday
259 ¾
Work 6:30-9:30
Finished Philosophy paper
El Rey Taco taquitos with extra guacamole, ground beef soft taco and green quesadilla
4 rounds of diarrhea after taking one Ex-Lax

April 29, Saturday
258 ¾
Fast
Cleaned, organized in my room
Weights, ab 40
Dad gave me cans of tuna. Maybe he wants me to eat?
45 minute treadmill, .8 mile, 48.6 calories

April 30, Sunday
258
Attended Julie's birthday party. Cool to see some of the old gang.
Doritos, fruit, carrots, broccoli, ranch dressing
2 roast beef croissant mini sandwiches, potato salad
Pepsi, cake, fruit salad
45 minute treadmill, .8 mile, 48.7 calories

MAY

May 1, Monday
258 ¼
English – book talk
Biology test next week
PoliSci lecture
OJ (240)
Saw Arnold for the first time since last December. It was obvious he noticed the weight loss which was pretty damn awesome. Made it really easy to get back on the treadmill even though didn't totally want to.
45 min. treadmill, .8 miles, 48.2 calories
Ab 40

May 2, Tuesday
257 ½
Bowling 154 – a new high score!!!
Prepare for debates
Pretzels, slice of cheese, 4 crackers, 3 oz. tuna
45 min. treadmill, .8 miles, 46.7 calories

May 3, Wednesday
257 ¾
Skipped English (Larissa skipped Algebra)
Fire drill during Biology
Skipped PoliSci
Supercuts $11 well spent
Payless socks and 3 pairs of shoes, all tan and cream

Pasta/pretzels/cottage cheese
45 min. treadmill, .8 miles, 48.3 calories
Ab 45, 1 EX

May 4, Thursday
257
Yeah!!! Down 50 pounds from where I was stuck for the longest time like four years ago. Feels so good.
Cran-grape juice – 240 calories
Reproduction quiz
Won Debate!!!
Handful of pretzels

May 5, Friday
255 ¾
Definition essay due
5:30-9:30 work
OJ (small), 3 bites of cottage cheese, pretzels
10 p.m. El Rey Taco – chunky beef burrito, green quesadilla
45 minutes treadmill, 1.0 mile, 60 calorie

May 6, Saturday
255
9:30-1:30 work
Green quesadilla, Tostitos nacho cheese, olives, lime sherbet (ate late)
45 minutes treadmill, .9 mile, 53.8 calories
Ab 55

May 7, Sunday
256
10 powdered donettes, milk
Work stand nachos – cheese, beans
Cottage cheese, slice of bread, lime sherbet
10-4 p.m. work
Redo definition essay

May 8, Monday
259
Definition essay due
Bio/PoliSci

Pepsi – almost all 2 lts
Copied Geo notes, punctuation test Wednesday

May 9, Tuesday
256 ¼
Fast
Bowling – 3rd place trophy
Archery score improved 30 points from beginning of semester
20 min. treadmill, .4 miles, 24.8 calories

May 10, Wednesday
255
English test
PoliSci test
Geography test
Exhausted
Book meeting, reamed paper
Received USC Acceptance letter
El Rey Taco green quesadilla, rice, beans

May 11, Thursday
Practicum
Soraya Mire on campus!
Fire Eyes documentary – disturbing, enlightening
Green quesadilla, chips, nacho cheese

May 12, Friday
255 ¾
Work 6:30-9:30
Presentations start
Chips, nacho cheese
Toast with butter
Stopped by bakery to talk to Alice

May 13, Saturday
257 ½
Work 2-7:30
Nachos with shredded beef
2 piece KFC chicken, mashed potatoes with gravy, green beans and corn
Called Angela about USC and her birthday

May 14, Sunday
260 ½
Work 2-6:30
Wok Express – all chicken, one egg roll, 3 almond cookies
3 rewrites of paper, Larissa typing until 2am

May 15, Monday
Literary essay due
Bio test 83.9% = didn't NAIL it
Jason tried filing a complaint against Hunter and was told to stand in line. Nothing to be done. She's tenured.
Leftover Wok Express, rice and noodles. KFC chicken, mashed potatoes, canned green beans

May 16, Tuesday
Power out – no English
Lime sherbet, taquitos and chicken quesadilla

May 17, Wednesday
261
No geography, check grade
Orange slice, cornbread stuffing, lime sherbet ~ two bowls
English presentation
Bio - genetics
Timeline for PoliSci
Talk about USC
Geography grade on last test – 81 - disappointing

May 18, Thursday
260 ¾
Peer response, Archery final
Bean/cheese burrito, green quesadilla
2 eggs with cheese, lime sherbet
BIO 41L Final

May 19, Friday
260
Nachos, Pepsi
Eng – papers due Monday, journals were collected and I know I was missing 4 entries
Bio – genetics, Played cards

May 20, Saturday
259 ½
Laundry, Literary paper
Cheetos, Noodle Roni white cheddar shells, Fritos
Played cards and made cards
Start day

May 21, Sunday
258 ¼
Literary paper
Made flash cards (geo)
Finish Fritos
Oral presentation stuff

May 22, Monday
255 ¼
English presentation = A, kicked butt, filled the hour
Wok Express, rice, noodles and chicken, 4 almond cookies

May 23, Tuesday
257 ½
Essay 6 due
Essay 7 revised due – A
FINAL
Hunter said my essay was a "Masterpiece." She WILL haunt me for the rest of my life! Amanda's father-in-law died

May 24, Wednesday
BIO 41 FINAL
Why did I listen to Debbie?
1/2 + box of Parmesan Noodle Roni
Geog FINAL
Pepsi (s)
Talked to clueless guy – defeated ego
Work 6-9
Finished rice/noodles, grilled cheese
30 minutes on the treadmill, 39 calories, .6 miles

May 25, Thursday
255 ¼
Bio grades available

Pepsi (3 or 4), 3 crab – burgers, ¼ banana cupcake
Worked on room
30 minutes treadmill, .6 miles, 38.6 calories, ab (25)

May 26, Friday
255 ½
Fast, Pepsi (2 or 3)
English finals available
Started novel, did cleaning
NO STATS???!!!
30 minutes treadmill, 45 calories, .7 miles, ab (45)

May 27, Saturday
253
Work 2:30-7:30
After work 252 ½
Nice to go back to work. Sophia talked weight and future love and school – USC!
El Rey Taco – nachos, ¾ green quesadilla
Pepsi (2)

May 28, Sunday
253 ½
Fast (almost), 9 pretzel bits
Mom/Dad went to an event in Palm Springs
Read PoliSci/cards
2 Pepsi, 4 Diet Pepsi, 2 water
35 minutes treadmill, .9 miles, 52 calories, ab (35)

May 29, Monday
251 ¾
Called in to cover Amanda's opening
Worked 10:30-6:30 = 8 hours, no break
No-meat lasagna, cheese popcorn, 6 pretzels bits, fruit salad, slice of banana cream pie
Cards

May 30, Tuesday
253 ½
No-meat lasagna, hamburger buns with butter and garlic powder, cheese popcorn 1 regular/1 large bowl

35 minutes treadmill, .8 miles, 50 calories (with belts), ab (25)

May 31, Wednesday
252 ½
Poli Sci Final 10:40-1:10
Cottage cheese, El Rey Taco nachos, rice, sherbet
Bio = 86.7, Bio Lab = 90, notebook B+
30 minutes treadmill, .8 miles, 47 calories

Undated May – Mental dump

My third semester of college is almost over. Just one more final next week – seven done, one to go. Not only is my semester almost over, but so is my educational career at Long Beach City College. I should be happy, thrilled, excited; I'll be going to USC next fall. What a major accomplishment. Anyone should be proud, anyone would be proud. So why have I stopped sharing this information. Why aren't I bragging? Is it because I don't want to sound too pompous? No. I've never had a problem putting my ego on display – way up on the highest, most brilliant pedestal. Could it be that I'm scared? Could it be that I'm afraid that someone is rocking my pedestal and that I am heading for the biggest crash of my life? After the initial few days wore away, weeks of scared nervousness, questioning my ability and a touch of depression took over.

    I know why I question my own ability. It's an insecurity that will always exist within me. How far can I go? How long can I last with that touch of self-confidence missing? How can I regain it? Maybe if I tell my story. Maybe if I share I'll better understand myself and better understand the many abilities that I do possess. When Sophia encounters difficult situations with her teenage daughters she turns to advice from us - Rachel and I - her colleagues and friends. She was surprised by my mixed up educational past. It's that same past that haunts my educational future. I've ripped myself off, while gypping the system. She thinks that now that I have returned with new determination I have a story to tell. People need to know how to do it. I'm not entirely sure I "know" how I did it. But I am well aware of my pitfalls and my peaks. I have repeatedly come to terms with them within myself. But I haven't shared everything with anyone and if this is to be an effective and honest account of my educational trip then it is time to face some bitter demons. I hope anyone I may have lied to along the way can find it in their heart to take pity on my situation and the reasons for which I felt compelled to lie. If not, it was nice knowing you.

Please do understand that I'm not writing this to hurt anyone. Just the opposite. There are a lot of kids out there that need to know they're not alone and just as many parents that have no idea what is going on with their kids. Parents must have brave hearts. But my audience is really a bit more personal than all the parents and kids of the world. As much as this is a story about me, this too is a story about my sister. Although Larissa is her own story and in order to do her justice she may be next, but there is only room here for her story as it relates to my own. The number one person I am writing this for folks, let's not fool around here, is myself. There are reasons for which I don't feel I deserve the blessings I have been granted. And here's why…

I can't remember the last time I was truly happy. Just happy, nothing else but happy. I usually have several thoughts going on at one time, a point of confusion to anyone trying to read my reaction to something, and during what should be happy moments other thoughts creep in. I don't know how to be happy, to have all of my sensations, turned on to one emotion. I can't remember Happy ever influencing that much control over me, or rather I can't remember ever surrendering to Happy whole-heartedly. For this I think I have realized that I've never been in love. To me, love would be that kind of happy. Happy thoughts are the only ones that come to mind. I've admired, I think I've even obsessed, but there has been no love and there has been no mutual love. I don't think anyone has ever really been in love with me. At least no one I wanted to love me. If they did they hid it very well and never told me. If you really love someone wouldn't you feel you had to tell them? Taking the risk of not telling would be risking the loss of love. And if you've ever found love how could you afford to lose it? Although, maybe love is better when it stays in the heart and mind. That love is whole and pure, untainted by a troubling world that manages to tear down the good. So if I have ever loved that is where it stayed but I really don't know if I have. It's never been returned. I've never had anyone go to the limits for me. I've always been the one to sacrifice and that's not love. That's stupid being used to further someone's gain. That's not a genuine connection. Will I know love when it knocks? Will I recognize the sound, or will I have my head buried in my work and my heart locked below Grant's tomb? When will I know the answers to the questions I seek? When will the answers know me?

Great minds are never known if they can't communicate. You may have all the answers, know every truth, found the meaning of life, god and the universe but unless you can communicate that information in a manner that others can comprehend then the knowledge is wasted, useless and lost. And, to even a great extent, one must know how to effectively manipulate the audience to provide the desired results and realizations out of them. This is where my story begins. We must all have the ability to communicate, but we too must have something to communicate. We must have some opinion, some essence of ourselves to share with the world. Our writing is thinking on paper. It is a physical manifestation of a biological, chemical process. We must think to write. That is why I found it so troubling that my sister couldn't make it through an English 1 class to save her life. By the time she was attending her third college she had already made several attempts, but without success. The semester I decided to return to school should have been her last. But she dropped English 1 again. She took 15 units that semester and credits me with the motivation to do so. Still needing that English requirement meant enduring another semester at Long Beach City College. English was the only class she needed. She should have been able to do it, but she never even turned in the first essay. Instead she spent the semester taking Cultural Geography, Bowling and Badminton. Being a Geography major and repeatedly taking this one professor lent well to her "cranking" in the class, but another semester went by and she wasn't graduating. I had to break the news to our parents. I knew for a couple of weeks and it was eating away at me. Just as she lacked the guts to stick through English 1 she lacked the guts to admit it. When the subject of school came up during a family discussion it was more than I could bear. I had Larissa's permission and spilled the beans. They weren't even surprised. I think they would have been more surprised if she were actually going to graduate. In an off-handed remark my mother said that if we were smart we would make a deal, Larissa and I. A math class for an English class. Sounded like a fair trade to her. I always wondered what it would be like to have a brother, but at that moment all of the "you're twins" comments sounded like epistles from on high. My mother quickly retracted the comment, to her it was a flip remark made in angry haste. To Larissa it was a dreamy possibility to the graduation aisle. And for me it would relieve the unbelievable migraines brought on by anything mathematical. If Larissa took my math classes for me my grade point average wouldn't be affected by my attitude and lack of willingness to devote to math the time it needed in order to be absorbed. My mother's passed over remark preyed on my mind, and Larissa's. It took a few hours to figure out schedules for the next semester but as the days clicked it became a glaring possibility that neither one of us felt we could pass up. There were a few moments of "can you believe we're doing this?" and "Can we really get away with it?" But other than those few fleeting moments there was no doubt that we would try. I had gypped the system (and myself) out of math before, I could do it again. I could respond to Ally. I've been called Larissa, at times and in certain social situations, more often than I've been called Calliope. It's the difference between the common name and the unusual name. People are afraid of screwing up an unusual name, so they generally try avoid saying it at all, not realizing that everyone, especially we unusually named people, love to hear the sound of our own names. I am more impressed by people that attempt it repeatedly (right or wrong) than those that avoid it altogether.

 Trying to work out our schedules was probably the most difficult task of all. It also almost got us busted. Karen, from my film class, was registered for the same English class that Larissa was registered for. Thank goodness she asked me to take it with her. Had she not I would have been showing up pretending to be Larissa with her in the class. Talk about busted! Plus Amanda, also from film class, was in there. There would be no way for me to go Tues/Thurs as Larissa and Wednesday to Geography (another class Karen and I took together, until she found out she didn't need it) as Calliope. So Larissa and I had to change her English class to my English class. Then there was a matter of finals. The school usually held all English finals at one time, so how would I take two English finals at one time? Fortunately, they had evening classes sticking to the regular meeting time, so instead I took two English finals on the same day. That was a strain I am pleased that I will never have to bear again. For Larissa's English class I would now have to petition because everything was booked. Since she was taking Math for me M-W-F 7:20-9 it seemed fitting that I take her English class M-W-F 7:40-9 so that is what we did. Being a petitioner I had to prove that I was eligible for English 1. A glitch we didn't anticipate. Larissa had suggested swapping registration papers but I didn't see a point. I had never been asked for it before. That was before Hunter. Before she added you to her roster you had to show it. When she asked for it I was drowsy and didn't think much of it, so I pulled mine out then returned to my chair. A few seconds later panic struck as I realized that the name was mine, not Larissa's so I returned to her acting confused "is that what you need to see? I'm not sure." She pointed to the Fully Prepared for English one and said she just had to be sure that I was. Fortunately she was old, with tired eyes and easily distracted. She never noticed that the names were different. I came within seconds of being caught, but I kept my calm, let those years of drama kick in and once again managed to act my way out of what could have been a devastating situation.

So what was it that drove Larissa away from English and me away from Math? We've always been opposites and that probably plays a part here, but I think there's more to it. Larissa was always shy. She in her own mind was expected to follow in my parents footsteps. She tried for a while. In middle school she took all of the home economics classes that my mother recommended. I don't think she ever took these classes because she wanted to. I think that she followed my mother's guidance because she had seen repeatedly what happened to me when I asserted my own opinions and personality and she was never so firm in what she actually wanted to stand up for herself the way I did for myself. Somewhere along the line I think she realized she didn't enjoy what she was doing. Maybe that revelation came her junior year when my mother got her a part-time job at House of Fabrics. Larissa would have never gotten that job without my mother's coercion. She only had the job a few months. It was a Christmas temporary job, but that's not the only reason it was short-lived. For most of our lives our parents took us to their adult social events. We were trained on how to keep polite company with adults, but when it came to peers we were pretty much left to wing it. Larissa's never been good at winging anything. So here she found herself in a new situation, new environment; no friends, no family, no desire to be there and no confidence. I remember there was a college night going on at the high school so Larissa, being college bound asked for the night off. Her manager, who apparently had been jerking her around, scheduled her. It was okay. We could pick-up Larissa and go late. But then her manager wouldn't let her go until around eleven or something. I don't remember all the details. The only thing that really stuck was the fact that Larissa let two people (my mother and the manager) walk all over her. She lacked the self-respect or confidence or whatever to speak up for herself and do what she wanted. I was never going to allow myself to get into that kind of situation. And I especially was never going to allow someone to exercise that kind of control over me. I think in some ways I got more out of Larissa's experience then she did. She just retreated into herself again and eventually emerged as a mathematician. Something our mother thought she would be good at.

I think what actually occurred was that my mother recognized that Larissa had become disinterested in sewing. House of Fabrics left a bitter taste in her mouth and she didn't care if she never set foot in that place again. So, needing a new goal in life Larissa turned to math. Math was real, logical, void of opinion, confrontation or artistry. Math was also a logical next step for Larissa – moving from one parent to the next. My father is an aeronautical engineer so math provided a tangible end result, which is something she wanted. She needed something to work toward only the decision was made in part by my mother who recognized her mathematical abilities. Larissa had a goal, but it was not entirely her own and her interest in it eventually faded into the bleak desert of undesirables. She stayed with math for quite a while though. Through her first semester of college. It was in college at Cal

State Fullerton that she finally came to terms with the fact that the life she was living was not her own. To hear my sister tell it and my mother tell it are two stark contradictions. My mother felt that she had to hold Larissa's hand. That Larissa wanted her there holding her hand. Larissa felt my mother's hand as a chokehold. I think Larissa didn't know what she wanted and had she been left alone she probably wouldn't have done anything at all. She's very inert that way, but in our house Larissa knew she had to do something so there she was attending CSUF as a math major. Unlike Larissa I didn't give a shit as to what my mother told me to do about education. Mom wanted me to take sewing, just as Larissa did. I didn't want to, so I didn't. Only nerds took that class and I had no interest in the subject matter or being a nerd. The third strike against it was that Larissa had taken it and I had already had a life time of, "Your sister was such a great student" and echoes of "Oh, you're just like your sister" that I devoted my energies toward being anything but like her. Oddly, the only times I've heard anyone contrasting us it was meant in a negative way towards me. Well, those people can bite me. I'll be whoever I want to be and sisters don't have to be the same. Besides, Larissa's really screwed up. I'm proud I'm not her. She lived a façade and to me that means she never really lived at all. Why would I want to put up a front? And to all those people, is a false front really what you're looking for? If it is I want you to know that that is just sad and I take pity on your Pathetically plastic existence. Instead, I moved into a world of Journalism and wood shop. I know woodshop really pissed off my mother, but it was real. I had fun and more importantly to me some of my friends were taking it too. It was a mindless, effort-full experience. The teacher was endearing and provided a classroom for growth. Mom was proud of my choice in Journalism, which I took in both high school and middle school. I know for a fact that she never read my work in my high school paper. I'm not sure if she saw my contributions to the middle school paper or not. I realize that it may sound strange that I wouldn't show my work to my own family, but if you were me it would make sense. It wasn't that I was afraid of ridicule. That I could combat. It wasn't that I was afraid of approval. That I could ignore. Although I might have been afraid of the influence approval would show, my true fear was in letting them in. I didn't and still to a great extent don't want my parents to know who I am. The more fuel they have the more they could set me on fire. If I were a stranger they could criticize me, but they wouldn't have all the information to do so and therefore their criticism would be unfounded and easily ignored by me. There is a security to be found in living in oblivion. I couldn't let them touch my core, so I built a fortress around myself. But in building my fortress I failed to realize that they weren't the only ones I was locking out.

In high school I took the ultimate plunge by signing up for drama. My mother forbade me to do so in middle school, so this time I didn't ask I just went to it. She considered it to be a complete waste of time, but it turned out to be the best thing I ever did for myself. In drama I found a group of people who were equally screwed up as I was and in that I found tremendous comfort. Also, in drama I found something my parents knew nothing about and something my sister was too scared to do. In drama I found myself, my voice, my personality and my dreams. Because my parents and sister had no experience in this field it was mine and mine alone. They had no recommendations, no notes of influence and nothing in their personal past to compare me too. I reveled in my solitude, my strengthened sense of individuality. I finally had something that belonged to me and me alone, and I was good at it.

As Larissa turned to math I turned away from it. Not that her interest in math was the cause of my disinterest, just as untrue would be the assumption that her immobilizing fear of English is due to my interest in it. Actually, I can pretty much pin point when math started frustrating me. Mr. Jones, my third grade teacher didn't like me very much. Not only was I a girl, but I was fat. He wasn't one to promote girls in general and he was particularly unkind to me and another fat student. He treated us like fat equaled dumb and we should be hidden or made fun of, something he never disciplined other students for doing. I think my existence frustrated him. He didn't want to keep me in the top reading group because I read, like I ran, slow. The only thing was I absorbed and analyzed better than his favorites who talked at super speed. Plus, the state testing always had me in the top 5% and sometimes top 1% of all California students and just the prior year I placed as the number one speller in the whole damn state. He had to keep me in the #1 English group whether he wanted to or not. But in math, he was cruel. He kept me in the #2 group even after I accomplished the posted guidelines for getting into the #1 group. He ignored his own rules to keep me from recognition. In fact there were tests for addition, subtraction, multiplication, division and fractions in those areas. Although I placed all the way through the multiplying fractions when the school wide awards day came my highest rank of achievement was announced as at multiplication. My parents were happy for me and dismissed my complaints that I had been dissed. I wanted them to fight for me. I had accomplished more than I was recognized for and that was unfair. They didn't understand how hard I had worked or how much the recognition meant to me. Mr. Jones is a bastard. He never apologized, of course, and acted like he had no idea what I was talking about when really he just didn't want his top student to be the fat girl. He never did move me into the #1 math group, an injustice even my peers recognized and commented on. Privately.

Although Mr. Jones blew my ego and rattled my respect for teachers he did not manage to blow my self-confidence. That was left to Mr. Fong. When I was in the fifth grade the top girl and boy math students from each class were to meet with Mr. Fong at lunch time to discuss participating in the annual math field day. Every day for weeks we met during lunch to practice. He told us repeatedly that we were only as strong as our weak link, so we had to be committed to the team. I was always first at his doorstep, eager to put in my effort and come home with a trophy. I even had to give up my chair in the student senate, something I truly regret having done. I was voted in and deserved to participate. Mr. Fong wanted us math field day participants to concentrate on our objectives though. Then as an advisor he skipped out on us to be photographed with the student senate, of which I was still a member and, too, should have been in the photograph but instead I was waiting outside of his classroom just as he told me to. He, too, was a bastard. During spring break Mr. Fong wanted us to meet daily for several hours to cover as much material as possible. I had to go to Arizona, there was no way my parents would allow me at age 11 to stay at home alone just so I could study math with Mr. Fong. I felt bad about missing the study sessions and relief that I wouldn't have to see Mr.

Fong. Mr. Fong had placed me as the Mad Hatter, which was a contest of time and accuracy. I liked the idea of sole recognition, but preferred to be the anchor on the relay team. No such luck, he felt my talents could best be used as the Mad Hatter. After failing to come home with a trophy we had a group lunch. This was supposed to be a thank you for your efforts kind of deal. Thanks and praise were far from my corner. He felt that I missed things I shouldn't have. Although it was too late to go back and take the test over he felt it was necessary to insult and berate me by using examples of everything I missed or didn't understand. I fought back tears, but a few managed to escape me. My teammates could feel my pain and were glad that his attentions were not on them. They looked away as I sat in tears and never questioned or made jokes about my failure. After that I didn't care much for math at all. I just stopped trying to get it. My disinterest had nothing to do with the statistical, father-proposed boy-interest thing at all. It was a direct result of one teacher's inability to accept his own failure at teaching a bright student. I never shared my humiliation before. If I had, I might have been better equipped to deal with it and may have found words of encouragement to replace the bitter sting of insult. But I kept my pain to myself and suffered miserably for it.

My story really comes in three parts: why I quit school to begin with, my growth away from school (which leads to) and why I returned to school. The focus being how I developed the determination to get into school and embrace it with the same open mind of a young child. It seems the key to obtaining any objective rests solely on one thing: desire. I have found this to be true in every case I've come across. One must truly want for themselves. Without that kind of desire, driving passion, there is no point, nothing pushing you forward, no reason to do anything at all.

I quit school the first time primarily because I didn't belong there. I should have never received an acceptance letter. It was a computer error, which they later caught. By that time I had already registered so I called. Some faceless, nameless lady informed me politely and as gently as she possibly could that I had not met the math requirement of the university. She even recommended that I enroll at a community college and apply for spring. Instead I choose to ignore the letter and her words of advice. I attended the first two days of class. The campus was huge, so was I. I felt lost and intimidated. Other people seemed to know each other. They were all having a good time, laughing. And as I walked by I felt as though they were laughing at me. Maybe they were, but they probably weren't. I was scared, I had no one and I had already been told that I didn't belong there. I never went the second week. I would drive down to the school, sometimes hanging out at the campus or the park across the street. I had no goals, no desire. I was depressed and felt ugly. I didn't want to talk to anyone and I didn't want anyone to talk to me. My poetry writing increased and so did its dark reflections. Fortunately, I have an attitude when it comes to suicide or else I might not be here today. Suicide is a chicken shit way to die and I wasn't about to let anybody say I had a chicken shit death. I allowed my parents to believe that I was in school for a year and a half. During the third semester I think my Mom knew somewhere deep inside that I wasn't attending but she just couldn't bring herself to fully believe that because it would hurt too much. When I broke the news that I wasn't going to continue with school it hit my father rather back-handedly. He didn't understand, he thought I was happy going to school. He was often naïve to the home situation. Because Larissa had so screwed up in her educational career Mom was ultra paranoid about me. Had I really been attending it probably would have bothered me even more than it did. Knowing that her questions had a founding was a source of brief amusement when I passed another one over her eyes.

Getting a job was probably one of the scariest things I'd ever tried to do. Larissa was working for Remedy Temp and she influenced me to also sign up the summer between my "freshmen" and "sophomore" years of college. She had barely started working for them herself but if she signed me up then she would get so much money after I worked so many hours. But there wasn't too much work available for two fat girls with limited skills. They never did use me and it wasn't long before Larissa got tired of them giving her an arm full of excuses for the lack of work. I tried again with ProStaff. I lied on the application saying that Remedy Temp had used me. I was a young idiot and the person interviewing me saw that. They never had work for me and then finally they did, months later and Mom told them that I was in school. I wanted to kill her. I mean that very sincerely. I moved on and turned in an application at a clothing store in the mall just in time to be hired as Christmas help. I was actually a bit surprised by the opportunity. I had been extremely nervous before the interview and there was a thing about checking references. I had given them both ProStaff and Remedy Temp, but what could they say about me? I had never actually worked for them. Whatever they said I really don't care because I got the job. I was really quiet at first. It took some doing to get me out of my shell, but I worked hard and had an availability that any manager would love. Right before Christmas one of the permanent staffers was fired and a temp quit. I got the other temps hours and was asked to stay with the store after the holidays. It was the best Christmas present I could have received.

After having my first taste of money I wanted more. I went through a Teller Training coarse thinking I would get a job as a bank teller and keep the mall job as part-time work. I think the greatest skill I acquired at the Teller Training Academy was confidence. I was the number one student in my small class, but I worked to insure that position. After our brief, "Yeah! You made it!" it was time to job hunt. I had two job interviews. I thought the one in Montebello went well, but they never even called back to let me know how it went --- if they filled the position or what. Citibank never called back either. She took notes during the interview. Things seemed to go really well. I mean that too. This interview was way better than the one at Montebello. But my resume had an error that I didn't realize until she asked about my 1 ½ years of experience with the clothing store. I accidentally typed the wrong year and instead of catching it I let it go. Well, they usually required 2 years of experience, but since I had 1 ½ they would let it go. Of course a work reference would indicate only a half year of service. It's no wonder they never called back. But that is still something I would never do. I guess a lot of people are afraid of even minimal confrontation, but if someone gave me a good interview and I couldn't hire them for some reason I would tell them why because if I were them I would want to know. And the worst possible thing to do to a person is leave them hanging. It's stressing to go a couple of days with hope in your heart, which quickly turns to self-doubt and frustration. Then as you realize that you obviously did not get the job it is easy to slip into a depressed state. All interviewers should indicate when the decision will be made so hopefuls don't go through the cycle and even more importantly I don't care how many people had to be interviewed for a position, all should be called back and notified as to whether or not they got the job. It's simple common curtesy. You weren't the only one to take time out of your day. In fact, you didn't even have as much at stake. Be the bearer of bad news. It really won't kill you.

    I received a summons to do my time at jury duty. I was secretly hoping that I would be placed on the first case that I was seated on. It was scheduled to last six months and at least that would give me something to do. But they kicked me off. In fact, I went eight days and never got seated on a panel. Maybe I looked too young. There weren't too many young adults roaming the halls of the Superior Court – not as jurors anyway. I amused myself by listening to my headset. In fact I listened to the same album over and over. REM's Life's Rich Pageant. It somehow seemed fitting, or maybe ironic. Anyway, it made me think. I met a woman that had worked at the clothing store in Montebello. She seemed rather nice and she really made me appreciate what I had a bit better. It was during my jury service that the Rodney King riots broke out. Thank God I wasn't there that day. Tuesday they dismissed me until Friday. When Friday was still a war zone I called in and the courts were closed. The courts would be open Monday. And when Monday came, I went. It was the closest I hope I ever come to seeing the aftermath of war. It was awful. There were still tanks and national guards armed to the hilt. When I was transferred to Traffic Court that was even worse. Another girl and I spotted a Pizza Hut across the street and that sounded way better than Cafeteria food, so we ventured over. The establishment had been burned down during the riots. The sign was the only thing left. A cold, hard reminder of where we were and what we had to deal with. We ate at Burger King instead. It basically was the only thing around that was still open, so it was packed.

    It wasn't long after jury duty that I decided to go into management for the clothing store. It seemed to be a way to get guaranteed hours and a steady paycheck. It took some time, but about six weeks later I had the full time job I was looking for.

OUTLINE FOR SUBJECTS TO WRITE ABOUT – ARRANGE LATER

Not supposed to graduate
Skipped more than attended
Not allowed to send out announcements
Didn't tell them about scholarship
Sneaking out
The sophomore party
Told coach to fuck off and die
Stole YMCA van
Couldn't register myself – the RDM
First day jitters
Stressed out car tow
Second jury duty experience
School – work combination
The study group from hell
You mean you don't have a computer

JUNE

June 1, Thursday
254 ½
Larissa graduates!!!
Finish rice, green quesadilla, beans
Rusty Pelican ~ crab stuffed salmon, Long Island ice tea, garlic bread, whipped topping, coffee ice cream

June 2, Friday
256
Fast
Work 6:30-9:30 (switch from Thursday with Sophia) Wore black/cream dress
Cards, Pepsi
25 minute treadmill, .6 miles, 36 calories, ab (35)

June 3, Saturday
254
Fast – well, almost
Work 2:30-7:30
Fruit punch, 2 biscuits, Snapple Lemonade, 7 McDonald's mushy French fries
Big Shit FINALLY!
English = A!!!
Should write a book – long day at work. Larissa went to Kristi's Installation. Cards.
Ab (25)

June 4, Sunday
Work 10:30-6:30
7 licorice pieces, Casa nachos with guacamole, fruit punch

June 5, Monday
252 ½
Fast – sort of
Bite of cottage cheese, 1 powdered doughnut, Pepsi
35 minutes treadmill, 1 mile, 57 calories, ab (35)

June 6, Tuesday
250
Fast
Finished Pepsi, Lemonade, Grape
Wash windows, scrub bathroom floor, launder curtains/bed
Ab (40), 40 min. treadmill, 1 mile, 60 calories

June 7, Wednesday
249
First time to break the 250 barrier!
Grape soda
El Rey Taco :/ Mom bought!
Nachos and chips, Licorice (2 servings)
Nasty – wet – green BM + 2D

June 8, Thursday
251
Worked 9:30-12:30 with Rachel
Helped with Libby's review
Cards
Wok Express – chicken + 2 egg rolls
Sherbet, popcorn with butter
2 slices of toast with butter

June 9, Friday
253 ¾
8:30-10:30 work (set-up for party)
Good all day
Slight fever
HIVES or MEASLES! Mom thinks it's a reaction to eating a LOT of real licorice on an empty stomach

Finished E's review
Then… after work, Porter's salad with bleu cheese dressing, small bread, finish noodles

June 10, Saturday
253 ½
WORK WORK WORK
Sunflower Party Picnic
El Rey Taco nachos with chips, rice, Ice cream (praline and cream)
Cards

June 11, Sunday
255 ½
Work 10-3
Finished nachos, green quesadilla, cheese popcorn, chicken, rice-a-roni, more ice cream
Cards

June 12, Monday
257 ¾
Open Registration.
Almost made it, but NO! Stew, 3 biscuits & Cheez Its
Car got and still needs oil – rinse down
Letty called for me to cover her Wednesday shift

    I think I've discovered over the past few days that during my "down" time I really need to maintain my food diary. The last several days have been fairly disastrous diet wise. I was doing okay. Knew I would have lunch the day of Larissa's graduation, but thought I would fast after that. After all I did buy (or rather Mom bought) some clothes that only sort of fit that day. So starting on the 2nd I was to be in Fast City. Well I lasted until Sunday. Knowing I had to work all day I ate 1 serving of the See's licorice Mom gave me, but planned to eat nothing else. Ended up eating Casa nachos. That's what happens when you have to work through a whole day on your feet. Things were cool Monday and Tuesday, even thought I'd make it Wednesday but spent too much time in the family room and gave Mom the opportunity to offer El Rey Taco. I love El Rey Taco. Why do I love food? And hell she was going to pay, so yeah I'll go. On the way out the door I farted.

Hadn't had one of those for a while. It was wet. Went to the bathroom. Nothing to come out. It was all over my leggings and my butt. Worse of all it was violent green. After eating nachos with chips went diarrhea twice and yes it was still an awful green. Then later that day ate 2 servings of licorice. Come to find out the spots that are appearing all over my body are not flea bites but probably hives – an allergic reaction to the strong licorice oil from this high quality product hitting an empty stomach. I wonder if it caused the green burst. Thursday was a bad day. By my own instigation went to Wok Express. I didn't want to have any more meat for the month, but there I was. I could hit myself. Also had 2 egg rolls. Then Friday made it all day. Went to work. Didn't get home until 11:40. Saw a piece of Porter's garlic bread on the counter. Had been offered salad before going to work. Mom and Dad were in bed. They left the bread out on the kitchen counter to dry out so I ate it. Then it was like I already had the bread so why not have the salad. Larissa came home and had salad then I decided what the hell might as well finish my Wok Express noodles and rice. After all I did pay for them and I have so little money I should get the most out of my dollars. Why offer it away? So anyway I go to work Saturday and it's the big sunflower party. I looked too cute! Had dreams of El Rey Taco nachos and figuring I had already pretty much blown the week I thought I might as well dig in then start clean on Sunday. I am such a pig that I decided to get rice and a quesadilla for later. Took a nap after eating the nachos. Mom gave me a hard time about the smell -- did I have anything to offer -- they have no money to go to Mimi's after the theater -- blah, blah, blah. Larissa went to the grocery. Ate the rice and had a little cheese popcorn and a large bowl of pralines and cream ice cream. What a cow I am, force feeding myself. Went to bed swearing that no matter what I wouldn't eat Sunday. I'd start fasting again. Even though I had El Rey Taco in the fridge. It was going to be a test. Started the day great. Skipped Jack In The Box, skipped the fries that were calling when I got Susan and I Icee's. But then I went home to an empty house. I crumpled, ate the remaining nachos which was virtually nothing and the green quesadilla. Unfortunately I also had three small bowls of cheese popcorn. Took an extended nap. When I got up Larissa and I had Rice-A-Roni. I ate most of it. Then had pralines and cream again. No wonder my weight jumped. I'm such a cow! Mom said one way to make sure the licorice caused the hives is to starve a couple days then eat it again and see what happens. That I can do. Today is going okay. Apparently Mom forgot about the licorice test though. She had an eye appointment. It went bad. She came over to my room whimpering and said she was going to go to El Rey Taco before coming home, but was too depressed. She later asked me what I was doing for lunch -- if anything? I told her I wasn't doing lunch. I'll bet I could have gotten an El Rey Taco run out of her but I need to save those for after I can fit into the short-alls and black dress she just bought me. I'll bet she plans on seeing those on my body sometime soon. They probably won't fit until 235, maybe 240. The only thing I'm eating between the 257 ¾ I was this morning and 240 is that damn licorice. And that is final!

Later… Boy, that final didn't last very long. I was fine until El Rey Taco was mentioned again. Larissa was going to go, but then Mom decided Oops! 7 p.m. is too late for El Rey Taco. Beef stew instead. I was fine, even happy with the change because stew doesn't usually get me. But then I sat out in the family room with her. Big mistake! The vegetables seemed like a good idea so I had some stew and took the biscuits out of the freezer. At least they are gone now. Then I had a small bowl of Cheez Itz. That was two hours ago and I feel nauseous. I think I would be willing to do El Rey Taco tomorrow, but that's it. School starts Wednesday, June 21st so the fast starts Wednesday no matter what. It would be nice if it would start tomorrow. I need soda. I feel like puking. That might make me feel better, if I could, I don't need to eat. I don't deserve to eat. Mom can buy me El Rey Taco when I'm thin, when I need substance. Tomorrow is a new day. A day to start over. A day to be stronger, firmer, more me. No El Rey Taco -- no temptation. I can do this again! Another 50 -- here we go!

June 13, Tuesday
255 ¼
Work 9:30-1 p.m.
Somebody left go backs from Monday.
Mom hit El Rey Taco without me

Sav-on, El Rey Taco nachos, green quesadilla, Cheez Its, Pepsi
Change registration – add Astronomy, drop STAT/ENG 3
Cards
Karen called, we'll talk tomorrow

June 14, Wednesday
256 ¼
Fast, did drink Pepsi though
Made day 1 – Thank God
Work 6-9:30 covering for Letty; Stayed until 9:45 at least

June 15, Thursday
254 ½
Work scheduled 9:30-1:30, but worked until 3:30
Mom and Dad left for Solvang
Larissa picked up Wok Express – Chicken + 2 egg rolls
Angel food cake, finished the Pepsi
Cards

Paramount Pictures announced that they lost money on Forrest Gump with 61 million at the domestic box office? Yeah right. They need a new intern -- like me. Tuesday turned out worse than it should have been. Wild Girls Club – Anka. Back to Tuesday. After Monday's suggestion of El Rey Taco from Mom, I thought she might go for it on Tuesday. I was okay with this. Start fasting Wednesday one week before school starts. But I had to work Tuesday and when I came home she had already gone to El Rey Taco and didn't get me anything. Larissa and I ended up going after Sav-On's. Mom was supposed to pay though, damn it. Then I find out the Monday before it was suddenly too late to go, Mom wondered if she had enough money and Larissa told her how much nachos were. Apparently Mom didn't realize how expensive they are. Way to blow it for me Larissa. Made it through Wednesday without a hitch. But then Thursday I was originally supposed to work until 1:30 only Stephanie was supposed to ask me to stay until 3:30 but didn't. So Rachel and I agreed to play mean. Mom and Dad going to Solvang helped. When Stephanie mentioned my staying I said that we were doing Father's Day lunch because they would be gone Sunday. I was good. Laying it on thick, but realistically thick. Then Larissa calls. I faked it like she just came back from lunch. She wanted me to pick-up Wok Express. I had no money and hoped she would say never mind. Instead, she offered to go. I felt like I didn't really have a choice. I didn't really want to say something about it in front of Stephanie so I had to just sort of go along, which sucked. I also then had a slice of angel food cake. It felt like a good movie/popcorn day. Never did either one though. Played cards until 2:20 a.m. Should have been an easy day to starve. Didn't even eat the Twinkie and had to put up with Larissa sucking chocolate in front of me. Actually, her eating it doesn't bother me so much as smelling it on her breath. Man, now I've eaten meat three times this month. I planned to go totally meatless. Oh well, that worked real well. So far today has been cool. Larissa finished my Wok Express – which I offered and now it's almost 8. I won't see her for two hours and by that time no one should be eating anything so I think I'm cool. Tomorrow shouldn't be so bad either. Larissa works from 12-8 and I have the house to myself. I always do better when mine are the only demons to fight with. The weather reminds me of my dreary December/January when I first plunged into total starvation. Not that I believe in signs but hopefully this means, or is somehow a personal indicator that I am or can do it again. I wanted to start summer school at 240 – that may be a stretch considering we start next Wednesday. And then I wanted to be roughly 200 by the time I'm going to USC. That would be really nice. It will also mean having a lot of inner strength and endurance – to pull the determination out and ignore interference.

June 16, Friday
256 ¼
Fast (for the most part)
Slept in late, cards
Started reading On The Road
7 Cheetos, Pepsi

June 17, Saturday
251 ¾
Fast, sort of
12 Cheez Its, 3 licorice, Pepsi
Mom and Dad came home about 8:30 p.m.

June 18, Sunday
250
21 licorice, Minimal popcorn
Braveheart with Dad and Larissa (for Father's Day)
KFC – 1 Chicken, mashed potatoes, biscuit, watermelon
10 Cheetos
1 Ex-lax

June 19, Monday
250
Fast, Pepsi
Cleaned bathroom, laundry, Crossword puzzles
Diarrhea day – several times
Ab 40 (25 r 15 k)

Made it through the 16th and 17th eating only 10 Cheetos and 12 Cheez Its. Pretty damn good if you ask me. Larissa working most of the time, Mom and Dad in Solvang and not having anything that is grossly tempting around helped a lot. Since Mom and Dad came back on Saturday that meant a Father's Day spent together. I ate 2 servings of the licorice. Let's see if I break out in hives. I sort of hope I do just so I know that's what it was. Took Dad to see Braveheart. It was good. Had very little popcorn and a gulp of Sprite. Then Porter's was closed so we ended up getting KFC. I had one piece white meat – extra crispy. Mashed potatoes with gravy and one biscuit. We played cards then had watermelon. KFC chicken really grosses me out. Or maybe eating meat is grossing me out more. A little more each time I do it. The veins and mush, oh it's disgusting. Going to bed I asked Larissa for a handful of Cheetos. The ½ biscuit I noticed earlier was gone and I wanted something breadish to go behind an Ex-Lax. Those things taste nasty. I want to move this crap out. I haven't shit the last two days – I don't think. And I don't want to climb the scale fully loaded. I took several dumps today. Most of which were diarrhea, but at least it isn't around now. I hope it didn't screw up the licorice experiment. I don't think it would and I am already getting major itches all over so I bet I'll be breaking out soon. Oh man I'll be really miserable!

June 20, Tuesday
248
Fast
Pepsi
Oil in car, read
Debate over, English 3
Ab 45 (30r 15k)

June 21, Wednesday
Fast
Summer School starts – Attended Astronomy – Oh my god!
Pepsi pt. melon berry cocktail
Gray leggings/sweatshirt
Work 5:30-9:30
Ab 60 (35r 25k)

June 22, Thursday
245 ½ (after school)
Fast
Jean shorts, taupe/cream tee
10 baked Tositos, 3 with salsa
Ab 55 (35r 20k)

June 23, Friday
244 ¼
Fast for the most part
5 Baked Tositos, about 15 more plus salsa
Mom moans over loan application
Work 6:30-9:30

June 24, Saturday
244 ¼
Mom "found" me a USC friend majoring in Film Production
Blueberry Muffin 8 oz. and Lowfat Milk before work
Nausea, fever
Work 3:30-7:30
El Rey Taco nachos, olives

June 25, Sunday
247
Work 2-6:30

3 Midori Sour's, ¼ Rachel's chicken quesadilla, chicken wing, nachos, artichoke dip
Maggie's Pub for meeting at 7 pm
Potato skins, Slice of boysenberry pie

June 26, Monday
249 ¾
School
Blue rayon pants, multi-color top
Didn't make it - Wok Express + boysenberry pie with vanilla ice cream
4 shits – explains the headache

June 27, Tuesday
251
Finish Wok Express noodles
Moved couches and front door
Spent 1.5 hours in library
Jean shorts, cat eye cardigan

     Made it to Thursday without eating anything then I had a few chips and maybe a spoonful of salsa. Nothing major. Friday I had about 20 chips with salsa. Then Saturday I decided since Sunday I'd be doing the Maggie's Pub thing with the people at work I had better eat something or else it could be scary bathroom runs. Saturday I worked so I decided to have a blueberry muffin and glass of lowfat milk early so toilet calls would occur at home. It didn't settle very well. I had some toilet calls here. Got to work. Felt on and off nausea and fever. Ended up in a gut roar. Had a diarrhea experience. Before that I hadn't planned on food until the Pub, but then realized I could be setting myself up. Came home from Sav-On. Almost went to El Rey Taco, but decided not to because I didn't want to pay. Ended up going with Larissa. Damn I hate paying for food. Never again! Sunday I ate some rice before work. At the Elephant Bar I had 3 Midori Sours and some of Rachel's drink. We all shared nachos, chicken quesadilla, chicken wings, potato skins and artichoke heart dip stuff. I ODed. Alice dropped me off. Mom had given me money for the day, but Alice ended up footing the whole bill. She is quite a generous lady. Monday is what really pissed me off. Larissa said she was going to Wok Express, asked me if I wanted anything. I didn't have to get anything if I didn't want to. I said no. Then she didn't leave. I buckled. Later Larissa said she was surprised I called her back to my room. She didn't expect me to get anything. It was evil triumphing over good and she was mocking me. I really wanted to hurt her. But there's only one way I can do that. Then today she had the nerve to call me baggy britches. Then she said it was a compliment when she called me tight buns. I weighed in at a hefty 251 this morning. How dare she call me any of those things? I'm fat – so fat it's disgusting. Larissa got her graduation pictures back. I'm a cow. Yeah, so I lost 60 pounds, but the picture sure doesn't show it. I still look enormous – sub-human. I'm a fucking whale and she's calling me tight buns. I could throw up. I finished my Wok Express. There is no way I'm paying for it and letting that bitch finish it for me again but I need to reaffirm myself. No eating! NONE! ZELCH! NOTHING! I just don't need it. My short-alls still don't fit quite right and I should be wearing them soon. Plus, I really don't want to be waddling around the USC campus. Went to school tonight. Didn't see Shawn. Maybe he's not in History 8AH. Oh well. I know I will be seeing him again. Tonight would have been good though since I had a legit reason for being there. Mom flea sprayed getting ready for a planning meeting. I'm just going to have to stay away from Larissa and those cruel food temptations.

June 28, Wednesday
251 ¼
Fast
Khaki rayon pants, fall leaf blouse
Saw him and choked, Mom's planning meeting
Jessica scheduled to visit, but ended up skipping our store
Work 5-9:30

June 29, Thursday
250
Fast
Blue sundress, curly hair
Did some Jack reading
Short day for Astronomy, out at 11:45
Took Donna home

June 30, Friday
247 ¼
On-call 11-6. Didn't go in, Christina's okay!
Fritos, Pepsi, tuna twelve inch sandwich from Subway
Handful of celery sticks
Played cards

JULY

July 1, Saturday
247
½ cup lowfat milk, 4 powdered donut gems
3 bites of cottage cheese, 2 slices of Wonder Bread with oleo,
Mozzarella sticks, lemon cake sample, Chips, salsa
Work 4:30-7:30
20 minutes bike, 4.5 miles
Ab 30 + 10
25 chin

  I guess my pukey mood really started on Tuesday. I was ready to put all the blame on Wednesday, but now I think that would be unfair. Actually maybe it really started Monday. It really bothered me that Larissa offered me Wok Express. It shouldn't have. She was just being polite, I guess. It's just that when it comes to food in this household it's used as a weapon. There is so much jealousy and game playing that I felt like Larissa was taunting me and tragically she won. Later when she said she was surprised that I decided to join in she seemed almost smug. Like she knew she had knocked me. What made this even more difficult to bear was how I had decided that Monday would be an easy day to return to fasting. I enjoyed myself Sunday – drank, even ate some chicken and here I go. A day to avoid food and not only do I eat, but I eat meat. Then Tuesday the remains were a reminder of the day before and just what would I do with them? Went to school and when I returned Mom was into some heavy duty cleaning. I asked if she was inspired and she shot back with "We're only expecting

40 people here tomorrow." She's the woman in charge and with a planning meeting scheduled it was time for everyone to inspect her (and her daughters) puke! Well, I was still in a cravits mood. Wok Express sat like a bowling ball in my stomach and I wanted it out. Mom and Larissa were moving the couch out to the garage. Mom was in one of those I need help and I just want you to do it kind of moods. Really stressed out. Larissa called me baggy britches. I was wearing my denim shorts. It really pissed me off, especially because of the day before and the noodles and rice that waited in the fridge. She had a lot of nerve. What mixed signals! Then she called me tight buns. I kicked her twice. It made me feel a little better. I didn't want to see either one of them so I stayed in my room. Then the couch thing turned into a three person project. The front door had to come off its hinges. That wasn't exactly fun. Putting it back was even a bigger bitch though. We all got bruises from the ordeal. Mom then said she would be flea spraying. That stuff makes me nauseous so I took it as an excuse to go to the library. I thought Shawn said he would be taking 8AH, but I never saw him. That's not to say he didn't go in though. I really didn't want to be there for the first class meeting, but it just worked out that way. Actually, now I'm glad that I did. Went home and could still faintly smell the flea spray. I gave in to the noodles and rice. King of "figured I might as well – otherwise they'd just sit there upsetting me" or I'd give it away and do I really want to pay for someone else in this fat family to eat – NO! So I ate the goddamn noodles. Having gone to the library and studying astronomy really made me kind of cranky and irritable so I went to bed early and planned to get up early, shower and head off to school. Naturally, when the alarm went off though I wasn't quite ready to face the day. Not having shit was starting to bother me because I had a double dose of the Wok Express and Sunday's events. Eventually, I felt my hair. I couldn't remember having showered the night before and that got me up. The, oh my god look at the time and I need a shower. I just didn't want to. Hell, I didn't want to get dressed. I ended up throwing on my cream/khaki/brown leaf blouse with my big baggy khaki rayon pants and my brown loafers. I barely even did my makeup then put on Different Rose lipstick which could be kind of much considering. Then I put on those big almost leaf looking

earrings. At first I thought I looked pretty good, but in retrospect I feel terrible about how I looked. My day was okay. Not really all that bad or all that good but when I arrived at school it simply plummeted. Walking up to the corner to cross the street I approached a girl, she looked at me. She kind of gave me a strange look I guess. She wasn't really attractive. Anyway, the light changed. There were a lot of people coming at us. I prided myself in swerving to the outside to avoid the crowd. I think she rumbled through people. Then after I passed the bulk of them I noticed a guy and a girl stopped at the corner. It was Geo Boy/baseball cap and some young blond. They're probably the same age. She was several inches shorter than him. He wasn't wearing his baseball cap. I panicked. I wasn't prepared. I didn't know what to do. Should I say hi? Should I smile? Will he acknowledge my presence? Would I be embarrassing him? Did he have a thing for this girl? My mind was racing and my confidence was lost. I walked face forward, never giving him a chance. I did note that he was in the middle of asking her a question. I could tell by the tone and it had something to do with parents – or at least I heard that word. I wondered if he looked at me. I wondered if he snubbed me like I snubbed him. I am almost for certain that he noticed me. How could he not? I'm a huge thing coming right at him. I know he would have to remember me because ya know, I'm so damn memorable in the worst possible way. He now probably thinks I'm crazy (I had a feeling) and a royal bitch. I mean, he was a nice kid. It was rude not to smile. That could have gone totally unnoticed by the girl. I was afraid that he wouldn't want to remember me and I didn't want to have to deal with that, so I never even gave him or myself a chance. I noticed he had started knocking his backpack back and forth so I think he was nervous – but nervous why – nervous how? Nervous he would have to endure another encounter. Nervous that he might have to explain how he knows me. Nervous of what Miss Cutie would think of him knowing me. Or just nervous about talking to this girl. I think he was nervous about me. He was probably worried about what I would do. Anyway that brief – few seconds – almost encounter really brought me down. How could I be so insecure? And why should I invest so much into what other people think? Why would I be so rude? What could make me abandon my normal perkiness? Is it that I'm just so used to people ignoring me? Looking away, pretending they don't know me that I just didn't want to face that kind of rejection again. Those few seconds were eating away at me all through Astronomy. It's all I thought about. When I got home I was nearly in a state of depression. In fact, a state of depression might have been an upliftment from where I was. I had to work Wednesday night too and as if that weren't enough we were expecting a visit from Jessica which meant I needed to look cute and perky and be ready with answers to anything and sell, sell, sell. Me – I didn't want to do anything. I wanted to curl up in my bed and die. I didn't want to do my make-up. I didn't want to look cute. I felt ugly and wanted to look just as ugly as I felt, but duty called. Hell, I even put the Hot Rods in my hair. I was turning on the charm as best I could. Then it turns out we had no visit. It was canceled last Friday. Supposedly Allison told "the girls." Now this is pretty pertinent info. I think Stephanie and Susan would remember, so we bitched about how Allison is a bitch and just doesn't remember what she says to whom. Jewel, Alice and Rachel were going to see Pocahontas and Rachel gave me permission to get someone to finish my shift so that I could go with them, but Amanda and Isabella both didn't have transportation, Becky wasn't home, and I just couldn't bring myself to stick Susan with Donna. Susan even said that it would be okay. I guess she really had a sense for how much I just didn't want to be there. But I thought calling Amanda in was cruel enough. There was no way I would call Donna. Susan would say it's okay, but deep down she would really kind of hate me for it... and I wouldn't be able to blame her. So I stuck it out at work, which ended up probably being a healthier choice. I opened up to Susan and it helped. Going to the movie would have been an escape. It probably was yet another tiny maturity step – dealing with myself and my feelings – doing what I have to being there for my job. Besides I really need the money.

July 2, Sunday
J. Paul Getty Museum with Mom and Dad, Garden Tea Room
Tuna stuffed avocado salad with ranch dressing, Pepsi, carrot cake and some lemon quiches???
20 minutes bike, 4.75 miles

Ab 30 + 15
25 chin

July 3, Monday
Apollo 13 for Dad's Birthday
Cream short set
Frosted Flakes, toast with butter, popcorn, Pepsi
Potato salad, quiche, chips, salsa/cottage cheese, pickles

    I think in my last entry I was discussing that I was glad that I stayed at work last Wednesday. I should really explain why. Susan is a large girl. We are probably roughly the same, although I may have twenty pounds on her. Anyway, apparently she used to be skinny. I remember her mentioning that she had lost a lot of weight using these all natural pills and when she stopped taking them she bounced back. Now she's taking them again. They supposedly increase your metabolism while suppressing your appetite. But, to me, there's a real problem if you turn around and gain it all back. If that's the case why put yourself through the hell. Anyway, I told her how Mom was having people over and how I hoped that they would be gone by the time I got home. At first she was curious about how they were friends, but she caught on to the fact that these were people I just didn't want to see. Recently, I think she said her aunt came over with her daughters. Maybe it wasn't her aunt. And the woman yelled, "Oh Fatso! Look at how you've" whatever. Basically she called her a fat cow and well, Susan is kind of like Larissa when it comes to sensitivity. Apparently this woman had always told her daughters how pretty she was, what a good body she had and they should be like her. Now she was yelling in Spanish – "What happened to you?" I'll bet Susan doesn't like any of the attention, good or bad. Susan had been a cheerleader which kind of surprised me just because of her personality, but it does explain why she likes these particular skirts so much. She really likes them short too. Anyway, the lady so bothered her she locked herself (or wanted to?) in her room. She didn't want to come out. And it was like, okay tomorrow I go right back on that diet. Which is too bad because we should never go on a diet, let alone go on one just because some bitch calls us a fatso. My heart went out to her. I can see why Richard Simmons has devoted his life to helping the obese. Point being, she admitted how she doesn't like seeing all of those people that knew her when she was thin. Because even though they may not say what this lady did it's on their faces. I understood. I've never been thin, but my weight has gone up and down and I've seen that look. The words hurt, but the looks kill. Her confessions made me more comfortable in sharing what was really bothering me. The whole crossing the street thing. She understood and that made me feel a little better. At least I wasn't alone. I'm not any happier about where I am, but at least I have good company. She thinks she probably would have done the same thing I did. She seemed to think it would have been worse if he had been with a guy, but I don't. I think if it had been a guy or if he had been alone I would have greeted him. Then we both agreed if the girl was ugly or fat I would have said hi, but she wasn't. She was cute and it killed me. We both recognized the change in our behavior, the lack of confidence. I didn't act like myself. I didn't act the way I want to, the way I think I should. I felt awkward and uncomfortable and responded accordingly. I don't like that. I never want to have that feeling again. It was awful. To tell Susan about the street encounter I had to tell her about the day of our final and how sticking around afterward was more aggressive than I would normally be, but how I didn't want to regret anything. It really did take some guts. But he was completely clueless. It amazes me how smart people can be without noticing the people or things around them. He's not the only one. Hell, if everyone remembered people like I do I wouldn't have a diploma right now, so I guess I should be happy people like him and Larissa exist. Anyway, I admitted something I never anticipated hearing myself verbalize. I confessed that he made me nervous. Of course, I only admitted to this in the context that he didn't know what I was talking about and that threw me. I had been so sure of myself and he blew it all away. He was polite, but the conversation drug and he eventually said, "Yeah, well, gotta go." I felt stupid. I stopped some poor guy going merrily on his way – for what? Just to make a blooming fool of myself. Yeah, he had a History & Anthropology final the next day, but basically I absorbed more of his time than he wanted. I was really down on myself about it and I'm thankful that I saw Arnold afterward because talking to him about USC and school in general made me feel a little better, but I still felt like an awkward idiot. I want to go back and say hi. I snubbed him and that was mean. Maybe he snubbed me too. But if that was the case at least I would be the better person, but as it is I just don't know. Now he probably thinks not only am I crazy, but I'm a crazy bitch. Susan thought that was pretty funny. She told me not to worry about it. How can I not worry about it though? It's not so much about him. It's about me. I let myself down. I didn't respond to a situation the way I would like to think that I would. And that really bothers me. Why do I care what he or anyone thinks? I should just be me period. Why impress anyone other than myself?

July 4, Tuesday
No School! (Obviously)
Work 10:30-6:30 (time and a half – yes!)
Frosted Flakes, Pepsi, taco, 2 beef meximelts, combo burrito, hot dog with bun, popcorn with butter

July 5, Wednesday
Study? Nope.
Pepsi, slice of toast, Stouffer's Pizza with extra pepperoni and shredded cheese, watermelon
Jean blouse, jeans
Received Counselor approvals to take English 48H
H = Honors (even in college we differentiate?)
Con-current enrollment – need registration card

  Had to work from open to close yesterday then Rachel invited me to participate in the Disney, corn dog, fireworks experience with Jewel and Daniel, but I declined. Mom and Dad said they did leftover spaghetti for dinner which sounded just awful to me, but after Taco Bell for lunch I really didn't want to go out and spend major money to bring food in. Also didn't want to spend major money to eat and then see oh, wow, fireworks. Like that's a thrill. Plus, I was kind of tired, so I nipped that idea. Rachel's at the beach today with Jacob and Stephanie is being fired. She came to work late on Father's Day, bought cigarettes in the only 5 minutes they had to go to the bank and then sent Amanda to the bank by herself with $1100 in cash. Like that was really smart putting trust in the ultra-gimpy woman. She could have simply disappeared and Stephanie would have been responsible. Then on top of that she tried to cover it up. She signed in at 10:30 and acted like everything clicked like clockwork. Apparently Amanda gave Rachel an inkling that something was going on. Then Monday Rachel spent most of the day in the office buried in paperwork and noticed when Stephanie opened her entry time was usually late. Rachel called Amanda and said she knew something was up and it would be better to let her know everything. At first Amanda kind of tried to skirt the issue, but eventually let it all out. Supposedly Donna, who also worked that day, doesn't know what's going on. We don't know whether or not to believe that. It doesn't seem likely. Then Rachel gave Stephanie the opportunity to come clean and her response was, "Well, I think I know what your talking about, but why don't you tell me what you know first." When I related this to Mon and Dad, Mom cringed and spiked her neck. Sounds like something Calliope would say. Dad agreed. What jerks. Then I got the, "oh, not lately, but there was a time." Yeah, I guess there was and you know they still don't know all the shit because like Stephanie I never fessed up. I let them bust me and I never felt that I was skirting my responsibility for my actions. I just didn't think my actions were necessarily any of their business. When Stephanie realized she was caught she tried to shift the blame to Rachel saying Rachel is simply too hard to deal with. Since when? Rachel and I agreed "when did this become about me, this is about you" which is something Stephanie just wanted to avoid. Stephanie then wanted Rachel to lie and cover for her and promised that she in turn would cover for Rachel. Only Rachel doesn't have anything she needs to be covered for, but even if she did Stephanie doesn't exactly have any integrity left so why on earth would anyone trust her with anything. Then Stephanie proceeded to whine that they can't fire her because she needs her job, her Mom just had a second stroke. You know, if she knows she really needs this job then she really shouldn't be so massively screwing up on such simple tasks. It had been a long time since Stephanie had a job. For someone that needed something as desperately as she did she sure did a lot to screw herself out of it. And like, two minutes after she was promoted to management. She's a cookie. She spent time in a mental hospital. She's a felon for having carried a gun through an airport radar machine. She said she used to carry because she also used a lot of cash. She used to hang with truckers and bikers. Had an affair with a married man. On Prozac and her parents are her legal guardians. She's 41 and lies to her parents about seeing our security guard George whose 29. At our evening out, her cousin's attendance was probably mandatory by her parents. Oh, and now Stephanie is trying to say that Rachel made everyone go out and drink. Isabella didn't drink and if she asked me not to I probably would have acquired my own table. Then Alice paid, like that was bad. Stephanie told Rachel how no one paid her back for the plant that "we" gave to Rachel after her return from Cerritos/vacation. Hell, Rachel got a "hey" out of me and that was plenty. But why would you say that to the person you gave it to, especially when you presented it like it was just from you to begin with. Anyway, a thank you card was bought for Alice and I guess we might be pitching in to help pay for our fun night. Bottom line, Stephanie got caught doing wrong then lost her shit all over Rachel and now all these crazy things she's been sharing all along sound a bit more scary than they used to.

      Donna hasn't had much work lately because Stephanie and Susan both have commented about her lack of professionalism and about how she doesn't accomplish anything. Susan confronted the situation but Stephanie has not. Stephanie has allowed Donna to believe she was not getting any hours because we had none to give. Then Saturday Donna noticed how we recently hired Susan to which she responded, "Oh, now I'm pissed." Stephanie had the opportunity to address her issues with Donna to Donna, but didn't take it. Now Donna wants to talk to Rachel so I told Rachel that I doubt Stephanie has confronted Donna the way she has made it sound like she did to you. That didn't make Rachel happy, but really I doubt Stephanie ever said anything to Donna. They are just too buddy-buddy. I told Rachel about the whole road trip idea. She wants to go. She thinks I should go for it now because if I wait when will I have the opportunity again. And she's right. She named a few places to stop. She told me I have to stop and see her Aunt Maye. That I could write a whole book on her alone. She didn't know we owned property in North Carolina. She agreed that I would appreciate it more now if I made the journey for myself, preferably by myself. I told her about Larissa wanting to know how I know what I know, how I got into philosophy and how she wants to read/discuss philosophy along the way. We laughed about how other people want to pick at our brains. We don't want to be picked over, analyzed, because then you may find answers we don't want you to have. We want to know what you know and know what we know and really don't care to be questioned about that knowledge. I told her about school starting and the concert (Live) I wanted to go to but even I know that living life is better than being a spectator at a concert, for which I don't even have tickets yet. She didn't know about our land, or homes. She said she would have to keep it in mind for a vacation. I'm not sure I want to travel with Larissa. I probably won't hate her as one of her customers suggested. It's just that she doesn't have too much to offer me. I want to travel with someone that has something – like Rachel or Amanda – to talk about. Rachel thinks I should just do it and worry about the money later. (I have a gas card.) I think I'm going to do it. Three days to Dallas. I'm going to do it. New Orleans, Macon, Miami, West Palm Beach. New York and everything I can hit in between. Southern soul food, Texas chili. I'm going to experience it so I can write it. And that is what it's all about. A lot of order so we can have a little disorder. Better buy a journal for it.

About having her brain picked over, Rachel and Daniel had an argument last night. They've been arguing a lot lately. I've noticed that I've picked up their joy for all things free. Rachel says her mother-in-law has more money than she knows what to do with but ripped off a ham because the grocer wanted to charge too much for it. And she wanted ham. Somehow, and this is probably a negative thing to admit to, I could see the in-laws point of view. But then again I guess I've done some pretty questionable things. Not the point. The argument was about control. Daniel likes to order, do it his way. Rachel likes to be sweet talked. Make her think it's her idea to change, but instead he bullies and she punches back. Just like me. Daniel taped the argument to prove how wrong she was. He'll play it back for her tonight. He doesn't realize that even if she does decide that she was wrong he has pushed her to the point that she will never admit to it. It's not a sign of weakness to say you're sorry or to forgive. She really loves him. He complains about hating his life and hating being with her and she's dumb. He could do things so much better. She believes him and loves him so much she's willing to let him go if that is how he will find happiness. Basically he blames her for his life. He says he could do, but he doesn't do and I know all too well that difference. Sometimes we see how things can be done better, but when we get in there to do it ourselves the hard work of it all overwhelms us and just... We might do it differently, but not necessarily better. We are not always as good as our mind leads us to believe. He may think he can do things super good, but then he needs to do it. He has to get out there and prove it because no one will believe him until he does. That too, I know from my own experience. I have to figure out what is going on with my summer. I have to get my orientation thing going. I should go visit my campus. That first day at Long Beach was nauseating because I didn't know what was going on. I need to get as comfortable as possible. I would really like to register before I take off for the East Coast because I won't really want too much stress after I come back from my de-stress vacation. I also have to register for LBCC which means talking to my counselor and knowing a little something about the honors thing and what will fulfill my requirements. Rachel let me know how my high standards of buttoning and zipping, checking each piece influenced her. I had an impact. Our first night closing together she noticed. She had never seen anyone do it before and she's done it my way ever since. I never knew that she picked that up from me. That was really cool for her to say. It really kind of made my day.

July 6, Thursday
Study before class, drowsy in class
Pepsi, El Rey Taco nachos
Shopping with Mom: glasses, dictionary, music
Jean shorts with white tee, blue/green plaid shirt
Cards, chores, read
Amanda called and we talked for 3 ½ hours

July 7, Friday
10:02 called into work ☹
Stephanie fired today
Worked 12-4

Rice-A-Roni broccoli and cheese
Turkey sandwich, toast, popcorn, butter
Read

July 8, Saturday
250 ¾
Work scheduled 12-4, but stayed until 7:45 = 7.5 hour day
Nachos with beef, Pepsi, cheese popcorn
Cards – avoiding Astronomy

     Mom's new saying is "am I the only one on this planet?" I hope it dies before it becomes annoying. It makes for a great title though. It's just that she has a way of abusing a once, twice, sometimes three times funny saying. She beats them to oblivion. The "on the jazz", "I'm so excited" and "BTSOMs" become weary. Mom shared some amusing tidbits about the wedding they went to. Larissa, I guess, spent some time realistically thinking about the road trip and the expense involved and I think is pretty much deciding against. I wonder if money is her only reason. She may be concerned about my lack of desire at stopping at motels and maybe she, like me, realizes we are different and are looking at this differently. I'm looking for an adventure. I want some experience and she's looking for vacation, see some relatives. Quite frankly I could care less if I see relative number one. I just really need to step away from my life. Rachel noticed my breaking out. Over cards even Mom looked at my face and said you are nervous. And she's right. I'm a bundle of stress, strain, nerves, pressures. It is a constant state of fear and exhilaration. If you've ever had to go on stage and perform there is a certain state, a rush of adrenaline, a tension of muscles, a mind race I've been in this stage for several months now and it's been taking its toll. Mom thinks by the time I graduate I probably be 125 pounds. Which graduation?

July 9, Sunday
251
Fast
Worked on Astronomy
6:30-10:30 priority pack at work
30 minutes bike, 7.5 miles
35 reg Ab, 15 knee, 40 chin ups

Oh man, I just took a dump. I needed to but man my gut she is a moaning. I keep telling myself that I'm going to go back to fasting. That went really well this week. Really it hasn't been going very well since the Elephant Bar trip, then that Wok Express thing, but seeing that guy put me back on track only with Dad's birthday coming and going to the museum I knew I had to eat something there and not wanting to have any problems while I was out I decided to eat on the 30th and first. The museum trip was nice. Pretty sure Billy Zane was another museum visitor. He was holding hands with a simple, attractive woman. It looked like he had a buzz cut hiding under a baseball cap. Naturally food was pretty hard to avoid on Dad's birthday, but actually I probably could have gone without. I could have skipped the popcorn at the movie. Afterward the family had hot dogs, which I didn't. I ate potato salad, then munchies. Then the Fourth, I worked all day with Rachel. She wanted to do a Taco Bell run so I figured okay. I'll even eat beef and then go back to fasting on Wednesday. That sounded like a deal. I even went to school, saw a counselor afterwards then I came home. Should have been free and clear. Larissa was going to the grocery. I wanted something, despite myself. We did pizza with extra pepperoni and cheese. Mom joined in too. Then I told myself Thursday would be a new day.

Well, it was for a while. Went to school early to study with Donna. I bought a Pepsi. She had coffee. Did class. Came home and Mom and Larissa were waiting on me. Not that anyone told me beforehand that we would be doing something. It really bugged me. I was looking forward to a nap. I haven't been able to sleep for a while and getting up early spending even more time on Astronomy I was both mentally and physically tired. Mom said we could go whenever I was ready. I asked when she wanted to go, she apparently didn't understand that I wouldn't be ready later. If I sat down and relaxed she wouldn't be able to roust me to go anywhere. Anyway, Larissa and I helped her pick out frames at Lens Crafters. Then we had an hour to burn. Shopping was not part of the deal. We went to Walden's. Renewed that card. I got my dictionary finally and an Alice work. Larissa didn't get anything. Then we went to Sam Goody's to renew that card. With renewal you get 25% off so I ended up getting both of the works I was vying for plus a cheapy little one. I got three things, Mom 2, Dad 1, Larissa 0. Mom spent about $60 on me and zippo on Larissa. That was cool, for me. I really made out. Anyway Mom mentioned food. I didn't want to eat mall food and I especially didn't care to eat in the mall. So I mentioned waiting for El Rey Taco. It worked out well for me considering I had thought about going earlier, except I didn't want to have to pay. Friday was supposed to be a bum at home, do nothing day, but they fired Stephanie and needed coverage or the hours would be wasted. I cleaned up and went to work. Made it through the whole day, but something happened when I came home. I was like, I figured I've eaten so far. Let's start over with a new week. I knew I had to work Saturday and Rachel said my hours wouldn't change, but then while I was there she said I could stay as long as I wanted because we had 5 hours still. I had weighed in at 250 ¾. That's almost 4 pounds up in a week which really isn't that bad considering I had really been eating. Then it got to be 3:15. I was scheduled off at 4. I said I would stay if I could get something to eat. Of course, she let me. I got nachos with beef. I never ever want to go in that food court again. The lady asked about Stephanie, if she was off for the weekend. I sort of said, oh yeah. The beef was great, but it still didn't satisfy the craving for steak that I've had for over a week. After work I went and bought one. I figured this was it. Then I had cheese popcorn instead of ice cream which is fine because I'm not such a fan of vanilla ice cream anyway. So now it is Sunday and I weighed in at 251. That surprised me. Steak and nachos – only up a ¼ pound. The road to a smaller me is in sight again. Better hit the bike before going to work.

July 10, Monday
248 after school
Fast
Jean shorts, CSLB tee shirt
Pepsi 16 oz. + ¼ lt.
Astronomy
30 minutes bike, 7.6 miles, 35 reg AB, 15 knee

     Last Wednesday I finally got off the dime and did something I've been meaning to do. Every day for quite some time I've been meaning to go see a counselor. Well, Wednesday I was telling Donna during our break that I wanted to take a certain English class and that it was only offered as an honors class. I didn't know if you had to be entered into the honors program just to enroll in one honors class. I mean the program wouldn't really do much for me now, and my grades are certainly there to be entered. Anyway, due to that conversation she felt I should see a counselor right after class or else I'd probably keep putting it off and she was right. I would. So I waited and I saw a counselor. At first I was disappointed that Jordon wasn't doing the 10-minute drop-ins, but it worked out. I presented my case and she called to leave a message with the professor. She gave me permission to take the class without reconfirming my GPA, which was nice, but a little too trusting. I guess that's why she took my name and number, in case there should be a problem. When she asked about my major she was taken aback. That's very competitive. I concurred. Then I just got this gaze. It was like a star struck thing, which is weird because I haven't even made it yet. Maybe she recognizes that I will and that's where the look came from. Or maybe she thinks I'm delusional, in which case, she can suck it. I informed Larissa about it and she was typically just listening. Me, I was walking out of the administrative building a little taller, a little prouder. Maybe this will satisfy the taste I craved and was denied in high school. In any case, I was really excited about it and lately I haven't been getting too excited about classes. Mom doesn't think I should take any classes at LBCC at all. She said something like "don't think you're saving us any money by taking a class there." I know I'm not because actually I have to pay to go there whereas if I took more classes at USC its already in the tuition; however, if I can cut it down to taking more units, cramming it into three semesters that will be saved money. Mom has prepared Dad for six semesters. For normal people that would make sense but six semesters to me means I should be a semester away from a master's or two or three from my Ph.D. and unless it is proven to me to be physically or mentally impossible then I will be doing it. Besides, I don't think she realizes that I need to take classes here. I need three to graduate and one unit of computers. Sure I don't really need an AA degree at this point but why not secure it while I'm already so close. And really, why I need to go here has to do with my own insecurity. I know people here. I'm fairly comfortable here. I'm established. Doing both will give me the opportunity to get my feet wet over there while the people over here check up on me to make sure I'm going for it. (Inverse squared — drawn to action at a distance)

July 11, Tuesday
Fast, sort of
Pepsi, 17 reduce fat Better Cheddar
Cream/taupe tee, JK pants
25 minutes bike, 6.4 miles, 40 reg AB, Knee 15, 50 chin

    Although I told myself not to I did it anyway. I weighed in. I told myself to stop torturing myself and to just weigh in once a week. Yesterday I couldn't help myself and headed for the scales after stripping down from school. I weighed in at 248, which was 3 pounds from Sunday, but not enough for me. I don't know when it will be, but I wanted that little thing to go down. That's such a good feeling when that little weight meter slides down the leveler. I exercised Sunday, yesterday and today. I weighed in around 9 and it registered 248. That was so disappointing. Maybe because I exercised I was building muscle or maybe I just had too many fluids in me. I shouldn't have weighed in. Then I got a phone call from Mrs. Nelson. Sounds like she wants a free Alice cake. First phone call from a board member in I don't even know how long and it was for a fucking hand out. Maybe she did plan on paying but if she did she certainly didn't mention or even hint at it. Thanks Dad for opening your big trap and sending a leach my way. The only time I would think to ask Alice would be for Jessica's reception maybe. Or something big like that. Not a ½ sheet deal.

July 12, Wednesday
245 ¼
Fast (Handful of peanuts)
Linen outfit
40 reg AB, 15 knee, 50 chin

    Weighed in today. Boy do I really listen to my own advice. I weighed in at 245 ¼, which was great. I mean almost 3 lbs. down from last night, but I have great expectations. I guess that means I should keep fasting BIG TIME!

Later… Boy do I really listen to myself. Went to school. Oh, I looked cute and wanted to see what's his face until I cut a wet fart. Fortunately it stopped in a way that you couldn't see it on the outside of my shorts, but it was a mess inside. So yeah, that totally blew my day. After cleaning up in the bathroom I was sweatin' it because what would I do if something happened like that during class. I was miserable. In the bookstore with Donna I thought I felt something but not out of my butt. Went home and sure enough I started my period. Awesome. With my crazy eating habits I'm surprised I've been so regular. I cleaned myself up and weighed in. Registered at 244 ½. That made me feel better. I never had the feeling that my period caused any emotional disturbances but maybe this puts a new perspective on the stress and frustration of yesterday's phone call. My gut suddenly feels abused. Yesterday when I exercised I barely started and my legs felt sore. I'm tearing my muscles and not feeding them protein to rebuild themselves. Maybe I shouldn't exercise every day. I'm not going to today. I really can't afford the time. I should be memorizing Astronomy, but tomorrow I will. Definitely, yes, tomorrow I will. Maybe the treadmill. That's kind of less – something. It's just less. I need to call Alice.

From another source… I decided to really get dressed today. Having dropped a few I realized that soon my linen short outfit would be simply too big for me to wear so I decided to go for it. I even got up early enough to curl my hair and do full make-up. Had to leave early to go get photocopy work done. Saw Mrs. Stevens. She didn't know who I was and that was fine by me. I was feeling good. I even had a nice drive to school until I pulled off the freeway. I felt an air bubble and pushed to pass it, which I did. It was warm and I felt a panic over its contents, but it really was only air. Then I felt another. The first went okay so I didn't think much of it. I released and my panic was realized. I squeezed the cheeks together and felt the warmth come up my crotch. I was scared. Nothing to change into. Nowhere to go. No time to go back home and change. Did I have anything showing or was it all in my mind. I changed lanes to park closer to the school. Today, the day I'm dressed, have to meet Donna because our first midterm is tomorrow, planned to see him 'cause I look cute and damn. Then I was afraid he would see me hunting for close parking. Then I was concerned about what the rear side view had to offer. I went straight for the bathroom. It was as bad as the first time. There was spotting. In front and I don't think it was in an area someone would notice but the stuff – definitely in my pub is just disgusting. Fortunately, the other times this happened there wasn't an immediate reoccurrence. Which going to class was of major concern right now. Plus some crud came out so I was hoping that I got rid of it all and not at the beginning of a diarrhea spree. My high confidence was pretty much shot, and Donna saying "oh you're cute" and "that is such a pretty outfit" really didn't do much to make me feel better, but it should. Maybe I need to always wear something. Maybe I just need to relax and enjoy life a little more.

July 13, Thursday
Between 244 and 244 ¼
What a bummer
Did okay on Midterm, Monday will tell
Played cards which was stupid because it turned into an El Rey Taco dinner
Bean and cheese burrito, green quesadilla, Pepsi and Slice
1 Ex-Lax

July 14, Friday
246 – Ugh!
Fast
Work 3:30-9:30, 6 hours
Shouldn't have even bothered weighing in
Work dragged
3 French fries, 5 bites of Spanish rice, Pepsi and Slice
Victoria Secret's shoes arrived

July 15, Saturday
244 ½
Fast
Work 9:30-4, 6 hours (1/2 lunch)
I can't believe 1 El Rey Taco could hurt me so much especially with taking an Ex-Lax
Pepsi, ½ waffle

40 minutes treadmill, 58 calories, 1 mile; 50 chin, 40 reg AB, 10 knee

I hate my life. I really do. My mind is restless and my heart alone. I've been beaten and broken by none other than myself. I've abandoned myself and I now have no where to turn. I have so much in me and it's not able to adequately come out. I'm alone in myself, my frustration. This should be a very exciting time in my life, but I just want it all to stop. I don't want to do anything. I don't want to be responsible for anything, including myself. I'm tired of other people 'understanding.' I'm tired of other people being jealous. They have no idea what they are jealous of – pressure, stress, enormous responsibility. Hell, if I could I'd give it all away gladly. I have no one to talk to. My sources are tapped. No one really makes me feel better about the situation. Everyone seems to offer some comfort but not nearly the peace of mind I so desperately desire. Oh life, it's bigger. I'm in the middle of taking Astronomy. A class I am learning to hate. Donna dropped leaving me to fend for myself with Janet "the kook", Frasier and the Mr. I am Wonderful Darren Ferguson Brit. I think I did okay on the first midterm. I no doubt passed, but I hardly think that I aced it. I haven't really been eating, but I also haven't really been losing any weight either and it's really pissing me off. I guess it might just be that my body is fighting to maintain its huge mass. I've never been this low that I can recall, which is just so sad considering I weigh 245 pounds. Last night I came home and there was a bowl of Spanish rice on the counter. I ate about five spoonfuls after eating three French fries. While playing cards Mom offered me some and I said I had some. She didn't even think twice. I mean I was in the kitchen a max of five minutes. How much could I have possibly eaten? Anyway, she had her answer and put the bowl away. Later I belched and said, Spanish rice. Mom got a real look of concern and asked if I had eaten today and I said yes and then she asked if I had anything before the rice. When I said three French fries she mumbled something about what a great welcoming mat that makes. Then after cards I asked Mom to check out my plaid dress to make adjustments in order for me to continue to get some use out of it. I'm tired of giving all my clothes away. Some of them I don't mind, but the stuff that I consider distinctively me I don't want to see on anyone else. Especially Larissa. Dad said something about my work showing off then said something like I just hope you're not hurting yourself. It was the first time he seemed to show genuine concern. Then he oddly added something about my exercising and that was good. Which it is, but he made it sound like it's okay to fast if you counter balance it by exercising. Fasting = lost muscle, so you exercise. He should know better than that. Sophia mentioned that when Monica wasn't eating she would have gobs of hair fall out and it's just now growing back. That is very scary. I feel like I lose a lot of hair already. Now I'm in an even greater panic attack over losing hair, which is probably causing even more to fall out. And I'm not as young as Monica, so who knows if mine would come back. Mom thinks I should keep my hair short. That I seem to do more with it (I was thinking the opposite) and that it is a more sophisticated look. And yeah I guess I should look my age and push myself, but I still want to be a little girl. I've never been a pretty little girl before. Susan thought that I was older than Larissa and she thought that when I said Larissa was graduating that she was getting her BA. Susan is only one year away from hers, but dropped because of accumulated bills. I guess I need to get back to Astronomy, it's just that there is so much more to say.

July 16, Sunday
243 ☺ A New Low
Fast
Work 1-6
Mountain Dew
Could have done Target, but DIDN'T
Monster Radio, Astronomy questions
40 AB (30/10), 50 chin, 15 butt, 15 leg
$220 Sale at work ☺

July 17, Monday
242
Fast
Finished Mountain Dew, Grape Slice
Melissa B. got married Friday. Her Mom saw Larissa while shopping at Lane Bryant. She gave Larissa, to give me me, Melissa's new Kentucky address.

Poppy tee $5, B+ on midterm
Work 5:30-9:30
40 AB (30/10), 15 butt/leg, 30 chin
I'm OBSESSED

July 18, Tuesday
242
Fast
Grape
Black/cream dress
Potato Bake, but didn't go. How can you go to a potato bake and not eat?
30 minutes treadmill, 44 calories, .7 miles; 40 AB (30/10), 40 chin
Pooped green clumps. Awesome.

  Today is probably going to be rough. I had been pretty firm about not going to the Potato Bake. I don't really want to see people and I don't really want to eat. In fact, I told myself I wouldn't go no matter my weight. Then yesterday Rachel kind of was going off on me about my stressing out. She thinks I've become obsessed and she wants me to stop while I can. She can't just hang out, neither can I. I can't remember the last time I was happy go lucky. She seems to think it was three months ago. I don't think I was happy three months ago. I was just hiding it better. It's been a long time since I just hung out. She seems to think I'm even keeled and she sees extremes. She is sort of right, but she doesn't know about my year as a bum. She doesn't see my extremes and yet she understands my feeling like if I let up for one second I'll blow it. If I cut loose for one night I'll lose control. Of course, that won't happen, but it could and I'm afraid of that possibility and I'm afraid I just don't know how to hang. She came running over to my car just to make sure we were still on for REM. I guess she is afraid of losing me, even though I am now officially her Sunday Girl. Anyway, Rachel had me thinking that I shouldn't be so hard on myself. I should relax. Then last night I indicated to Larissa that I might go to the Potato Bake, which was stupid. I have Astronomy questions to do and today I weighed in at 242 again. In fact today it seemed to be edging up, but I didn't even eat yesterday and the more I think about it I should just stay safe at home and if I feel I have the time or I'll make the time I should take the opportunity to exercise while I have the house to myself. Which reminds me, I need to listen to my blank tapes so I can record over them. Anyway, it will be hard making it through today without eating. Larissa didn't make it easy yesterday and I still made it so maybe I just need to keep faith in myself. Be proud! Rachel told me I don't want people to be proud of me because then I have to deal with that burden. She's right.

    Later… a change to commemorate my toilet experience before going to school. At least they're before school now. Odd little clumps though. Sort of a different experience. I actually made it through the day. Thanks to Astronomy I really couldn't afford to not go. And I did answer two questions. I also took the time to exercise. That felt good. All by myself. My stomach is starting to hurt though. Like it's reeling over, looking for some lost morsel or shriveling and dying. I'm starting to get headaches too. I'm surprised it took this long actually. Maybe my body is getting used to the routine. That would explain the slow change in numbers. But really, in ten days one bean and cheese burrito, one green quesadilla and three bites of rice. I expect results. And I guess nine pounds isn't bad, but I am demanding and royally impatient!

July 19, Wednesday
241 ¼, afterschool 240 ¼ ☺
Fast
White tee/plaid skirt
30 minutes treadmill, 45 calories, .7 miles
Study, study, study

    Still pretty bummed out that I haven't broken into the 30s category. I'm awfully close. Had a diarrhea dump before school – note the color. (Written in green ink.) Oh man, and my stomach is begging for substance. My headache is getting worse. I thought about eating to give my brain fuel, but I don't think so. It'll just send me to the bathroom and make me nauseated and sluggish. Besides – to match March I have to starve like six more days.

July 20, Thursday
240 ¾?
Midterm

I don't get it. Scoop of cottage cheese, 10 Triscuits and I'm only down a half pound. That's bullshit.
El Rey Taco nachos, Pepsi, Mountain Dew
30 minutes treadmill, 45 calories, .8 miles
Headaches, gut pain, diarrhea

July 21, Friday
242
Fast
5 kernels of Cracker Jack, 1 powdered doughnut
Work 5:30-9:30
45 minutes treadmill, 65 calories, 1.1 miles; 45 AB (35/10)

  Sometimes Dad has a lot of nerve. Watched Quiz Show after work. In the kitchen Dad asked me how I was and I said okay I guess. He said good, keep it up. I asked what I was to keep up. He said something about being good, to which I told him that he was too easily convinced. He said he expected to hear the truth. I wanted to slap him. I debated to attack or not to attack the powdered donettes. Mom and Dad had some during the movie. I ended up going for one and Dad re-entered the kitchen. He said something about being good to myself. What a joke. I eat one donette at 12:30 and he's concerned, but I go a week without anything of substance and no words of wisdom or worry. I hate the mixed signals. I hate the fact that food will forever be a part of my life. I hate the fact that after six months of hell I'm down more than 75 lbs. and still a fat cow. Allison asked why I bought a 14-16 tee for the denim promotion. Bitch. I don't want my weight to be a focus. Good or bad and yet it seems to be an impossible thing to avoid talking about.

July 22, Saturday
241 ½
Work 1-6
2 eggs, 6 oz. milk, 6 donettes, slice of cheese, 2 slices of toast with butter, ½ Noodle Roni parmesan, Pepsi
Large salad with blue cheese dressing from Porter's
Cards

July 23, Sunday
244

Slice of buttered toast, 1 ¼ waffles with butter and syrup, scoop of cottage cheese, 10 saltines, Pepsi
30 minutes bike, 7.4 miles; 50 AB (40/10)
Monster Radio

July 24, Monday
244
Fast
Work 6-9:30
Pepsi, 3 waters
242 ¾ after school
Black tee, jean shorts
50 minutes treadmill, 71 calories, 1.2 miles, 50 chin
Walking along Carson

 Today was the deadline for the USC Orientation application. I mailed it today. I only received it late last week though. It's a good thing I called for it otherwise I would be SOL, which I may be anyway. And I'm not so sure if I would be upset if I were. Sophia did some probing on Saturday. She wanted to know if there was more pressure to do well, if now because I'm going to USC that I was expected to perform. Basically my answer was YES!!! But what she wanted to know was if Mom and Dad were putting on the pressure or if it was just me. And you know something. This whole time it's been me. It's only been me. I mean, sure, Mom told me not to fuck it up but that was more of a 'you better really do this and not flake out and ditch' than 'you better ace this.' I'm the only one that has demanded high performance and zooming speed from myself. I'm the only one to bitch about getting a B instead of all A's. In fact, everyone that is closely associated to me is both proud and impressed. But I haven't impressed myself. I know what I have accomplished and I'm proud of that but I don't understand why it's not enough. Why do I feel like it all has to be perfect for it to be okay? Why do I feel like I have to push myself into the grave or lose everything that I have accomplished? Nothing can take away what I have. I need to understand why I'm driving myself into insanity and an early grave. I suppose I'm just afraid. Afraid of letting up, afraid of going back to the other extreme. Afraid that I'll allow myself to be intimidated by the whole process we call life. I definitely need a vacation.

July 25, Tuesday
243 ¼
Cream see through outfit
What a bummer! Midterm B- ☹
Guadalajara Inn – beef taco, Tamale, margarita
Try on formals
2 diarrheas
30 minutes bike, 7.8 miles; 25 chin +25 more, 60 AB, Arms

    Seems so different. Why have all of my friends gone? Why do I miss them? Was it me that left them? What have we learned from each other and were we ever really as close as I thought we were. Why do I feel so different? Why do I now write and speak my mind more freely than I did then? Was I simply too afraid of being rejected and hurt? Why am I so much stronger now? Or am I even really? It may very well be my greatest illusion. I still don't let too many people get too close. As friendly as I am with Rachel it turns out that I am more able to share my insecurities with Susan. With her I have been able to share things about myself I never thought I could possibly share with anyone, other than – maybe – Larissa. We had a pretty extensive conversation about losing weight. She asked if it was a conscious thing. Part of me wanted to say no, but I was totally aware even when I went those couple of weeks in February without eating it was because I choose not to eat. The decision–making process, to decide what to eat and what was too much for me to be eating, I'd like to say that it all just happened for me, that I didn't think about it so much. But I was so stressed about school, which is odd because at that time I didn't have much happening, but I was also very depressed. That is what started it in January. I told Susan that it was the stress of going back to school. I didn't want Mr. Judge to look at me as Larissa – just as fat, just as homely, just whatever. I was always fighting for my own identity with him. Funny thing is that I probably had it all along. I didn't need to differentiate myself for him. I needed to do it for me. I needed to change for me. I still need to change for me. I'm not happy with myself, the way I am and I'm the only one on the planet that can do a damn thing about it. At Julie's party Felicia said she needed to lose forty pounds by August because she was going to be a bridesmaid. I wonder how she's doing. She told Julie that she wouldn't even be able recognize her. I sat there both gritting my teeth and laughing. I, at that point, had lost over fifty pounds and not one person said anything. Now it's true they may not have wanted to say anything, out of politeness, which I would actually appreciate. And it's also true that I was wearing my blue sundress that was probably hiding the fact and sometimes we forget exactly what other people look like when we haven't seen them in a while. I lost a good twenty-five to thirty pounds before I started exercising and now it seems impossible to break a new barrier. My July seems to be equal to my March in number of days of fasting and I think I'll be exercising even more in July, so why is the weight not coming off? In fact my measurements don't seem to be doing much. I need to stick to my AB isolator and watch that darn video. The buns of steel chick also has an arm video which I totally need. My arms are still huge and nasty. Rachel mentioned to Allison about how during our sales promotion that we didn't receive enough 14-16s and Allison was questioning it. Rachel said that she and I had bought the only two our store received. I can wear a 14-16 especially when it runs so big, but not in pants. Oh my no. My size 20 scooter shorts are barely breathable but six weeks ago my black sundress was a heck of a lot tighter than it is now so if I keep doing my thing the shorts will be roomy enough soon enough. Anyway, Allison flipped her lid. They talked. Next thing I know she was in our store checking me out like a rack of meat. She even admitted that when she heard I had lost a lot of weight she just had to see me. She asked how many sizes I had gone down, then she asked about how many pounds. I wondered how long it would take for her to share this information with the whole fucking company as she walked away. She just looked at me funny. She was eyeing me. I don't mind attention, but not like that. It was creepy. It's not even that I don't want to talk about it because it's such a big part of life it's hard not to. And I guess there in lays the fascination. When someone changes such a big part of themselves we want to examine the change, what caused it, how it was achieved. But my whole life has dramatically changed. I'm not the same person I was a year ago and yet I am exactly the same person. I still like the same things. I still have the same overall opinions. I'm just becoming harder in my decisions and more set in my own personality. I feel like I haven't really accomplished all that much when I look at all that is possible for me to do and all that I want to do, but looking at where I was and where I've come from I deserve to be proud about what I have done. I've changed. I've allowed myself to change and that's a hard thing to do. I'm fulfilling my seventh grade dream. I just don't want to be so scrutinized for fulfilling my dreams. I want to be admired for being me by people who are friends, by people that care about my well being and want me to be happy. Allison made me feel like a lab rat. She doesn't give a shit about me, she just wanted to see what the commotion was about. Sophia told her that maybe they should go back to school. That's only been a part of it. There have been a lot of little changes in my life and the biggest was being receptive to change itself.

July 26, Wednesday
244
50 Cheetos and Fritos (leftovers), cheese enchilada, beans and rice, Pepsi
Brown outfit
40 minutes bike, 10.3 miles; 90 AB, 50 Chin

  Before I ever met Amanda several people had forewarned me about her quirks. I heard about how her son Isaac conned Rachel out of $75 by giving her car a passing smog check – never mind the fact that the documentation was obviously falsified. I heard that she moved often. Usually living with people she babysat for and moved when kicked out. A few years ago her husband divorced her and essentially left her with nothing and now she fills her day with positive hype to get through the day. I sincerely believe she has convinced herself of the positivity stuff, but she still masks a real hurt. Or maybe I would so I transpose that on to her. I just can't see how she can find love in her heart for a man that screwed her out of everything, everything her life was. He has two families and has completely disregarded his first. She was a mother by the time she was twenty. She raised their young children and worked to support the family while her husband attended Whittier College. I don't remember what his degree is in, but he's into politics. She talked about being taken to functions and how politicians consider themselves to be a superior breed. She does believe that politicians are a breed to themselves, but I don't remember her ever acting or talking that way herself. She gave him the best, including the best of herself. That might just have been part of the problem and why he went to another woman. She gave her best and eventually had nothing left to offer. She was also always willing to play second fiddle. She was willing to dress in rags and so forth so that he could afford club memberships and such, so what did he leave her with? The rags. She didn't demand better for herself, so she didn't get it. She didn't require equality in the partnership she was engaged in. She was a part of the 60's scene, but I don't think she was a hippie. I can see her smoking a joint though. She believes in vibes. I'm still not very sure what exactly that is supposed to be, but it makes me giggle every time I hear her say it. I must say when that embarrassing encounter occurred with Shawn I felt more comfortable talking to her about it than Rachel. She understood that I sensed something. That I thought I was receiving or picking up on something. And I probably just didn't want to share it with Rachel because I'm used to Rachel seeing my strength. I'm not sure how I would feel if I let her see my weaknesses. She'd probably tell me to buckle up and get a grip. That I shouldn't let my weaknesses stop me from making the progresses I seek. She would give me all of the sound advice I can give myself, but it would require sharing. She knows I'm human and everyone is, but showing self-doubt when I've always been so confident puts me in a very vulnerable position. It's not so much how she would react to my vulnerability but how I would respond to her afterwards. Would it suddenly be all mush? Would she always be concerned about it afterwards or would I feel like less of a person? Would I then wonder what she thinks of me as if I'm not doing that now? Amanda was going to be the issue of the day though so this really should get back to that. Amanda always comes to work with junk store treasures that remind me of the red house garage sale days. And hiding under the table covered with knick-knacks and magazines and dolls and make-up. In Amanda's face I see the pain of the sister I left behind when we raced and she fell. I was so bent in winning, no matter what. I didn't turn back to help her. At first I thought it was a ploy to trick me because I was winning and she would jump up and whiz beyond me, but when I got to the tree (our goal) I turned around and saw her blood. Even then I continued on around the house in the front door through to the back window. There I stood and watched her cry. Left all alone, left to her own defenses, buckling over in pain. I yelled at my Mom that she needed help. Mom wasn't worried. A matter of minutes felt like an eternity. Life was moving in slow motion and after she made her way in Mom cleaned her up, but I couldn't stand to be around her so I kept my distance. I wanted to brag that I won my race, but it seemed so inappropriate. But that face is the face of Amanda. The pain of being left and in such pain that one cannot even bear to sob because there is nothing there to flow out. All that is left is the hurt and pain. Amanda may mask such things with positive affirmations, but beneath that is the fact. The face of pain.

The Walking Mushroom.

Believes in letting go of her sons. Believes that she has not seen the best days of her life. That the good stuff is yet to come. Has a picture of who her ideal man is. The voice of Ferguson, body of Brian, the spirit of Steven – she has it down. She is happy with herself and that is all that really matters to her. Oh, two drinks and she's easy pickings. Right now she is loving the grandmother stage, but pronounces it as a temporary phase. She baby-sits all the time and plays, does the whole park thing. She considers it to be a temporary thing, though I doubt she has any clue as to what lies ahead and instead of stressing out over the possibilities like me she lives in faith believing the good times will come. We've never touched on religion, but I know through her vibe thing that she is a character with a deep sense of faith.

July 27, Thursday
246 ½ ☹
Midterm postponed, AFI tee arrived
Pepsi, 5 bites of cottage cheese, 3 celery, 1 carrot stick, 2 slices of toast with butter, finish Fritos & Cheetos, pickles, croissant, Cranberry sauce
45 minutes treadmill, 61 calories, 1.0 miles; 90 AB, 25 Chin

July 28, Friday
247 ½
1 diarrhea before going to Disneyland
2 eggs, cheese, OJ, 2 slices of toast, Pepsi, butter pecan ice cream cone, Pretzel, 3 piece Fried Chicken dinner with salad

July 29, Saturday
249 ½
Work 2-7:30
Struggled through work, 2 VS diarrheas
Baked chicken, mashed potatoes, celery/carrots, blue cheese, Pepsi

July 30, Sunday
251
Fast, Pepsi
Study for Astronomy all day
Mom and Dad picnic, Larissa at work
Mom and Dad had BBQ
REM Concert on the radio
Exercise

July 31, Monday
247 ¾
Midterm
Pepsi, Mountain Dew, 2 slices of toast with butter, cheese, ½ box mac & cheese, pickle
Taupe/cream tee, cream jean shorts
Exercise

AUGUST

August 1, Tuesday
Other ½ of mac & cheese, cottage cheese
Ice Cream Social – vanilla with butterscotch
El Rey Taco nachos

August 2, Wednesday
250 ½
2 eggs, 1 cheese, 4 slices of toast, box of Mac & Cheese, cottage cheese

August 3, Thursday
250 ½
FINAL
Sam Goody's, spent the night at Alice's, try-on party at work; Freeze out
Hot wings, celery, rice, beans; deli – roast beef and potato wedges

August 4, Friday
Car tune up $500
Made purchase at work
Rice, Pepsi, Chinese Taste – BBQ pork, teriyaki chicken
Bakery alone, 1 a.m. hit the wall

    Worked yesterday. Rachel said we would do Target for breakfast so be there at 10. Well, I'm always early. Should have taken my Plato because I was there at 9:45 and apparently Rachel forgot about our plan and arrived at 10:30. She also had no money. I decided not to say anything because for one thing

I didn't know how firm it was of a plan and I just didn't feel like being upset, especially not at Rachel over something like that. Jacob's breaking up with Tamarra. Rachel's concerned. Her Mom fell during the week. Really messed up her knees. Rachel's transmission went out so now she has to bum rides. Jewel stayed the night with Mom. We did Taco Bell for lunch. Now I have no cash. Dropped off Rachel. Met Kevin then Jacob showed up to drop off Jewel while I was there. Rachel and Jacob tried to tempt me with Mom's chocolate chip cookies. No go. Jacob wouldn't talk and Rachel really wanted to. I sort of felt like he might have had I not been there. Tamarra's not going to Vegas. School was the given reason. Went home and there were three slices of pizza left, which I consumed. Couldn't believe it. Today's been really drab. Too hot to do anything but I know there is a lot for me to do. I missed seeing Clear and Present Danger. Watched The Client, though. It was better than I thought it would be. I better read for school tomorrow. Had two days of doing nothing and one day of work and hanging out. That was cool. I wish we had more to talk about though. Doubt = wisdom. In education comes a growing gap. She has such faith that I have educated myself away from. Thursday was the big night out with Lisa at Denny's and the hair has been cut.

August 5, Saturday
Spanish Test at 11:30 in Taper Hall
Diarrhea
Rice/celery, Del Taco – 2 chicken quesadillas, regular fries, Pepsi; mozzarella sticks, blue cheese dressing, popcorn
Water World with Alice

August 6, Sunday
"Early" arrival for orientation, Pardee Tower
Pepsi, 2 piece chicken, rice, beans, potato salad
Call from Rachel – scheduled 12:30-6:30

August 7, Monday
USC Orientation
OJ tour registration
Lunch – cheese enchilada, rice fruit salad, salad
El Rey Taco nachos, 2 Pepsi, Nilla Wafers

August 8, Tuesday
246 ¾
Fast, sort of
Surprise!!!
Came home from orientation, showered, then packed a small bag. Told Mom I was leaving, she said I wasn't, then I did. Left at 1:15 and hit the bank. Dinner around 8 PM in Arizona. Went for the salad bar and then picked at it.

August 9, Wednesday
Woke up in my car in El Paso around 6 am after having only pulled over around 2.
Coke, lemonade, Fritos, 2 Zingers
TEXAS dinner – ribs, roast, sausage, rolls, peach cobbler and bread pudding, fried zucchini
Made it all the way through Texas in a day. Who said it couldn't be done? They just weren't driving fast enough.
LIVE on repeat

August 10, Thursday
Fast (ish)
Woke up in Louisiana and hit the French Quarter
20 oz. Coke
Flat tire in Alabama. An angel stopped to help me change it.
12 oz. Pepsi
11:30 p.m. rest stop for sleep
Mountain Dew, 2 Zingers
2 shits – mucky

August 11, Friday
Down and up Florida's Turnpike $11.80 each way. Ridiculous and shocking!!! The drive up = massive down pour. I and many others pulled over to wait it out. Even that was scary because you just couldn't see a damn thing which meant neither could anyone else and one person slipping up would spell disaster. Walked West Palm Beach and met myself in the water.
Grill cheese and 1 major diarrhea
Spent the night in a hotel. Called home and you could hear Mom's chin hit the ground when I told her I was in Florida.

August 12, Saturday
Athens, Macon
Car went for 8 hours straight, poor baby.
Southern Fried Chicken 2 pieces of a 4 piece meal. I just couldn't keep eating.
Sleeping in South Carolina

August 13, Sunday
Spent all day driving.
Tossed the leftover fried chicken. Just wasn't confident if it'd still be good. Tuna 6 inch sandwich at Chapel Hill
Went to sleep at 1:15 AM in Georgia

August 14, Monday
Visited Emory University
Ate at Loretta Lynn's Kitchen
Called Rachel
Sleeping in Memphis, Tennessee
Chicken, meatloaf, country fried what??

August 15, Tuesday
2 O's and still spotting
Graceland
Taco Bell – burrito and meximelt
First cup of coffee
Stopped just east of Oklahoma City

August 16, Wednesday
Stopped at an unfamiliar southern fast food type restaurant and had to ask what their menu item 'Corn pup' was. That made the cook swing around to see who was asking. It's just a different name for corn dog. Go figure. But watching the clerk try to describe what a corn dog is was hilarious. Tried to make it home, but there was no way. Slept in Kingman, AZ. McDonald's, Denny's tuna and mozzarella sticks

August 17, Thursday
245 ¼
Home by 12 NOON
El Rey Taco nachos, buttered popcorn, Pepsi
Mom said Larissa was depressed. Wind down.

Dad's home

August 18, Friday
248 ½
After O & P 246 ½ - much better. Mom and Dad dined at Porter's and brought back pizza. Four slices of XL sausage. What a pig.

August 19, Saturday
247 - wow
Pepsi, cottage cheese, buttered toast, cheese, grilled cheese, buttered popcorn

August 20, Sunday
247
Pepsi, cottage cheese, buttered toast (2), more cottage cheese, 2 cans of tuna, chicken breast, carrots, corn (butter), Angel Food cake
30 minutes bike, ?, 3 miles; 60 AB

August 21, Monday
School starts
246 ¼
Banana, cottage cheese, chicken breast, rice, Pepsi, Chicken tostada with extra chicken breast, beef and cheese burrito – almost all
45 minutes treadmill, 1 miles, 60 calories

August 22, Tuesday
248
LBCC starts, stopped by work
Pepsi, Nilla Wafers, watermelon, El Rey Taco nachos

August 23, Wednesday
248 ¼ - ½
Finished Wafers, watermelon, 4 slices of buttered toast, 2 eggs, 1 slice of cheese
USC Registration conference
30 minutes treadmill, 70 Ab Isolator

August 24, Thursday
246 ½
Registration starts
Toast?, Cool Ranch Doritos – 1 serving, Pepsi, chicken breast, tuna melt with cheese, coffee cake
Eng 2 Professor can be super annoying
Skip English 48H, but didn't drop yet!

August 25, Friday
246 ¾
Mountain Dew, toast with butter, 2 eggs, 1 slice of cheese, coffee cake, rice, Fritos, cottage cheese, carrots/celery
Maverick
Work 4:30-9:30 Expected Jessica again? But NO!

August 26, Saturday
247 ½
What!
Finished Fritos and Dew, Pepsi, El Rey Taco nachos (didn't finish), watermelon, popcorn with butter
Getting Even With Dad
Dumb and Dumber
Stargate

August 27, Sunday
Work 10:30-6:30
Sammy's Tacos – nachos with shredded beef, Pepsi, 1 slice sausage pizza, garlic bread, salad, 4 margaritas
Jacob's Birthday Party

August 28, Monday
250
USC New Student Reception 2:30-4
Wok Express – chow mein noodles, rice, teriyaki chicken + 2 egg rolls, red quesadilla, Pepsi

August 29, Tuesday
252 ¾
Bowled 2 games – 92/96
Eng 2 – writing sample due, but not collected
Finished chow mein noodles, red quesadilla, olives, Pepsi,

sausage and pepperoni pizza with extra pepperoni and cheese
Pepperoni, sausage, 1 Tropical Freeze, Almond praline ice cream

August 30, Wednesday
254 ¾
USC Classes start
3 BMs before going to classes and 1 after
2 bowls of ice cream, tuna melt with cheese and tomato, STEAK, broccoli au gratin rice
cards

August 31, Thursday
253 ¾
Alice's Birthday
Turn in Chry. Response
El Rey Taco nachos, cheddar cheese, shaved cheese, finish rice, finish ice cream
Mute Witness

SEPTEMBER

September 1, Friday
252 ½
Fast, 2 Pepsis
Time to start Mr. D again
Went to Cultural Anthropology. Professor is a Harvard grad and also teaches at UCLA. Looks maybe 30.
Visited Alice. Wished her Happy B-day, received an open invitation
Bakery 8:30-11:30 icing pillars

    Today was the first time this year that I did my monthly stats and showed an increase. Especially disappointing since last month did not garner a weight loss either, but at least in July I maintained. The months were very different. I starved most of July and ate meat most of August. Decided that this needs to be the start of a new month of real dieting. (Dream Academy – Life in a Northern Town, REM – Stand) I noticed a decline of the obese at this new school of mine. I mean there were definitely other portly people there, maybe even a couple larger than me, but I increase the ratio and don't want to. I don't want to be the largest one in class. I don't even want to be close to that category. Cutting meat out of my diet seems to be a definite plus, so I've really got to get back to that. I decided to starve for a while since exercising seems to be an impossibility in this heat. Today went well. I drank 300 calories in Pepsi and had some icing (not much) while doing pillars for Alice. She offered pizza, asking me if I was hungry. I declined. She said she wondered if I ever eat. I reminded her, as she also remembered, my eating on the 24th at Jacob's birthday party. Turns out the pizza she was offering me had jalapeno peppers on it. Like I would even eat that. I think it also had meat and I gotta stay away from that shit. Rachel, Daniel and Jewel stopped by. Kim was promoted to South Coast Plaza. Mission Viejo is now open and Rachel wants it. I don't want to see her go, but it would probably be good for her. Jacob went out on Tamarra. Went to Pepper's with Brian, Noah's brother. Brian lost him. Jacob was with some Downey girl until four in the morning. Made Alice worry. Put Brian in an awkward position. Apparently, a few days ago Jacob confessed his love for Tamarra to Alice so Alice is doubly frustrated. Rachel seems to think he's going through a thing, just turning 21, finding out that he's attractive, and can get what he wants so is testing the grounds, but doesn't think he slept with the girl. Jacob called Rachel for advice. Rachel and Daniel are arguing yet again. Rachel called Jacob a male slut. The problem is being honest with Tamarra. Going out isn't really the problem, all parties agreed. It took Alice by surprise. I'm only surprised that it happened so soon. I was giving them a few more months, but even I saw the end coming. I hope tomorrow is a low temptation day. Rachel offered breakfast at Target on Sunday, which means I'll definitely be eating something. I hope it doesn't make me sick. I thought about eating tomorrow just to avoid any embarrassing situations at work on Sunday. I guess I'll go easy on myself. I won't do anything but won't deny myself if something free – non-meat comes up. Maybe I should just go about my days like that. Not focus so much on food, but it seems that I can't help it. I'm obsessed. It doesn't matter if I'm eating or not, food is what I think about. What I'll eat, when I'll eat or not eat, what and when others are eating. I don't really care as long as I keep losing weight, but it is annoying. And I have so much more to lose.

September 2, Saturday
248 ¼ = Yeah!
What a difference a day can make. Down 4.25
L's been sick since Wednesday
Dinner with Mom and Dad
1 ½ servings of pretzels; salad, bread and pizza at Italian eatery; Strawberry Tropical Freeze, Marshmallow Munchie

September 3, Sunday
249 ½
Work scheduled 10:30-4:30, stayed until 6:30 because Amanda called in sick
Dropped Rachel off, met Kevin
Taco Bell – combo burrito, soft taco, meximelt, Pepsi; 3 slices sausage pizza; Marshmallow Munchie

September 4, Monday
252 ½ ouch
Broccoli and au gratin rice – whole box, slice of toast with butter, slice of cheese, 4 Marshmallow Munchies, Tropical Freeze Strawberry Daiquiri

September 5, Tuesday
252 ¾ - 252 after nap
Fast, Pepsi
Response due Thursday
Sav-On for soda, Wash down car, parking tag
Film class – no AC, long drive home
Band Wagon

September 6, Wednesday
248 ½
Fast
Slept in, found parking center
Classics room changed – discussion groups – leader
Spanish – my pronunciation sucks
Typed up response
Mountain Dew (little), Pepsi (12 oz.) Pepsi over ice

September 7, Thursday
246 ½
Fast
Finished Mountain Dew
Dentist – need to replace filling or creative dentistry
Turned in response
Lord of Illusions with Clive Barker and Jane Sellars
1 diarrhea and 2 spouts

    House of Little Daggers. I'm so fucking proud of myself. I turned down El Rey Taco. That is just so fucking amazing. I was pretty bummed because for a couple of days I was back in the 50s. Two days of starving I dropped six pounds. The only thing is that a couple months ago I hit something of a plateau. Beginning of June I was 247 and now in September I'm the same. It's pretty safe to say I really didn't do much sacrificing during August, especially there at the end. Now it's time to get back on track. I had meat like 18 or 19 times last month. My goal for this month is the two I've already had, but I'll accept two more. I really don't see why I would need them, but I don't want to close the door on myself and having meat once a week is reasonable. Anyway this morning I weighed in at 246 ½ which puts me back past the 70 pound mark which I like. Then, right before going to school I took a dump. It wasn't exactly diarrhea, but it was, or maybe I should say there was some with some significant clumps. That set me to worrying about farts. I know my period is coming which usually brings more gas and more opportunities for an embarrassing situation. I had to go to school a little early to photocopy my response to "Sonny's Blues" which I finished late last night. Example of procrastination costing money. Anyway being nervous about that didn't help my gut situation. I went to the bathroom before leaving the library. Had a couple put-puts, but not much appeared. Saw India girl from Hunter's English class after English 2. She's not taking Hunter because she's teaching M-W-F or something like that. She's a nice girl. I bet she doesn't remember my name, which in this case is a good thing. Anyway, I weighed in after coming home, thinking maybe with my toilet experiences I might have gone down a touch. No such deal. In fact it registered at 246 ¾ which is odd because I didn't even drink much in the morning. Anyway, what else could prompt me more to avoid eating than the stress of being so close to that barrier? When Mom asked about El Rey Taco I didn't even really think before answering which is a good thing because if I had I probably would have rationalized caving into it somehow. Like I bet she was willing to pay. So after that I avoided her and now I know I'm safe because she's eaten lunch. I passed up El Rey Taco and I'll do it again damn it! Those bastards with their nasty sour cream and red shit sauce – yuck! I'm getting ill just thinking about it. I'll stick with my Mountain Dew and Diet Pepsi – Thank You! What it all boils down to is that I haven't got it figured out just yet. Apparently, I wasn't really in the clear as much as I thought. Mom bitched earlier today about Larissa not doing anything yesterday and then snuck out of her room just to tape a space show. Mom feels like she's avoiding her – and she is – even if that isn't her intent. I think Larissa is scared to mention NC to Dad. I don't think she has but Dad's very negative about the idea. Anyway the flu thing that started on my first day of school has kept her down for a week. She had to work this morning so it was easy for her to promise Mom that she would get up in the a.m. Anyway, I suggested that Mom call Larissa for El Rey Taco. She ignored me, but Larissa called before leaving work. At 2:05 Mom called me to the phone and Larissa asked what I wanted from El Rey Taco. I said I had a dentist appointment. She's getting Mom something and wanted to include me. How nice. It would surely have me running to the toilet with a bout of diarrhea. Amazing how quickly I came up with a reason not place an order without actually saying no. I guess I was right about doing it again. I said no to El Rey Taco and I'll do it again.

September 8, Friday
244 ½
Stiff Wild Cherry Pepsi, 1/3 serving pretzels + salt (6), 3 bites of cottage cheese, 5 bread/butter pickle chips
Dad came home @ 7:10
245 ¼ ☹
Porter's salad with blue cheese dressing, 2 slices of sausage pizza, 1 Marshmallow Munchie
4 diarrheas then another at 12:40 a.m.
Sore butt

  Apparently, saying no paid off faster than one would normally think. After going to the dentist I decided to weigh in again and I was down two pounds. The dentist was annoying as usual. Curled hair. Wanted to look cute. Clive Barker is an – diminutive returns – interesting man. A little off, but who isn't. Weighed in this morning at the same 244 ½, which was a little disappointing because I thought maybe I'd go down a touch more, but that is two pounds from the day before, so that's cool. Saying no really does pay off. Dad's home early. Started my period like clockwork and I have the seminar and work this weekend. At least I don't have anything today. Slept on my back – real stiff – last night. That's kind of strange. I probably need to start exercising again to help take care of that. Dumped magazines. Read Spanish/Plato and pulled out CNTV application stuff!

September 9, Saturday
Film School Seminar
9-6 Chaplin Theater, Raleigh Studios
245 ¼
After the above 247?
½ + Rice A Roni pouch, Marshmallow Munchie, Pepsi, Plum

Went diarrhea like six times yesterday. My gut was in a total uproar. The seminar was good. I made it through the whole thing without eating. Came home, went back out to Broadway for Clinique bonus, then napped. After that I was feeling very lethargic and a bit bad for not spending time out of my room. I guess I wanted to prove I was awake. Should have popped a Pepsi and stayed in my room. Instead, I made Chicken Rice-A-Roni. I ate a Marshmallow Munchie. They have a lower % of fat than that noodle stuff Larissa likes. Anyway, I probably had three servings of rice or 600 calories +200 for munchie + 300 for Pepsi. Damn! Definitely should have stayed in my room. I think maybe tomorrow I should take a lunch just so I'm not tempted when I'm out. But, then again I made it through today. So maybe I'll be fine because tomorrow night I have to work.

September 10, Sunday
246 ½
Work - Major Priority pack 8:30-11:30
Seminar 9-6
Coke (20 + 12), Pink's polish dog, 3 Strawberry Daiquiris, 1 Midori Sour, Chips, buffalo wings, 2 eggs, cheese, salsa, chips, Pepsi (20 oz.)
Stayed over at Alice's

September 11, Monday
248 ¼
Came home to shower
Marshmallow Munchie, Pepsi (24) ½ serving pretzels (9)

On the Edge journal
RENEW
Bike 20 minutes, 4.65 miles, 15-10-10 Abs

September 12, Tuesday
246 ¾, after school 246
Fast
Caffeine free Pepsi (1/2 2 liter)?
Engl 2 – trans on my response
The African Queen
Ab 15-10-10-15

September 13, Wednesday
243 ½
Spanish quiz, 100% sure I did poorly
TV 8-10
Caffeine free Pepsi, Mac/Cheese, real Cotton candy (Mom went to the County Fair and brought it home)
3 diarrheas

September 14, Thursday
243 ¾, after school 243 ¼
Fast
Pepsi (almost all 2 liters)
Fun – movie in film class
Attack on the response
25 minutes treadmill, 33 calories, .5 miles; Ab 20-15-15-15
Internship?
1 diarrhea?

September 15, Friday
242 ½
Fast
Finish Pepsi, lots of water
Thelma & Louise
Anthropology
Stop by Alice's, no one there
Rachel call or ride
30 minutes treadmill, 42 calories, .7 miles?

    It's been a long week. I pretty much discovered that if I do something on the weekend it means I don't study. I was really beat. I hope I'm becoming adjusted. Yesterday Jay called my writing disjointed and underdeveloped. Actually it was one because of two. I know I didn't spend a lot of time on it and I really didn't spend any time thinking about it. He thought I had great ideas. The seminar seemed cool, but I'm wondering if I can afford the writing one. I don't have the time, plus he said you basically write those two days. That'll be such a drain. Go just to have someone telling me to write. I'm thinking of backing out. Plus then I'll have money for that stereo.

    Dad just came in to find out my breakfast plans. He's thinking of Denny's. I politely declined. I got my diploma for the seminar and it has emeritus on it like I'm retired. What a dumb fuck that guy is. Anyway I gave in and went to Pink's. When in Rome I suppose. Then at Acapulco I had buffalo wings and four drinks. They kept ordering rounds. I should pay Mia $20. Monday I should have gone from Alice's to school, but no, I decided to come home which meant I ate a marshmallow munchie. Mom was a little ticked because I left my alarm on. I went to school without eating anything else. At school I was really on the edge. Whether to eat or not. I was driving myself crazy. I came home had ½ serving of pretzels and biked for 20 minutes. I was really sluggish. Tuesday after English 2 I collapsed in bed. I had no strength. I slept for a couple of hours. Had a Spanish Quiz Wednesday. I think I failed. I know I didn't ace it that's for sure. I was pretty bummed out and Classics I have all this reading. When Mom came home with cotton candy from the fair it was more than I could handle so I had some. Then I figured what the hell and made Mac and cheese. Mom had a cat food bowl portion and Larissa got a few bites, but I ate most of it. Had three rounds of diarrhea. And I had told myself to go home and exercise. If I had done that I wouldn't have been in the living room watching TV with Mom and her cotton candy. Another case of stay in your room! Thursday was cool. Went to school. Had my writing attacked. Gassed my car. Came home, exercised. Listened to music. Showered. I don't remember napping. I did listen to music between coming home and exercise. Went to the dentist for a replacement filling. What a drag. Mom said I deserved a nice cool shake. I shook my head. Got ready for film class. Saw Emma. Turns out she wasn't avoiding me last week, she was absent. The movie was FUN. The producer/director was there. He's the one looking for interns. I thought about it, but there was a crowd so I decided to call if I really wanted to spread myself out a little more. Anyway, I made it through the day. Today I have Cultural Anthropology for which I have not done the assignment. Oops!

September 16, Saturday
240 ¾ at 8 a.m., 240 ¼ at 10:30 a.m.
Phyllis' Visitation
½ oz. max. mild cheddar cheese, melon and corn bread refreshments after visitation
Met up with Rachel, talked her into a Stateline run then hit the road
Taco Bell – bean burrito, tostada, Pepsi, Dairy Queen Blizzard

September 17, Sunday
Drop off Rachel
Work 10:30-6:30
Drove back from Stateline to arrive at work just in time
Coke, rum and coke
3 eggs, white toast, hash browns, apple fritter, Twister pretzel, ½ grilled cheese, mozzarella sticks with blue cheese dressing

September 18, Monday
Almost skipped Spanish but didn't and glad
½ grilled cheese, fries with blue cheese dressing, Dr. Pepper, Doritos, Cheetos, Zonkers, slice of banana cream pie

September 19, Tuesday
Skipped Engl 2
The Brothers Karamazov
Met with Nicole for Spanish dialogue work at SFS theater
Finished Cheetos and Zonkers, Dr. Pepper
2 Taco Bell tostadas, 1 cheese quesadilla, 1 bean burrito

September 20, Wednesday
Classics lecture
Spanish – dialogue activity went ok
Pepsi, Werther's (1), Anaheim El Rey Taco nachos
No Rachel/Daniel - housesitting
Larissa and Dad arrive after 11

September 21, Thursday
Slept on couch
Did Engl 2
Good discussion
Faulkner – Miss
Left Rachel and Daniel's
Beans and rice, Pepsi, green quesadilla and rice
Stars Fell On Henrietta – Cox and Heny

September 22, Friday
247 ¼ at 12
Green quesadilla, side of beans, Pepsi, 12 pretzels
Clean up room
30 minute bike, 7.5 miles; Chin 50; Ab 20-10-10-10 or 15?

September 23, Saturday
244 ½ at 12
Fast
Nope! ☺ Didn't eat
Mandatory work day
Ava's Reception, Amanda was a Marshal. Saw Mrs. Matthews for the first time in forever. She beamed at me, which made me feel awesome. Dad offered to go out to eat after and I passed. Sort of felt bad about it because we don't have a lot of just us time, but I really didn't want to eat and that part of me won.
30 minutes bike, 7.5 miles; Ab 25-10-10-10;

    I think I threw away the phone number for the film internship. Shit! I am sooo proud of my damn self. Dad offered dinner, if I could decide where to go. We came home. I can't make those kinds of decisions. If I choose then I'd have to eat. It would be like saying I want to eat when I don't. Sure it would have been a free meal, but it probably would have included meat. Anyway, I did a lot more eating while watching Rachel's house than I thought I would. I thought I'd be able to not eat at all but I had something like every day. No meat though. I bounced back up a bit and now I'm coming back down. I was really lucky last Saturday. I didn't eat much Wednesday then nothing on Thursday and Friday so by Saturday I was primed to have a mess after eating. Thanks to Larissa I had refreshments after the visitation. Only went for the melon and cornbread though. Nothing happened between there and home. No El Rey Taco other than what I picked up in Anaheim and took to Rachel's. We did Taco Bell. That shit usually goes straight through me under all circumstances, but no problems on the road. Even had a blizzard. Didn't go to the bathroom again until we were leaving Stateline. Anyway, I got a lot of compliments today and that makes it easy to let down your guard, but I didn't. I have a long way to go still and I have this plateau to break through. Please don't waiver until I break the plateau!!!

September 24, Sunday
242
Work 10-6:30, Friends and family day at work
3 cinnamon donut holes, 1 buttermilk donut, Chinese Combo – BBQ pork
30 minutes treadmill, 46 calories, .8 miles
Major BM

September 25, Monday
243 ¾
Skipped Spanish, in library
Called Rachel – she fell at work
Tuna melt, whole can and 2 slices of cheese, Mac & cheese, 2 chicken breasts
30 minutes bike, 7.7 miles; Ab 30-10-10-15

September 26, Tuesday
244 ¾
Discuss "A Hunger Artist"
The Big Combo
Finish Mac & cheese, ½ after class, chicken fat, potato with butter, slice of cheese, pretzels
35 minutes treadmill, .7 miles, 42 calories
2 BM

September 27, Wednesday
243 ½
Spanish comp due
Writing cycle due – test
p. 37/38 due

Milk and gram crackers twice; Taco Bell – tostada, bean burrito, cheese quesadilla, Mac & cheese at 12
45 minutes treadmill, 1.0 miles, 57 calories

September 28, Thursday
245 ¾
Midterm question passed out
Response due
2 hours of sleep
The Holly Chronicles
½ baked potato with butter, Frosted Flakes with milk, olives, slice of cheese, 2 waters
30 minutes bike, 7.4 miles; Ab 25-10-10-10

September 29, Friday
244
Vacuum hall/bathroom, changed light bulbs, laundry
Buttered bread, Mac & cheese, El Rey Taco small nachos, green quesadilla, 3 Pepsi's, Larissa's popcorn
40 minutes bike, 10.1 miles; Ab 35-15-15-10
2 BM

September 30, Saturday
243 ¼
Pepsi II, 3 waters, deli – potato wedges, mixed cheese ½ + some from the other half
Vacuum
Bike 20 minutes, 5 miles; 45 minute treadmill, 1. Mile, 58 calories; Ab 35-15-15-15? Or 10?
Yeah, that's right, I exercised twice!

OCTOBER

October 1, Sunday
243 ¾
Mom and Dad's Anniversary and I'm cooking, oh no!!! ☺
No BM?
2 Pepsi, 2 or 3 Tropical Freezes, Cornish game hen, yellow rice/black bean stuffing, Veggies, chips, salsa
Smoked cheddar muffin that were THE WORST
One of Alice's amazing cakes
Bathroom call while entertaining – darn it
Work on Plato paper. Because nothing wraps up a successful dinner party like Plato.

October 2, Monday
247 ½ - Holy shit balls
Classics paper due, Spanish Quiz
Finished paper, Bombed quiz
Pepsi III, stuffing, cheese, chips, veggies with Ranch dressing, cake
30 minutes treadmill, .7 mile, 43 calories
BM

October 3, Tuesday
244 – That's better
Engl 2, Good news on Emily response
Film – The Hustler
OJ Verdict announced – acquitted on all counts
Cake and milk, buttered bread

Start then Dad finished
Stuffing, cheese, chips, veggies, Pepsi
30 minutes bike, 7.3 miles; Ab 25-10-10-10

October 4, Wednesday
244 ½
Spanish Oral presentation ← bomb. Well, okay
page 80 Ex. A due
Classics – discuss OJ
½ peanut butter & butter sandwich, Pepsi II, rice (5 Minute) most of, slice of smoked cheese, Skittles
30 minute bike, 7.9 miles; Ab 25-10-10-20

October 5, Thursday
243 ½
Engl 2
Pepsi, finish rice + other rice, milk, buttered bread, two powdered donuts, El Rey Taco nachos with extra chips, banana cream pie
Dead President's with the Hughes brothers

October 6, Friday
245 ½
Anthropology midterm
Review
Response due
Pepsi II, Jack in the Box – stuffed jalapenos 6, bacon cheddar potato wedges, rice with butter
3 BM

October 7, Saturday
246
Study for midterm
Pepsi II, buttered toast, Frosted Flakes with milk, Nerds, El Rey Taco nachos with extra chips, start green quesadilla, 6 sodas, Almond praline ice cream
45 minutes treadmill, 67 calories, 1.1 miles

    Boy do I keep going back and forth on this food thing. I can't seem to set my mind. I'll plan to skip a day, but come home hungry and tired and end up caving in. It's disgusting. Maybe because I've been approaching it the wrong way. I've been exercising so my weight really hasn't changed much. I'd say I'm a pretty stable 245, but is stability what I'm looking for? No, I don't think so. Well, I am sort of. I'm looking for a stable intake or rather a stable condition of non-intake. Anyway, it's been quite a while since I've had any noticeable change. Even my hip measurements fluctuate but never beyond a certain point which would indicate the change has more to do with my inadequacies in measurement taking. I don't just want to change my body - I need to change my body – I need to change my life. I still have so much going for me, but me. I have such a big ego and I manage to throw it around enough, but still, every so often I lose that confidence and when it's gone I'm naked. Nothing. At LBCC I'm still not totally comfortable in those little desks and that still has a power to reduce me, make me feel internally small and worthless. I don't want people to see me the way I am. I want them to see me the way I see myself. I want them to see me the way I want to be seen. I need acceptance. I need tolerance. We accept more from those who fit in. I need that reassurance sometimes. Like when no one understands what I'm trying to say in Spanish, or Jay is analyzing my paper.

    Larissa came home with our El Rey Taco. Mom and Dad went to the theater. Larissa and I talked. She's thinking about going to North Carolina in November with Mom and Dad. I think she should. I think she should know what she's getting into should she actually decide to move there. Besides, it will give her a visual image to focus on and a greater sense of security in her decision. She admits that she's unsure of what she wants to do there. I told her how the Alice thing hurt me. I said I wasn't looking for a response. I think I got what I was after though, it was in her eye. She admitted to shunning other people's ideas, especially those she had for herself, because if we think she does something for us than it's not like she's doing it for herself. She recognizes the immaturity of this, but it doesn't make it go away. I told her to go to church, get married and have kids. She admitted that marriage and kids have always been a constant desire – now, 10 years ago, but where can she meet a man? Indeed, she goes no where. She also apparently ignored the church part of my comment. I see myself with kids, eventually. I never really admit that though. It's an on and off thing, more off than on. She asked where I see myself or saw myself going. Writing has always been a thing. Famous not so much. But maybe. And movies. I want to do something with film. But marriage? Children?

Later… Back to me. I always saw myself as being thin. Thin and physical. I guess that's what this fasting thing is all about. I want to be on the outside the me I see on the inside. I just want to be me. In "A Hunger Artist" it is made clear that to him fasting is an art form; it is how he obtains his spirituality; it is what brings him closer to God. What moves the spirit? I know on days that I feel thin I feel as though I've obtained something. I have something I never had before. I feel more complete and in that I feel satisfied. When I get a pure compliment I know that I have something I didn't have before. Anyway, I think maybe fasting is my way to spirituality. It may be my way of understanding the world better. To want to have that aching need. I finished the green quesadilla I started yesterday. I think, change that, I know it's the final flush. I'd hate to pay for something to see it sit as a continued temptation and no one else deserves what I work so hard for. It's kind of fitting that I choose today as my start day. Start right NOW! because I also started my period. The cramps are killers, but will subside the general ache in my belly from lack of food. I'm a little concerned about that fart at work though. I didn't see it coming. I guess Susan didn't hear. Thank god!

October 8, Sunday
246 ½
Worked 10:30-5:30 with Susan, Courtney and Donna
Pepsi I, water II, finish green quesadilla
45 minutes treadmill, 64 calories, 1.1 miles

October 9, Monday
244 ½
Spanish midterm
Got Classics paper back A- !!!
Acapulco – 3 strawberry margaritas, nachos, chips and salsa
5 sodas, 1 of which was Pepsi, mango
BM

Today seemed like it would be an easy day. A midterm to worry about and when that's done a paper due Thursday, a story that needs to be read for tomorrow and a paragraph on "extent" plus I should read that Film book for my paper. Anyway, so much to do, plus should fit in exercise and stomach/guts in uproar so not eating would be easy. Then Rachel calls. It's Monday Margarita night at Acapulco, which means they're only a buck a pop. There was a mention of buffalo wings. I pooh-poohed that for me. I didn't really like them anyway, but they serve chips and salsa. Plus, do I really want the calories in a margarita? Oh well. I'll get to see Angela and Rachel. I'll just have to steer clear of the chips. I wish I went to school early today. Well, I knew today would be impossible and it was. Made it through Classics and Spanish and even told myself on the drive to Acapulco to stay away from the food. Yeah, well, that didn't exactly go so well. A few chips later, a few nachos later and then, yes, three strawberry margaritas. So much for all that fasting and spirituality mumbo jumbo, but how could I not partake. I mean how could I not celebrate? Seeing Angela again, A minus on the Classics paper, Spanish midterm, hanging with Rachel. We have spirituality so we can be immoral every once in a while right? Well, that's my cover. Now it's back to my road to spirituality. Let the fast begin.

October 10, Tuesday
244 – Amazing
Fast
6 soda, 1 Pepsi
Engl 2 uneventful
Electrician here, 4 hour nap, missed taping
Anthropology p again
Catch 22
Major BM
Stomach crunch
Headache

  I made it through the day. It's been a long time since I have. Offered Jack in the Box. Already did that once this year. Besides Larissa ended up leaving at the same time I had to leave for school. I was really surprised to weigh in ½ pound down from yesterday, especially since I felt so bloated. I meant to go to the library after class, but watching Catch 22 proved to be more mentally exhausting than anticipated. I feel bad for not participating in the discussion, only I felt so drained afterward. Renew the faith, I can do this. I know I can. I will.

October 11, Wednesday
241 ½
Fast
6 soda, 2 Pepsi, 1 water
Spanish page 74 ex B
Classics – nothing going
Walk 1 mile

    Weighed in at 241 ½, which is the lowest I've been in about a month, since house-sitting for Rachel. Now comes the truly difficult part. I have yet to break through to the 30s. I always seem to sabotage myself when I'm right on the edge. But not this time. I'm going for it. I need this. I really do need this. I'll endure smells, headaches, my stomach crunching in on itself and the fear of diarrhea accidents for this. I don't care if it's not healthy. I don't care if it hurts my body. Like weighing what I do is a good thing? I just want to be thin and I will be thin, at whatever cost.

October 12, Thursday
239 - Wow! YES!!! New low!
Fast
2 black olives, 6 Diet Pepsi, 2 Pepsi, 1 water
Film midterm due
Skip Engl working on Film paper
Running late – then needed gas
Now and Then with Lesli Glatter ☺

October 13, Friday
237 – Wow!
Fast
6 sodas, 2 were Pepsi, 2 water
Midterm Classics discussion session (optional)
5 p.m. weigh in check up = no change
Rough day no energy
2 BM

    Yesterday was a hell of a day. Woke up at 5 a.m. Skipped English to work on Film paper. Finished the paper within a half-hour of leaving. Running late and needed gas.

Not much of a turn out for this Film. I'm surprised, although it was a film about adolescent girls and friendship, so… Christina Ricci, Gaby Hoffman, Melanie, Rita, Demi, and Rosie. Director Lesli Glatter spoke afterwards. She's cool. Did some Twin Peaks and apprenticed under Steven. Received an Oscar nomination for a short. While I was typing up my paper Mom offered me olives. Turned her down cold. Impressed myself. Drank eight sodas, two being Pepsi and one water. Today I was down another two pounds. It's a weird sensation to break through a new barrier. That's when you feel it. That's when you see it. I've now lost over 70 pounds and that's a lot, but I have so much further to go. Woke up to one noisy stomach. Larissa made rice and it smells good. I wonder what I would be if I hadn't had the Pepsi's. Just took a dump. Real mushy. Time to worry about flatulence again. Some people are sooo sensitive. Mom's been trying on outfits having Larissa and I giving thumbs up or down. I, yet again, went through my closet and ended up giving her some of my 26/28s. I never wear them anymore, so why not? And a pair of pants I gave her match a blouse she recently purchased. She made a comment about how bad she would look without us so I said like a JC Penny bargain basement shopper and she told me not to throw that in her face. I thought it was an inside joke, but she was clearly hurt by the comment. She's the one that told me that story. Hello! She said, "not today." Yeah, okay, sensitive much? Earlier today she asked who was going to get her lunch. Larissa just ate and volunteered me so I told Mom she didn't need me to. She thanked me through sarcasm. I did save her money though. She should be happy. She eventually fixed a PB sandwich.

October 14, Saturday
235 ¼
Fast
6 sodas, 2 were Pepsi, 2 waters
Major headaches
Anthro/Film/Classics

Made it through another day. Had no umph to do anything though, like reading, reviewing notes or writing a rough draft for a paper that is only due Tuesday, like Hello! When are we going to work on that? Got a hip measurement of 51, which is nice, but I was hoping for more. Or less, rather. Went down almost another two pounds. It was a little high for two or I took 1 ¾, but that brings me to 235 1/4, which is getting there. Pretty cool. In the last week, I've dropped over ten pounds. Only half a green quesadilla and some of those nachos and I bet half of the ten is just water. That's why I can't stop. There's no way. Last night I had this total nightmare about food. Man, I was chowing down and buying high fat shit. I want to know how Rachel stays so thin while eating that shit. Maybe I will be able to, too one day, but will I even want to? What on earth am I ever going to eat?

October 15, Sunday
234 ¼
Fast
Water 2, Pepsi 2, soda total 5, Coke 1
Work 10:30-3:30
Allison came in just to ruin our day (and make a purchase)
30 minutes treadmill, 41 calories, .7 miles; Ab 40-10-10-20

Day Six. Things are really starting to get rough again. Soda tastes fuzzy, stomach almost continuously hurts, non-stop frontal headaches, dry eyes and no energy. I'm even pouring in the Pepsi. Farted at work – no mess, but boy did it smell. Tried on wool coats. 18-20 looked great. 14-16 just a little snug around the butt. Can't decide if I should go for leather or wool or both. Larissa thinks the more sophisticated wool would be more appropriate and I totally see her point. But leather is fun. Although there is the whole animal issue and I don't know where I am with that. I keep thinking of outfits to buy that only look good on flat stomached small people. The determination must be in me again, or else the November 4th party proposal would not have scared me. I mean, I'm really nervous about it. A room full of people who know what I do, Amanda cooking for us so there's going to be pressure to eat and I don't want to. The concert on the 3rd is going to be hard enough, but two nights with Rachel? She's going to be all over me to eat. And what about Mom and Dad going to North Carolina? What am I going to do with Larissa? It could go either way. Stay focused! Maybe I should exercise – and what do you know. I got myself going. Larissa picked the music and I had a half hour on the treadmill. It wasn't especially great, but

I did sweat. Kind of got a lightheaded feeling, but kept going. My legs don't seem to rub together quite so bad, but they still do. I noticed walking into work today that my feet point straight, which has been an issue in the past. Used to have too much turn out. I've been taking it easy on myself this semester. I haven't really studied much and I certainly haven't kept up on the reading and every paper just doesn't seem to get done until the day, within hours of being due. I need to snap out of it. I'd produce even better work if I'd just get over my bad self. The fart after exercise alarmed me, but not to worry, I was clean. Although it did quickly lead to a BM; kind of clumpy, very dark brown.

October 16, Monday
233 ¼
Fast
5 sodas, 2 Pepsi, 1+ water
Classics midterm, Spanish quiz skipped
3 compliments ☺
Black jeans – smaller size – yay!

    Starting the day with a nasty, juicy, mushy fart. Fortunately, I was on the toilet at the time. I was down 1 ¼ pounds which is okay but what a rip. I even exercised yesterday. Although I did have three sugar sodas. But man I want to hit 230 now, like right now damn it. My lower stomach is sore – all tight and my butt's not really a pleasant field of work either. Put on my black jeans and what do you know – no problem zipping those puppies up. Got a notice from Superior Court – grrreat! Mom said I looked good. Then asked what I was tipping the scale at these days. Classics final wasn't that great, but could have been worse. Girl on tram complimented my Obsession, said I smelled great. Then in turning in my midterm the person after me said 'good writing' and I had noticed a change of expression in my professor when I put the paper down. I said thanks and got a look from Prof. that said Yeah. Bookstore – no tees. Purchased four books. Only one is actually needed for a class. That is assigned. The other three are film books though and will help in writing my paper. Left school around 4:40 after studying for Spanish. Go figure. I guess I realized I needed more time on my paper. As it is I don't really have a draft and its 11 p.m. – bed time. At least I do have five pages of notes. Only I'm not really sure if I'm answering the question or not. Now I'll have to make-up that quiz. Have to play make-up in English 2 tomorrow too. Oh Life! At least after my paper all I need to do is review for Spanish quiz and do my Anthropology thing. Made it through another day and sitting in the USC park was hard. All those smells, especially the meat. My stomach feels like its curling over and I worry about farting or having BMs. Major headache. Eyes are really "tired" from dryness and soda is tasting funny again but I guess it should. It's officially been a week. But sort of nine days.

October 17, Tuesday
232
Fast
Film paper due
BM slime
Great day in Engl = boost the ego
Work on film paper all day
George stopped by
1 bite of rice, 3 crackers, 4 oz. milk, 4 soda, 2 water, 2 Pepsi
Feel a cold coming on, pushed the Vitamin C

October 18, Wednesday
232 ☹
3 crackers, pretzels, orange, 4 soda, 1 Pepsi, 1 ½ water
Spanish oral presentation?
Guest speaker in Spanish
No BM

    Yesterday was quite a day – full of stress. The prior night I went to bed with wet hair – not smart. English 2 of all The Hunger Artist paragraphs mine was the only one the class agreed was any good. Good deal! I think Joanni's was getting there. First draft due Tuesday, like I needed something else. Came home to work on paper non-stop. Larissa did the typing for me. It needed to be six pages and mine came right down to the bottom of five. I wanted to scream and I definitely wanted to kill her. She didn't seem to care. Plus I'm even more stressed about referring to that Film History book. I mean I also refer to the lectures so I guess I should just let it go. Donna called on me in class. I should see His Girl Friday.

Class was so cold I could feel a cold growing in me. Mom recommended an orange but I took a vitamin C. Larissa asked if I had eaten and I said not today and I got this "oh well, no wonder" response from all three of them. Dad told me to have a couple of crackers – consider it medicine. Mom said it was to push the shit out. So I had 3 – that's ½ a serving or 30 calories plus 4 oz. of milk. I was bummed about weighing in the same today, but in going back through my calendar that happens. I just need to hold fast. Last night I could feel snot and fluids draining. It was so gross. A couple of times I had to sit up and cough or swallow. I'm not sure if it's just a cold. I was afraid of water going in my lungs. Maybe I'm paranoid of dying, choking in my sleep. Midterm Friday. Need to see videos. Midterm Tuesday. Need to read and copy notes. Paper Tuesday. Need to write responses as well as paper! Ouch!

  Later... Thought yesterday was bad, but man who knew what today would bring. Ate 3 crackers this morning to help push out the acid. Went to school. Left my water in the car. Read outside Annenberg and suddenly couldn't focus. Real nauseous. Went upstairs. Felt like I was going to have a problem and the prior class hadn't let out so I went to the bathroom. Peed, not much going. I told myself to get it together and go to class. Didn't last long. I felt hot. Sensation like I was going to pass out or throw up – neither of which I cared to share with a class audience, so I picked up my stuff and went back to the bathroom. Those Classics students probably think I'm nuts. I sat in the bathroom on the chair in the shower stall area for about a half hour, I'm guessing. I passed out at some point. I don't know where the time went, but I knew I didn't want to cause a scene by returning to class. Had to make a choice – home, health center or library. Didn't really want to miss yet another day of Spanish so I bought a package of pretzels and a Pepsi and went to Leavey. The pretzels gave me something to eat occupy my mind. I also realized that the nausea was probably from snot and the pass out was from not eating and pretzels was the sanest option provided by the conveniently located in the lobby vending machine. I ate them as if they were medicine. Necessary. Took a nap – that too helped the nausea pass. Made it to Spanish got 71 out of 90 on the midterm. Didn't make up quiz and didn't ask guest speaker a question so don't get participation points, but I was there. Got home still feeling like crap. Ate an orange, that seemed to help. At least the nausea/pass out thing has gone. Now I just have these killer headaches and snotty nose. Hope I'm better tomorrow. I need to watch videos at LBCC.

October 19, Thursday
232 ¼
Fast
1 ½ water, 3 Diet Pepsi
Engl 2, watched video's in library
Brown jeans – oh, yeah
Still no BM, major nose/snot issues
Could taste metal when drinking the Diet Pepsi
Headaches
Copy Cat

    Can't believe I went up. Even if it was only ¼ pound. I barely ate. I didn't have a BM though. Odd considering all the days I wasn't eating but had one.

October 20, Friday
232 at 8:30
231 at 11:45
Fast
1 ½ water, 3 soda, 1 Pepsi
Anthropology midterm
Major cold
Hard time focusing, headaches continue
No BM

October 21, Saturday
229 ¼
Fast
6 soda, 2 Pepsi, 1 ½ water
Reading for film
Sketch for English essay
Veg out
20 minutes treadmill, 25 calories, .4 miles
1 small BM

    Well, well, well, life continues. I love film class, but it's always so damned cold it's really annoying. Studying for my

Anthropology midterm was pretty rough. I had a hard time focusing. These massive headaches don't really help. Had an elevator experience. That was awkward. Oh well. I should forget about him and just do my stuff. I hit a new low again! Finally broke through the 232 I was stuck on for so long. Best part is that I've past through two major barriers this month. Shot through that 240 that was plaguing me and now I've busted the 230. I know for a fact that I weigh less now than I did when I was a junior in high school. That's really kind of scary.

October 22, Sunday
229 ☹
Work 10:30-5:30 - went well
Porter's salad with blue cheese dressing, 1 2/3 slice of cheese pizza, 5 Starburst, 3 soda, 1 Pepsi, 1 ½ water
Almost immediate BM, eventual total of five

    Well, I'm down on four. Man is Porter's boring a hole through my butt. Although it is high time that orange and the pretzels from Wednesday got pushed through – but ouch. Third round was mostly fluids. Susan's getting married in June. She and Arnold talked to the Priest. She can't believe it. I can, saw it coming. Surprised it hadn't already. Susan's putting herself on a diet because she has to have the perfect wedding, which includes a skinny bride. So now with the pressure she's putting on herself she gets nauseous if she eats or doesn't eat. Letty's getting married in May.

    And with the fifth round came fire. Oh man – burn, baby burn.

October 23, Monday
228 ½ - The 5 BM's did it
Fast, 5 soda, 2 Pepsi, 2 ½ water
Exercise before school!
30 minutes treadmill, 40 calories, .7 miles
Classics midterm pass, Spanish homework
Up until 1:30 working on paper, then couldn't sleep

October 24, Tuesday
230
Fast, 3 bites of rice, 1 water, 3 soda, 1 Pepsi

Film midterm :/
Engl paper due
Made scale adjustment then weighed in at 230
After class reading 229
DIDN'T collect essay, I'm PISSED – waste of my time
Oh Lord: it is time

October 25, Wednesday
228 ¼ - I can smile again
Fast, 5 sodas, 1 Pepsi, almost 1 water
Skip Classics
Spanish killer quiz
Chair fell on my head in garage

October 26, Thursday
227 ½
4 avocados with salt, chips and low fat psycho cheese
6 Sodas, 2 Pepsi, 1 Water
Response due
Discuss first assignment
Midterm back ☹
Sort dresses
No BM

October 27, Friday
229
Optional Classics discussion section
El Rey Taco small nachos +chips, green quesadilla, 2 slices of cheddar cheese, 3 Rice Krispy treats, 5 sodas, 1 Pepsi, 1 Water
60 minutes treadmill, 77 calories, 1.3 miles (break between two 30 minute sessions); Ab 30-15(3)
    Ate yesterday and today. Oh my. Major farting going on. All air. No BM's either day. Strange.

October 28, Saturday
232 ½ Ouch!
Still no BM
7 Soda, 3 Pepsi, 2 water
Avocado with salt, cheese 4 slices cheddar, handful of chips, 2 Rice Krispy Treats
Engl notes

30 minutes bike, 7.75 miles; Ab 40-20(3)

    I hate to think what I would have weighed in at today had I not exercised. I exercised for an hour and still gained 3 ½ pounds. I know part of it is the fact that I haven't had a BM yet. I keep farting though so hopefully that is a good sign. El Rey Taco nachos are a real killer. I'm not eating any more. Maybe Halloween. I haven't decided. I asked Larissa if she wanted to go to dinner before the concert and she seemed enthused but that would mean us paying. I'm not sure I like that idea. Besides, I should really skip the week until Amanda's dinner. I hope I make it through the concert with Rachel. Monday I exercised before going to school. Tuesday for English we were supposed to have our essays done. Well, they weren't collected or even discussed which really pissed me off because I was up until 1 in the morning working on it, skipped reading for my Film midterm and that midterm was kind of important. I feel like I'm setting myself up for failure. I have done nothing for my film classes and now I'm second guessing my ability. It's like I'm looking for a way out of what I truly want. Strange. Why am I doing that to myself? I still haven't done the application and so at this point I won't be putting much effort into it. What to do. Skipped Classics on Wednesday. Hadn't done the reading, not ready for discussion and just didn't feel like it. Chair fell on my head. I was out of it for a while. Thursday after English I ate an avocado. Went right for it. Boy were they ripe. Eventually ate four. Did homemade nachos with psycho cheese. It was nasty. Dad's trying to eat himself to death. He ate a half gallon of ice cream in two days and last night about 10 oz. of cheese in a single sitting. I wonder why he doesn't want to live? And he asks me to eat an ounce of meat every three days. Even Mom saw through that one. She recommended a complete protein to replace fat cells with protein. But even she said a glass of milk and slice of bread can do it.

October 29, Sunday
233
Work 10:30-6:30 with Melissa and Donna, markdowns & promos
Taco Bell lunch – burrito, tostada; Deli dinner of potato wedges and ½ mixed cheese sandwich, 4 soda, 2 Pepsi, 1 Water

30 minutes bike, 7.4 miles; Ab 30 (15)3

      Going through major stress about what to do with my life. To apply or not to apply. Man am I breaking out. And what to do about Film 466??? Need to do rewrite for English. Need to write for Classics. Have an appointment to see Donna on Thursday. I hope that class is going well. We'll see. Ate the last three days. Thursday – nachos. Friday – nachos. Saturday – avocado and chips and cheese and today Taco Bell and deli. That's four days and still no shit. I'm beginning to worry. I thought Taco Bell would do it for sure. It usually does when I don't want it to. Still farting so maybe that's a good sign. Maybe since I hadn't been eating it was converting to protein. I could hope. REM Tuesday – FINALLY – what am I going to wear?

October 30, Monday
235
Finished my deli sandwich, chunk of cheddar cheese, avocado with salt, Grilled cheese, toast with butter, watermelon 5 soda, 2 Pepsi, 2 water
Classics and Spanish
Up until 2:30 on Engl 2 paper
30 minutes bike, 7.6 miles; Ab 25 (3) 10
3 BMs

October 31, Tuesday
236 ¼
Haircut!
REM at Arrowhead
Engl 2 turned paper in
2 cheese & crackers, 2 slices toast with butter, 2 eggs, 1 slice of cheese, Jalapenos (7) with blue cheese, potato wedges with cheddar and bacon, Chablis/coke, 5 Soda, 2 Pepsi, 1 water
30 minutes bike, 7.6 miles
1 or 2 BM

NOVEMBER

November 1, Wednesday
236 ¼
No Classics class
Spanish – teacher didn't show by 5:15 so we left
Kurt Vonnegut lecture
Cheese and crackers (1), 2 slices of toast, 1 box of mac & cheese
30 minutes bike, 7.9 miles; Ab 30-15-15-30
1 major BM

November 2, Thursday
236 ½
Skip Engl 2
Graham crackers in milk, El Rey Taco small nachos, apricots, Cheese/crackers, Popcorn with butter
See Donna – picked up midterm paper
Johnny 100 Pesos

November 3, Friday
237
REM at GHB Pavilion
Rachel bailed at the last minute. Her fighting with Daniel has reached a breaking point.
Wok Express – teriyaki chicken, 5 cookies, Coke at concert
Taco Bell – 2 soft tacos, 2 meximelts, 1 tostada at 2 a.m.
5 soda, 2 Pepsi, 1 water
30 minutes treadmill, 44 calories, .8 miles

November 4, Saturday
239
Work party at Rachel's
10 powdered donuts, 8 oz. 1% milk, 3 pancakes, 1 almond cookie, cottage cheese, 7 sodas, 2 Pepsi, 1 water
30 minutes treadmill, 49 calories, .8 miles; Ab 30-10-10-20?

November 5, Sunday
238 ½
Call from Rachel for bodyguard services. We went to her condo to collect belongings. Really intense situation.
She's moving in with Alice so Alice changed her locks to make sure Daniel can't get in.
Tommy's – cheeseburger, chili fries; 3 donuts, 4 Tropical Freezes; Rice and beans
Work on paper
Up until 11:45
Home at 2

November 6, Monday
238 ½
Fast, 6 Sodas, 2 Pepsi
Classics paper due, finish typing at 1:04
Discuss Astante
Convo with Chris – scary
Spanish – tape oral
More homework, No exercise or eats
3 BMs

November 7, Tuesday
234 ¾
Cottage cheese, popcorn with butter, Apple pie, 7 sodas, 2 Pepsi, 1 water
Engl 2, Nap
The Carey Treatment
Mom's visitation, Larissa does Election Board
30 minutes treadmill, 44 calories, .7 miles; Ab 40-10-10-15
1 BM

November 8, Wednesday
233 amazingly enough

Fast
5 soda, 1 Pepsi
Classics, Spanish Composition due, finished at 1 a.m.
No Eng Lit! What am I doing?
Daniel went to hospital Monday
May be going to Saudi Arabia for a cake delivery

November 9, Thursday
231 ¾
Fast
6 Soda, 2 Pepsi + 8 oz., 1+ Water
Engl 2 Papers back A-
Things To Do In Denver When You're Dead
No call from Alice so stopped at bakery
30 minutes treadmill, 45 calories, .7 miles; Ab 30-15(3)

November 10, Friday
230
Fast
7 soda, 2 Pepsi, 2+ water
B complex and Vitamin C
Copy notes
Called on in Engl
30 minutes treadmill, 47 calories, .8 miles

November 11, Saturday
228 ¼
Fast
Took hip measurement – 47 ½ ☺
8 soda, 3 Pepsi, 1 water
Copy more notes
Had a BM - guess it's first in 3 days???

November 12, Sunday
227
Fast
6 soda, 3 Pepsi, 1 water
Work 10:30-3:30 with Melissa (she was 20 minutes late)
Bought 3 pairs of shoes, nobody at Alice's when I called
1 messy BM before work
Screenwriting cancelled

November 13, Monday
226 ¾
Fast
4 soda, 2 Pepsi, 2 water
Spanish quiz, picked up schedule of classes
Classics – graded, but no return
Spanish rough quiz
B & C Vitamins
@Alice's, didn't see Rachel though

November 14, Tuesday
225 ¾
Fast, 5S 2P 2+W
Engl 2
Topic passed out Thursday, rough draft due in a week
Heart Like A Wheel
Mom and Larissa left for Visitation & Stateline
Order birth certificates for passport
30 minutes treadmill, .7 miles, 42 calories

November 15, Wednesday
224 ½ - 223 ½ after 3
Fast
Work, Letty helped
Classics – paper B, grade so far – B? Huh
Spanish tape turned in, quiz returned
Make-up story
1 Diarrhea before school, another after
30 minutes treadmill, .7 miles, 42 calories; 40 ab 15(3)

November 16, Thursday
223 ½ - kind of bummed
Fast
7 soda, 2 Pepsi, 1+ water
Engl – paper topic passed out
Anthropology films
Last Summer in the Hamptons
Mom and Larissa return at 1
30 minutes treadmill, 41 calories, .7 miles; Ab 30 (15-3)

November 17, Friday
222 ¾
Fast
6 sodas, 2 Pepsi (at Arby's)
Anthropology
Family +1 response
Register for school
Attend class – midterm back 97
Powder at Lakewood with Rachel and Jewel

November 18, Saturday
222
Fast
6 sodas, 2 Pepsi, 16 oz. water
USC vs. UCLA 20/24 loss
The Santa Clause
Organized desk, laundry, unloaded bike
1 BM

November 19, Sunday
221 ½
Fast
5 Diet Pepsi
Work 11-4 with Jo and Susan
Feel like I'm starting to get a cold, headache

November 20, Monday
220 ½
Spanish Writing Cycle - Sections 13, 14, 15 due
Mac & cheese, apple pie, 8 oz. milk, huge scoop cottage cheese, 2 slices buttered toast, banana, 3 carrot sticks
3 soda, 24 oz. water, 20 oz. Pepsi
6 diarrheas (2 were at school, 1 during Spanish)
30 minutes treadmill, .7 mile, 42 calories; Ab 30 10(3)

November 21, Tuesday
221 ¾
Fast
5 soda, 16 oz. water
Engl rough draft + discuss
Who we identify with instead + poems

Moonstruck
30 minutes treadmill, 43 calories, .7 miles; Ab 30(10-3)

November 22, Wednesday
221 ¾
Classics class canceled/Skip Spanish
Shopping with Mom, made pumpkin pies
Combo King – rice and noodles
30 minutes treadmill, .8 mile, 46 calories; Ab 40 (15-3)

November 23, Thursday
222 ½
Thanksgiving Day
Made oyster dressing
At George and Kimberly's until 4:30. George applauded my weight loss. The way he went about it made me want to punch him in the face.
Went to Alice's for a while.
Home and a round of Trivial Pursuit

November 24, Friday
225 ½
Straighten up room, slept in really late, Sav-on for soda and magazines
Stuart Anderson's steak – oh so heavy
Flat city

November 25, Saturday
230
Fast
Classics notes – Spanish notes
Flat city
1 diarrhea, release on undie?!
30 minutes bike, 7.8 miles; Ab 30 (10-3)

November 26, Sunday
227 ½
Fast
Work 10:30-4:30. Store was Dead!
Film notes
30 minutes bike, 7.9 miles; Ab 50 – 15(3)

November 27, Monday
226 ¾
Fast, Pepsi
Classics library home
Skipped Spanish
Worked on Engl paper
Irritable, unfocused
2 rounds of diarrhea
Ab 30 (10-3)

November 28, Tuesday
224 ¾ at 6:30 a.m.
Fast
Skip Engl 2
Weigh in at 12 – 224
The Color of Money
30 minutes treadmill, .8 miles, 46 calories; 40 ab (3-10)
2 BM

November 29, Wednesday
224 ¼
What's the deal? From 12 went up!
Shower, 1 diarrhea run, 223 ½
Classics lecture
Skip Spanish again, work on Engl
Mac/cheese big bowl, buttered toast 1, graham crackers in milk
Ab 40 (2-15)20

November 30, Thursday
224 ¼
Fast, 3 bites rice
Final essay distribution
Anthropology videos
Engl. Review poems
Toy Story with director and others. They were really proud of themselves and the cinephiles who picked up on the carpeting being the same as in The Shining.
Ab 40 (3-15)

DECEMBER

December 1, Friday
223 ¼
Anthropology final review
Response due
(Classics 3rd paper)
El Rey Taco small nachos, green quesadilla, Marie Callendar's potato cheese soup, Coke, lemon pie
1 major BM
ER with Rachel

December 2, Saturday
224 ¼ - surprised it wasn't more
Wok Express – 2 egg rolls, teriyaki chicken & BBQ pork, 3 almond cookies
45 minutes treadmill, 70 calories, 1.2 miles; Ab 40 (15-3)
1 big BM

December 3, Sunday
224 ¾
Work 10:30-4:30; Additional 15% off employee discount at work two hours after store closes, made purchase
Plenty of baked potato skins, finish Wok Express, 3 almond cookies – ate very late
Work on paper

December 4, Monday
226 ½

Classics class
Spanish missed quiz and homework assignment
Work on papers
Potato with butter, 2 slices of cheese, Mac/cheese box

December 5, Tuesday
228 ½
Film – second paper due
In The Line of Fire
Engl essay due
Grilled cheese, can of olives, box of Nilla Wafers, small El Rey
Taco nachos with chips, Pepsi, pack of Starburst
1 BM

December 6, Wednesday
229
Spanish final review
Shopping for x-mas presents!
Ray Bradbury 12-3
Missed Classics for signing
Potatoes with butter, 2 slices of cheese, butter popcorn, Pepsi

December 7, Thursday
230 ½
Fast
1 Cheetos puff, Pepsi
Poetry Reading 12-1
Othello – no Chris; Brian Miller/Joshua director Oliver Parker
Watched ER with Mom and Dad, laundry
1 BM, no period yet

    HOT DAMN! Blink and your life is gone. Went to both REM concerts with Larissa. Rachel left Daniel. He was smoking pot and doing lines again. Of course, she found this out the day of our REM concert and couldn't go. I was incredibly disappointed, yet somehow not surprised. Schools been stress! Starved most of November. Exercised three times a week for the whole month. So far I've only exercised once this month. I've been eating too. I'll tell myself not to, go almost all day and then break down. I've eaten five days in a row now, once with meat. I need to stop or else my clothes won't fit me anymore. I don't really want them to, but I want it to be because they are too BIG for me. I have two weeks before my Anthropology final. I hope to be 207 by then, but I'll settle for anything close like 210 or 212. So basically I'm not touching food for at least eighteen pounds. I know I can do it. Want to go shopping with discount card and Mom. Want to be able to wear those clothes too. So now unfortunately I have to keep in mind the saying Mom related from some comedian – nothing tastes as good as wearing a smaller size feels. AMEN!

December 8, Friday
227
Fast
3 Cheetos puffs, 1 Little Caesars bread stick, Pepsi
Classes end
Classics Paper Review Session
Film Review Session
Shopping with Larissa – Bath & Body, Express, Victoria Secret's, Lerner NY $170
Ab 40 (2-10-1-15)
2 BM

December 9, Saturday
223
Fast
Pepsi
Slept in while Larissa went to Lori's
Recopy film notes and some film reading
Using Soraya essay for Classics

    Family certainly doesn't make weight watching easy. Thursday Mom came home from Sam's with Tropical Freezes, olives, graham crackers, apple pie, pasta boxes and a huge bag of Cheetos. She didn't actually offer anything, but basically it's all up for grabs. EVIL! She asked if I had lunch plans, to go somewhere. I said no. I asked her if she wanted me to and she grumbled about eating the money she just spent. Then Larissa called wanting to know if we want her to bring anything home for lunch because she was about to get off. Mom just chowed major Cheetos so said no. Then yesterday Larissa and I went shopping. Thursday we planned for the three of us, but timing kept Mom away. Larissa and I went to Cerritos. She thought we'd walk the mall, but I just wanted to go to certain stores. Spent $170. Got some goodies at Bath and Body Works. Two bras and thigh highs from Victoria's Secret. Didn't find anything I liked that would fit me at The Limited. Got outfits from both Lerner and Express. Neither really fit well. The black skirt from Lerner is barely zipable. The red top and cardigan are perfect though. They are incentive outfits. Larissa called herself a fat cow in the Express line. At Lerner she left and sat in the mall. When we were leaving she started to complain about not seeing other stores, which I thought was odd because I told her where I wanted to go, it was my idea to go shopping and she was going with me. Besides, what else did she want to see? Anyway, she then asked if I wanted to take anything home. I'm so glad that I was smart enough to drop my money in my bag in the trunk. I told her I would have if she was buying. That I don't buy food. She had six bucks. That rules out El Rey Taco. She mentioned Burger King or Jack in the Box, neither of which excited me of course. She mentioned I could get potato wedges. No dice. I told her if she really wanted to she could just go for herself. She did. Right before ordering she sort of asked something about being sure that I didn't want anything, but she didn't wait for a response before placing her order. In fact, what she said to me wasn't a question. It was a statement, like she was talking to herself. I pointed it out to her and she even agreed. The total – oh she got a shake, potato wedges and Jumbo Jack – was $5.27. Then she sheepishly asked, "You didn't change your mind, did you?" Was she really depressed about being a fat cow and respond by chowing on fast food? Mom and Dad did Little Caesar's. There was still pizza, but fortunately it had mushrooms and I don't even like their pizza, not that I heard an offer for it. There were also breadsticks that made the house smell like garlic. That turned my appetite on. I ended up eating one. Didn't really mean to but it simply worked out that way. Meaning, I couldn't help myself. I have to keep on track if I'm going to be able to wear the clothes I just bought. Stay focused. 223 this morning was a wonderful surprise. That's four down from yesterday. Didn't expect it, but man I'll take it. My lowest is 220 ½ so I am really close. Can't wait to hit the teens!!! I'm so close to hitting the 100 pounds lost, I can taste it. Literally. Probably in the next few days – Yay!!!

December 10, Sunday
222 ¼
Fast
Work 10-4, Mia was late
Also worked with Courtney and Donna who made some seriously mean streak comments. Saw old Montebello customer.
Wore jean/rayon dress & Express tights!

December 11, Monday
219 ¾ - so close
Fast
Pepsi
Finals
Classics paper due, dropped it off at 2:25 p.m.
Reading for film, Film Review Session
Recopy notes

December 12, Tuesday
218 ½ - Wow. Just wow. First 100 down, another 100 to go?
Fast
Finals
History of Film Final 7-9 ? okay
Paper = B+ (Engl 2)
Major BM around 4:45

December 13, Wednesday
217 – So happy. Merry Christmas to me!
Finals
Rice (beef flavor) with corn, can of olives, Pepsi, slice of toast
Spanish Final 11-1
Size 16 skirt fit!!!
30 minutes bike, 7.75 miles; Ab 30-10-10-20

December 14, Thursday
219
Finals
4 bites of spaghetti/olive free, Beef taquitos, small nachos with chips
Final Film essay due
Engl poem paper returned B- = say what now? Rewrite!!!

1BC
1Cran

December 15, Friday
220
Finals
Classics Final 2-4
Engl Final 8-10:30
Turned in Angela Ball response too
2 greenie beanie cookies, 2 butterscotch cookies, lick caramel spoon, 2 slices sausage/Canadian bacon pizza
30 minutes bike, 7.6 miles; Ab 20 (4)

December 16, Saturday
221 ½
Cut and wrap my homemade caramels
Watch Bugsy Malone
3 slices of pizza and salad with blue cheese dressing, caramels, Pepsi, Nachos with beef and beans, 1 Tropical Freeze
Hung with Alice, Rachel and Jewel watching movies and eating pound cake. Sleepover.

December 17, Sunday
? up early
Work 9:30-4:30 with Rachel mostly
2 bags chips pretzel, Captain Crunch, caramels, cookies, slice of toast, Rice bag, Pepsi, Cottage cheese, slice of cheese

December 18, Monday
228 - ouch
Fast, Pepsi
Passport picture done, saw Franny at Sav-On
451 Intro read
30 minutes treadmill, .8 miles, 47 calories; Ab 30 3(15)

December 19, Tuesday
224 ¾
Start Jury Duty
Walked during lunch
Applied for passport
Acapulco for gift exchange with co-workers

4 midori sours, nachos, buffalo wings, El Rey Taco green quesadilla

December 20, Wednesday
225 ¼
Fast
Pepsi
I feel a cold coming on
30 minutes treadmill, 47 calories, .8 miles; 30 minutes treadmill, 45 calories, .8 miles; 40 ab (3-15)
2 Anthropology videos and 2 rounds of exercise
Mom and Larissa went shopping

December 21, Thursday
223 ¼
Day 2 of Jury Duty
Snoop Dog in the elevator
Cut caramels, made marshmallows (not very well)
Bean/cheese burrito, green quesadilla, graham crackers, N.E. Clam Chowder, slice of cheese, cheese/tomato sandwich

December 22, Friday
226 ¼
Anthropology Final = FINAL final
Nachos with cheese and black olives, 2 slices home pizza
Visit Rachel at Alice's. Bummed out. Tommy Burger with chili. Shopped with them at Super Kmart
Sidewalk parking

December 23, Saturday
Get Rachel up – sleep in
Ice Skating at home
2 slices of pizza, Pop tarts, nachos with Larissa, tried a new batch of marshmallows
Drop off gifts at Montebello – what a mess. Saw Angela, Christina and Julie. Met Sue.
French Kiss

December 24, Sunday
230 ¼
Worked 2-6:30

Caramels, Del Taco Chicken quesadilla, Shrimp(20), Nacho chips with salsa
Cards, Batman Forever

December 25, Monday
231 ½
CHRISTMAS!!!
Home for lunch - Duck, Chips with salsa, olives, potatoes with gravy, stuffing, green beans, beets, Pepsi, wine, caramels
At Alice's for dinner - Turkey, more potato and stuffing, green bean casserole, pumpkin pie

December 26, Tuesday
232
Third Day of Jury Service
Duck, potatoes with gravy, stuffing, caramels
Walk with Dad
30 minutes bike, 7.4 miles, Ab 40

December 27, Wednesday
229 ½
Fourth Day of Jury Duty
Full plate of stuffing, mashed potatoes with gravy, shredded cheese, 5 olives, milk, Pepsi, Coconut cake, bread with butter
30 minutes treadmill, 43 calories, .7 miles; Ab 40

December 28, Thursday
229 ¼
Called Jury Duty – overslept
Milk, coconut cake, olives, chips and salsa, Pepsi
30 minutes bike, 7.6 miles

December 29, Friday
228 ½
Fifth Day of Jury Duty – all day, no panel
Move to Traffic Court on Tuesday
Chips and cheese, toast with butter, slice of cheese,
Beef/cheese burrito, beef taquitos
Visit with Angela, Ava, Julie and Christina
30 minutes bike, 7.75 miles; AB

December 30, Saturday
229
Work 9:30-5:30 or 5:45
Green quesadilla, turkey, Olive Garden, Denny's
Went home to shower and get my stuff together for Vegas and next thing I know Mom's coming along. We swung by Alice's to meet up with the rest of the gang and then picked up Tamarra on our way out of town.
Arrive in Vegas around 3:30 a.m.

December 31, Sunday
Cab ride
Breakfast – sausage, Lunch buffet – pork chop AND prime rib, Dinner buffet – prime rib AGAIN
Brought in the New Year on the downtown strip then drove home after. Drowsy and dangerous but we arrived in tact.
Home around 6 a.m.

YEAR TWO

JANUARY

January 1, Monday
229 ¾
Wok Express – teriyaki chicken, 2 egg rolls, 3 almond cookies, pumpkin cookies
Arrive back from Vegas around 6:30 a.m.
Puzzles, NO George

    Driving back from Las Vegas was an experiment in terror. I had a very difficult time staying awake. No thanks to the sleepers. That was by far the most annoying aspect of the trip – that the nappers never rotated. I witnessed a selfish, immature side of Rachel that would have been best left uncovered. She still really expects her mother to pick up the pieces. Arrived home between 6 and 6:30. Slept straight to 3 PM. Fortunately, George and Kimberly changed their plans so were not expected. Got up at 4. Stiff and sore, feeling like a bloated cow. Ate Wok Express anyway. Finished it off too. Plus 2 egg rolls and 3 almond cookies. Damn it was good. I don't know about this meat thing. I mean when I'm thin and maintaining my weight I'm gonna want my meat. I think I'm just a carnivore by nature. Mom had a meeting to go to. Watched Sneakers. It was a pretty good movie. Really didn't want to go to bed to get up for Jury duty. Chowed on Mom's pumpkin cookies. Did my Beatles puzzle.

January 2, Tuesday
230 ¼
Fast
1 Pepsi
6th day of Jury Service at Traffic Court

    Got up early and headed down to Traffic Court. 6th day of jury service in Boredom hell. Bought a Pepsi. Didn't eat all day. Called the Post Office from court. No help. Can't even progress unless it is a life or death matter. The girl didn't understand. Tried the long distance number and it was busy. Told Jury person about my trip and she postponed me until the 16th. I really don't see why she didn't just set me free. I mean, I served the five days – come on. Got home and called about the passport and no pick-up. Getting annoyed about being asked about it all. Sore subject. Decided I really should purchase my schoolbooks and get a calendar and this journal while I was at it. I find I generally follow my own rules when I set guidelines down in ink. Really this was a very non-productive day. Didn't hammer out resolutions or anything. I guess I was still mentally and emotionally and physically recovering from all that was this New Year and New Year's Eve celebrations. At least the rest of my vacation won't be ruined by Jury Duty.

January 3, Wednesday
225 ¾
Slept in
Purchased Oreo's, cheese, soda
Had stuffing and duck, olives
Puzzles, read mags, start cleaning

    Made a list of things to do today, but didn't do very well. Slept in pretty late and had no ambition to do or go anywhere really. Why I needed my journal and resolutions set can be made apparent by what I ended up doing. Let's start with the fact that I finished the X-mas stuffing and had a good serving of duck. It was my third. Me, the proclaimed herbivore has had three servings. I doubt anyone can say the same. I needed soda and craved Oreo's in a major way. Larissa and I went to Albertson's. I also got cheese figuring I might as well have something of relative nutritional value if I'm going to oink over Oreo's. Worked on a puzzle and maintained some conversation with Larissa and Mom. Actually didn't break through the bag like I thought I would. I hate vacation. I feel so awkward not really doing anything. No real goals to accomplish and even self-imposed goals like cleaning the bathroom seem frustrating and bring on a headache. I'm out of the sync of the world. It's times like these that I truly realize how uncomfortable I am in my own skin.

January 4, Thursday
229 ½
Definitely no passport – had to call Alice yesterday
Purchased books at school and put on Nations by mistake
Receive Anthropology final – A

It's almost midnight. Ming came to my room to sleep. It's the second time this week. I purchased this journal to fulfill my journal entry resolution, which I haven't even cemented yet. I really do need to work on my resolutions tomorrow. Went shopping for books for next semester and couldn't resist the temptation of charging personal use items to the tuition bill. Then came to find out that the stupid chicky put the whole bill on my MC instead of just the eight-dollar difference from my USC card. I could kill. So could Dad. Anyway entries for the $1^{st} - 3^{rd}$ will be done tomorrow. Thought today would be more productive but I've gotten the lazies. Not doing Jury Duty or going to Saudi. Got Anthropology final back. No personal note. An <u>excellent</u> exam. 33/33 on all three questions. Confused about exam average. Posted as 92.5 when I had a 97 on the midterm. Got an A anyway. If I didn't I would have been calling, but it means I earned a higher A than noted and maybe someone else got credit for my midterm score. I guess I should <u>let it go</u> because I got the grade.

January 5, Friday
231
Ouch! ODing on Oreo's, cheese, potatoes really hurt
One little BM and one normal one
Made resolutions, cleaning
30 minutes bike, 7.6 miles

The Oreo cookie made into cereal breakfast really hurt me. Or was it finishing the cheese at 12:30 am. Or the mashed potatoes or the entire yellow bowl of buttered popcorn that left my lips feeling dry and chapped. Feel a little bad because I never really said goodbye to Alice. I'm not really good at good-bye's anyway. She was probably busy. I hope she didn't miss me. I talked to her Wednesday after making calls about the processing of my passport. Spent quality time duking it out with one lady who then directed to call a number no one was answering. Also talked to Rachel. She was brief. I guess the store was busy. She didn't actually say. She has me off the schedule through the 13th. A little annoyed that she posted the schedule without giving me any hours. I do need the money. I think she could tell. But I'm also a bit relieved I don't have to work. Need to ask for the 14th off for the visitation. Better remember. Finally made my New Year's resolutions. Some major, some minor. The daily stuff will be difficult to keep up – like this. But so will ensuring travel plans. Everything's doable and possible and stuff I really want for myself.

January 6, Saturday
228
Thought this would be day 2
Melissa called, our store won a Chinese meal which is scheduled for 7 p.m. tomorrow
Rachel seeing Exhale tonight
3 slices cheese, bread, butter, olives, rice with and without corn
30 minutes bike, 7.75 miles
Bath

      Ming slept in my room again last night. Third time this week. What's the deal? Thought I was well on my way into day two when the phone rang and it was for me. It was Melissa letting me know that the store won some Chinese Food Dinner Contest that I was totally unaware of. Anyway the plan was to go to the Chinese Harvest tomorrow at 7 PM. Rachel yelled a hello over the phone then told Melissa to tell me she was going to see Waiting to Exhale tonight. My only response was okay. I didn't know what to say. I want to see the movie, but wasn't really in the mood to go anywhere or see Rachel. I think I've seen too much of her lately. And I wasn't about to invite myself. It irked me. Debated whether or not to attend the Chinese thing, but figured if I didn't I would get questioned about it and I just as soon go. But it means being social. It also means eating (and probably meat) which I hadn't planned on doing. It also meant eating today so I wouldn't be running for the bathroom tomorrow. I'm just really annoyed and frustrated. I don't want to be forced to have a good time. I don't want to be told I'm happy – or worse – that I'm not. Ugh!

January 7, Sunday
Read/dump mags, drop off car
El Rey Taco small nachos, side of corn chips, Chinese Harvest with work group (plenty of meat), Corn dog, butterscotch sundae
30 minutes bike, 7.4 miles

    Decided in typical Stephens dietary fashion to load up today. That is the only way I can explain myself. Went to El Rey Taco on my own, which meant I was paying. Decided that this would be the last time I ever buy myself El Rey Taco. Quite a challenge but it is such a downfall that I really should try. I did exercise but boy did I feel pooky doing it. El Rey Taco weighed heavy on my mind and stomach. Did the Chinese Harvest thing with work. ODed on meat. Really enjoyed it. Talked about weight loss. Rachel told people I'd lost 90 lbs. (because god damn it, I've gone up) and told me to pass around my driver's license. Thanks for putting me on the spot, girl. Pretty annoyed she threw that number out there. Others were shocked. They spent a lot of time talking about Susan and how she says she totally wants to lose weight before getting married but she really doesn't want to lose weight by her actions. Personally, I don't think she really wants to get married and she's willing to use her weight as an excuse. Amanda found jealousy in her heart when she saw someone else's family with four generations of women and she has no daughter. We all told Monica not to settle when it comes to men. Rachel missed the movie because she fought with Daniel and spent the night crying. Donna's older than me, which is scary consider how she acts. We think Courtney's gay and Isabella needs to find her life dream. Me. I'm okay, I guess.

January 8, Monday
229 ¾
First call about car came in around noon
Writing up papers

Another call around 2:30, the morons couldn't find car
Call about 4:30
Need 30,000 major tune up not 40,000 plus parts $930
Done around 4 PM tomorrow. WHAT?!?!?!
Puzzle, bath, clean, read

    Just like I thought. I didn't get up until McKenna called about my car. To my surprise that wasn't until about noon. The girl was calling to find out what I wanted done. Second call came in around 2:30. They couldn't find my car and needed to know where I parked it, which was really frightening considering I was parked at the curb. Mom said she was making a rice dish and asked me if I wanted any. When I said no she glowered at me for quite a while before she turned away in disgust and went to the back bedroom to sew. I know she doesn't really like rice so for her to prepare it as a meal is a deal. I know that she knows I like rice so was anticipating a resounding yes from me but I want to starve this week. How can I buckle on the first day? That's so wimpy. When McKenna called back the estimate was $930 to be delivered by 4pm tomorrow. She did a 30K major tune up instead of the 40K I think my car needed. (30 is more expensive). Didn't exercise today and definitely could have but my period has me feeling rather lackluster so I wimped out.

January 9, Tuesday
228 ½
Received passport in mail and wanted to SCREAM!!!
Picked up my car, went to Sam's with Mom and got new book bag, Larissa did NOTHING all day
Apple pie, milk, El Rey Taco bean/cheese burrito, green quesadilla
30 minutes treadmill, 44 calories, .7 miles
Talk to Dad on walk 1.25 miles

    The cat meowed me out of bed. That pig didn't even want to go out. He just wanted food and attention. What a typical man. Received my passport in the mail. I wanted to die. No! No! I wanted to kill somebody – and not with a gun. No, that wouldn't be satisfying enough. I want to do it with my bare hands. A little too late government fuckers. Rachel wasn't at work or home when I called. Picking up my car at McKenna was a whole ordeal. They were delinquent in bringing my car around. I probably waited a good 30 minutes. The Cashier and Daniel the driver could tell I was pissed. Too bad I wasn't in a fighting mood. My La Habra ticket, passport and NationsBank checks haven't cleared yet. I hope NationsBank doesn't ding me. Went to Sam's Club with Mom. I got my book bag, also munchies for the visitation. Mom went out for a fundraising meeting. I took to the treadmill. Just got back to my puzzle when Dad came home and asked if I would go on a walk. I agreed. Larissa needed ten minutes so was left behind. Passed Mom on the street. She later thanked me for going. Dad asked me about future school plans and career stuff. He's trying to plan ahead. He said something about maybe driving my car one day. That REALLY bothered me. Gave in to El Rey Taco. (Bean and cheese burrito & green quesadilla) but didn't have to PAY!!! Then topped it with apple pie & milk. Oh well.

January 10, Wednesday
228 ½
USC – First day of Classes
No Wednesday classes, slept in, cleaned, tidy bathroom, rearrange books, call Rachel
Thisclose to making it today – but NO! 3 slices cheese, bread, butter rice dish, apple pie and milk
30 minutes bike, 7.7 miles

Just when I thought I had it going on. Couldn't pass up El Rey Taco yesterday. Decided I'll only do fast food if someone else is paying. And Mom did, for me. Larissa had to cover herself. Yay! And to think I was lying about not having any money. Good for me. I'm finally putting me, not them or my appetite first. Anyway, slept in late today. Scary cause tomorrow is an early day and long day. Today was the first day of Spring Session, but I don't have any Wednesday classes. Thought I'd starve today but it occurred to me that I should eat tomorrow. I'm going to have a lot of dead time at school tomorrow and it's unrealistic to think I won't eat at some point. If only out of boredom. So why not plan. Have breakfast. Plan dinner. I've been wanting steak, so why not tomorrow. Make it a semester start tradition. Besides this weekend is the visitation. I should relax and enjoy, maintain. Let the first week of school happen. Then freak out. So I had a grilled cheese and extra slices. Then I went back for some of the rice

Mom made yesterday. She was glad she wasn't the only one to have some. She didn't know that Larissa had. The apple pie seemed to take the wind out of her sails as she chomped on a Butterfinger. Hit the bike after calling Rachel.

January 11, Thursday
228 ¼
School all day
Engl 261, 262, 430 and Spanish
2 eggs, 1 slice cheese, 2 slice bread butter, OJ, graham crackers, PB & butter sandwich, steak, salad with ranch dressing, 2 small potatoes with butter, chocolate cookie dough ice cream
Walk with Dad 1.25 miles

  Early day and full day. Felt almost surreal getting up and driving into LA. No smog day. All of the buildings were visible. It was fabulous and horrific at the same time. Classes were okay. 261 the guy is totally Republican and boasted over his four books. 262 the guy was wearing Converse and had a spot on his unbuttoned white shirt. This guy has some potential to be cool. I just hope we see eye to eye. Shakespeare lady was a bit dry and I have a thing for the subject. Scary Spanish guy made us do something, which bummed me out. I intentionally didn't take my book, which meant I had to share with some anal guy named Peter. I think I'm going to like this professor better than my last one. Ate like a hog. Up early to have eggs, cheese, toast. Took food to school. Graham crackers during my break. Peanut butter sandwich before Spanish but I didn't have the apple. Stopped at the grocery for my traditional start of a semester steak. Also had potatoes and salad. Nobody home. Then had some cookie dough ice cream. Took a walk with Dad. Talked about school. Watched NBC line up.

January 12, Friday
228 ½
Started Beowulf, calendars, bath
Graham crackers in milk, El Rey Taco small nachos, finish ice cream, 2 medium potatoes with butter
Called Rachel – Christina went to the hospital
30 minutes treadmill, 50 calories, .8 miles
Walk with Dad 1.25 miles

Surprised that I only went up a quarter of a pound after everything I ate yesterday. But I guess I shouldn't be surprised with my current double dosings of exercise and the general stress load. Slept in and had a graham cracker breakfast at noon. Since Mom was sewing I went to the family room to start reading Beowulf. Did my calendars for the upcoming months. Mom and Larissa ran errands. Brought home a late El Rey Taco lunch. Larissa paid. Cool, huh? I think I'm going to go to Spain and Portugal, maybe even France between my USC finals and LBCC graduation. Called Rachel. Alice and Joseph are doing a three day lay over (on the Saudi people) because of the New York blizzard. Poor dears. Rachel and I pouted at each other over the phone. And Joseph to be with her, of all people. Christina went (emergency at eight months) to the hospital. Next Friday work people are going to Safari Club. Rachel and Jacob are trying to set up Isabella and I with Bryan and Jacob. Rachel wanted to see if I wanted to do a movie, but changed her mind after hearing my schedule. Did the treadmill and walked with Dad. (I offered)

January 13, Saturday
228
Michelle's Reception
Up at 6:30, leaving at 7:30, flat tire near Buttonwillow
Huge turnout for reception
Cheetos, Tuna Melt with fries and blue cheese dressing, 2 Filet of Fish, 1 soft serve cone, chocolate kiss

Woke up at 6:30 to voices. I don't remember ever actually getting any sleep. Really surprised to go down half a pound especially since I had El Rey Taco and late night potatoes. Had a Tuna Melt. Bought some junk and soda in the gift shop. They had a decent briefcase for $20. Got maybe 2.5 mi. down the road before we were hit with a flat tire. Got the car jacked, but couldn't get the hubcap off. Turns out I was also attacking the rim. Called AAA. Had a nice jog to the call box. I definitely still do not have a jogger's body. Then we had a hunt for a tire. Pulled over by Mr. Dickhead CHP. Had Mom crying and me trying to calm her and answer his asshole questions. To protect and to serve? More like to harass and disrupt. Asshole didn't even offer any type of assistance. Two good Samaritans did though. They should be CHP. Did

McDonald's before reception. Can't believe I actually went there. The reception was packed. It was great. Jenny, Doris and Mrs. Statler came together. Jenny is ruling over Glendale. They recently added six new members. Wow! General theme for the day was love and friendship. Love Can Build A Bridge Between You and Me. Did McDonald's because Foster's was closed. Felt like a pig about it. Larissa wouldn't go with Mom to visit with her girls. Mom said she swore – a NO! NO!

January 14, Sunday
Check out of the hotel at 11, arrive at gym at 11:20
Cheetos, tapioca pudding, 2 beef meximelts, 1 taco, Starburst, 3 cookies, fruit drink
Drive home
Split Pea Anderson traveler special, 2 bowls; Jack in the Box grilled sourdough burger in the Magic Mountain area

Mom thinks I have a size 12 butt and that I'm trimming down nicely between waist and hip. Larissa commenting on my mustache really made me self-conscious. Rachel also mentioned (briefly/fleeting) a beard in Vegas. Now I'm all paranoid about facial hair. What to do? Arrived at the gym way too early – 11:20 a.m. And for what? Cindy arrived sometime after 1:30 – wearing make-up, but still looking like a slob. Megan and Mr. Anderson were the only other people from my year. Same as last year. This time Megan was wearing a formal though so I made her go for escort. Then she made me introduce her. I said "my" instead of "one" which apparently caught Sherri's ear. I didn't notice but Mom told me about it during the drive home. Sat by Jenny. Did a little talking. She's in charge of the adult skit. Doris wants Larissa or I or both to go to Phyllis' installation on the 3rd. I don't know what that's about. I definitely need a new job. Larissa is very focused on food. She was always concerned about the next food break. She was jealous of my sourdough burger I could tell. I was happy to get all the food stuffs that I wanted in so now I can get back to fasting. Arrived home around 2 a.m.

January 15, Monday
233 ½
Work 9:30-5:30; Set up clearance

Rough getting up
No scheduled relief, so we had lunch delivery from Sammy's – plain nachos and a Pepsi; potatoes with butter and cheese
Didn't finish reading, but went to bed anyway

    Had to work today which was cruel (not Rachel's fault – I volunteered) because I was dead on my feet. I knew I was scheduled for all day, but nobody told me that we wouldn't have any relief. At first I was cool with it because then I couldn't eat, but I was thirsty and there were cookies in the back. Ended up ordering from Sammy's Tacos. Talked to Rachel about tipping when they charge for delivery. Also told her I was going to Spain. She told me she doesn't want her life anymore. Why did she get married and have a kid? Also, that I needed a lot of money. I told her about my Anthropology grade. She said, "You thought about calling, just so you could talk to him again." I wanted to hit her. Not saying she was wrong, just that I wanted to smack her for saying it. And no way would I call over a petty dispute for a higher A. Rachel wanted me to invite Larissa to Safari Club. I didn't. Found out that she'll be working. So will Rachel for that matter. She was still annoyed that I didn't even ask. But I want to have a good time and these are MY friends. She said might attend a meeting, just to see me all dressed up. Daniel got a job. Waiter for Olive Garden. The other one he lost was IHOP. They found someone with more qualifications.

January 16, Tuesday
232 ½
Up at 6 to shower
261 – very dull, napped in library (L)
262 – technical dull started to nod
430 – no copy of Richard III or reading, felt left out
Skip Spanish
Raining after 4:30
Hit bookstore, home 6:15, BED!!!

    Had a very difficult time getting out of bed and into the shower. Even worse getting out of bed to get dressed. Didn't really want that chill or to get dressed. So I wore leggings and sweatshirt. Basically my pajamas. First two classes were okay. Took a nap in the library. I don't know if I made a noise or not. I think I did. Two guys were like, "What was that, a fucking cow?" But later they talked about hunger noises and one guy couldn't wait to have lunch. So it's a mystery. Started to nod off at the end of 262 which didn't really make me comfortable going into 430. Then I was about one of five that didn't bring the right text. Also, had nothing to say because I hadn't finished the reading. I hate being in that position. After class it was raining. Went to the bookstore. Spent more than I should have. Bought Spanish tapes. I hope it helps. Dad got some from the library, but hasn't done anything with them. Went for the tram stop. Too tired and miserable to think of doing Spanish. He's passing out a due date list, too. Maybe I should visit office hours. Took about an hour and forty-five minutes to drive home. Got home at 6:15 and went straight to bed. Slept solid for eight hours. Up briefly then out again.

January 17, Wednesday
228
Man did I sleep – 16 hours with a few interruptions
Read Beowulf and Richard III
Caught up journal from weekend, did laundry, called one potential job
Felt weak-kneed, major headache

One positive thing about yesterday. With all the things to do and being tired I never took time to eat. In fact, until 2:15 a.m. all I drank was water. Major farts yesterday and the day before. Had a BM after weighing in. Went down 4 ½ lbs. Need more of those. Rest of Jury Duty service put off until March 11th. They're taking my Spring Break. Awesome. They wanted my summer, but no way was I about to do that and potentially get paneled and there goes my whole summer. I need a job, but I'm wondering how much more I can handle. I realize I only have four classes, but it is a lot of reading. Still, if I got a job I could probably give up working at the mall or only be a Sunday morning girl. We'll see. Did several loads of laundry. Did some basic straightening in my room. Felt very nauseated and had a major case of weak knees. A real surprise considering this was only day two, but I guess it's been a dramatic drop. Did some reading but certainly didn't catch up. Called the number for the Reading Instructor position. Steve was out and didn't return my call. I think I'll call back Friday when I have time. I need to call Cal Fed about that service charge thing. Also need to produce a new resume. Major headache. Right eye really bugging me too. Mom did errands and picked up El Rey Taco. I wanted it too, but no. Mom's really kind of plumped up.

January 18, Thursday
224 ¼
Major headache at school – wondered if I could make it
261 – Viking ships
262 – scanning, boring
Cranberry Cocktail 11.5 oz.
430 – couldn't read because of different edition
Oral Presentation sign-ups for Spanish - eek

  Down to 224 ½. That's almost ten pounds in two days. No wonder I don't feel well. My body is trying to adjust. Thought about getting a snack bar at the parking center, but told myself I could at least make it through the first class. Viking ship pictorials and lecture – very dull. Had a Cranberry Cocktail after class. Figured it was better than something solid although it was 200 calories. Did my Shakespeare responses and scanned prose. 262 was very technical – dealing with sound. Dull. Felt really stupid in 430. Oral presentation sign-ups. Passed on these topics. They're flying somewhere overhead. My Richard III had no line numbers so I couldn't read when called upon. What a dork! Vegetated between 4:30 and Spanish. Didn't miss much Tuesday but everything today was beyond me. Most of the time I had no idea what was going on. I need to work on my vocabulary in a major way. Forgot to pick up Financial Aid packet. I really need to do that. Spanish has extra credit available which I'm really happy about. Watch a movie – nine points for a two page write up about it. Right on! Christy has everything pierced, but seems cool. Fine Arts and Theatrical something major. Mom went to the grocery and bought tasty stuff. I hate her.

January 19, Friday
222
Ladies Night Out with the co-workers
Tuna melt with tomato, Chicken teriyaki, mac and cheese, 4 almond cookies
Alice goes to UCI

30 minutes treadmill, 46 calories, .8 mile

  Figured I might as well eat something today since I was going out drinking tonight and didn't want to have a problem with alcohol hitting an empty stomach or having to run to the bathroom because of eating while I'm out. Since we had two tomatoes I made a tuna melt with one. It was really good. Then I sent Larissa out to Wok Express. I got a pint of chicken and almond cookies. I've been craving it for a while. Exercised on the treadmill; felt good. Called about the Reading Inst. Position again. I have an interview tomorrow. Need to do a resume. Also requested applications for the other two advertised tutoring positions. Called Rachel around eight just to be sure we were still on. More work people are going than I expected – like Courtney and Amanda. I thought it would be more select. Plus Jacob's friend Jacob isn't going. Neither is Isabella. And it's not Safari Club. Going to Cue's instead. A nine o'clock call changed it all. Alice went to UCI (Tracy took her). She passed out, threw up and soiled herself. Went to bakery. Let Rachel vent at me about the family situation. Daniel showed up – awkward. When we were done getting everything as ready for deliveries as we could we went to the hospital. Stayed at the hospital until around 2 a.m. Jacob took me back to my car. They think it might have been food poisoning. Also fatigue. Joseph never showed while I was there.

January 20, Saturday
227
Wrote/typed resume, interview at 2 p.m. went very well
Bumming around, watched ice skating
El Rey Taco – small nachos with extra chips, green quesadilla

  Major guttural cramps due to eating that plate at 2:30 a.m. It's like I'm waiting for the gas to come. Finished typing resume as I walked out the door. Mrs. Thompson stopped by. Mom's doing a dress bag plus more quilt squares for her daughter. The interview went extremely well. It's a real good thing I did the resume. I would have a job right now if my class schedule were different. She's looking for Tuesday/Friday 2-7 and I have 2 Tuesday classes that conflict, but some guy just finished his Ph.D. and got a job. He's only coming in on Friday and she's going to ask him if he wants to go (he's staying as a favor) so I might be taking his position. I hope he wants to quit. 5 hrs. a week. $10 per hour and I don't really have to do much. No lesson planning or grading. Just answer any question the students may have. Wasn't going to eat, but Mom offered to buy El Rey Taco. How can I refuse a free meal? I buckled. Then I planned to exercise but never got off my butt. Watched a lot of ice skating and shocked Mom by saying yes to helping her with quilt squares. She has five to do, hopefully by tomorrow, so I pitched in along with Larissa. Got a sore finger to prove it.

January 21, Sunday
226 ¾
Work 10:30-6:30 with Susan and Amanda
Jack In The Box potato wedges and large Coke, butter cookies; Dinner at Alice's – meatloaf, mashed potatoes, veggies, 3 Pepsi's, cocoa, ice cream dessert, home potatoes

Really didn't feel like getting up to go to work, especially didn't want to get out of bed after my shower. Couldn't decide if I was eating or not. Kept going back and forth. Was running out the door kind of late. Susan went to Jack in the Box and I got potato wedges and a drink. She paid. In fact, neither of us wanted lunch so I ended up never paying her back. She's ever frustrated with her relationship with Arnold, especially their sex life. Also worked with Amanda. Apparently, Courtney made a fool of herself at Cues. Amanda said I'm open to receive a man. There has been a change in me and I'm ready now. She sees me spending three months trooping through Europe, based out of the south of France. She thinks I am going to assume the professor role in Educating Rita. She, I guess, thinks I lost my professor. Rachel invited me over for dinner. Alice looked so much better. Jacob was more thoughtful than usual. Daniel is jealous of my relationship with Rachel. Made some comment to her about my hanging out a lot. At least I didn't go begging for an invitation. Stayed past 11 PM. Got home, Larissa was up.

January 22, Monday
230
Potatoes with 2 slices of cheese, almond cookies, noodles, green beans, bread sticks, chocolate brownie ice cream

Sell back books at LBCC, bath, called about a film job, left unreturned message
Larissa got a job as Taylor's gofer
30 minutes treadmill, .8 miles, 47 calories

  Man do I need to lay off the food and get my ass back into exercising. I think I should eat something on days that I have school, just because I don't want to have a problem there and if I always have a headache when I go to class I won't be able to concentrate, I'll have a bad experience and then I won't want to go back. Went to LBCC to sell back books. Almost given a hard time about my ID, but I nipped it in the bud. Got $44. They weren't buying back my Anthropology book though. That makes me wonder about things. Went to the grocery after picking up more almond cookies. Got large ones which was a mistake. Too big and dried out. Ate healthy. Thought about skipping dinner. Got my butt on the treadmill and eventually worked a hunger up. Didn't have any fruit today though. That's bad. I need to work on what I eat when I am eating. Mom saw Sherri yesterday. Grace is trying to find me material. What a motivator to keep going. Need to shed more, make a bigger impact. Enjoyed a bath, but didn't do reading for tomorrow. Why not?

January 23, Tuesday
230 ½
Graham crackers, milk, almond cookies; deli roast beef sandwich, potato wedges, 6 pieces of See's chocolates
261 Beowulf almost done
262 scan test
430 start Richard II
Skipped Spanish
Shopping at Robinsons-May for Clinique to get the bonus gift, Wherehouse
Almost had a BM at school
30 minutes bike, 7.4 miles

  I hate Larissa. Actually this should fall under yesterday, but the more I think about it the more I realize. She is such a lazy butt and has opportunity just fall into her lap. She got a job yesterday. No interview, no resume, no worry. Just a phone call to Taylor. George called Sunday to let us know she had potential opportunities for both of us. She didn't do anything for it and will be making $10 per hour. Taylor didn't return my call. It had something to do with the Cannes Film Festival so a brief thing, if I get it. Today I'll be at school all day so I guess I'll talk to her Wednesday. School was a drag. It's a pain in the ass when I don't keep up with the reading. Bailed before Spanish. Just didn't feel like sticking it out. Called home and got the answering machine. Went to Robinson's-May. Got gift, compact and brow shaper. Mia helped me – she was nice. Oh, Rachel told me our Mia is going to Express – good for her! Rented Educating Rita, they didn't have Richard III. Hit See's and the deli. Called Taylor again. Mom and Larissa went to El Rey Taco after going to Sam's Club. They bought a shit load of party type food. Damn! Finished my half plate Roast Beef and potato wedges. Watched TV. Felt like a bloated cow. Finally got my ass in gear to exercise anyway. Real good thing too.

January 24, Wednesday
232 ½
Finish graham and almond cookies in milk, finish chocolates and Ben & Jerry ice cream, crab sandwich, 2 avocadoes and cheese, 3 buttered breadsticks, 2 Pepsi, chips, salsa, cheese
Major gas finally pushed through Taylor
Cal Fed
30 minutes treadmill, 48 calories, .8 mile

    Went up two pounds. Back up to 232 ½. I'm glad I exercised or else it would have been worse. I've been doing too much eating when I'm not really hungry. I didn't really want to finish that sandwich. Ate some chocolates just because they were there. Watched Educating Rita. It was good. I'm not sure that I'm either character. Maybe somewhere between. I think the change Amanda sees is that I have discovered myself, or rather a part of myself. I'm not airy or earthy exactly but maybe have a pinch of both. Larissa says she's having a charley horse in her leg and back. She didn't know what to call it. Lots of moaning and groaning as she tried to stretch out. It reminded me of what I don't want to be. She wasn't sure if she could drop off my tape for me. What a lazy ass. I've been doing way too much eating when my tummy doesn't need it. I feel like a bloated cow and with reason. In two weeks I've lost and regained the same god damned twelve pounds. The jump up decreases the pep to get moving, but I put myself on the treadmill anyway. It was one of the first times I actually felt like crap after exercising. I felt like I needed to puke. Can't decide if I should start tomorrow or Friday. Talked to Taylor about Cannes. Finally. She's a hook up for an interview, that's all. Called Cal Fed.

January 25, Thursday
232 ½
Missing 261
Strained back picking up a Kleenex
Went to USC Student Health Service
Ordered to rest, no lifting heavy items, no exercise
Put on pain killers, muscle relaxers
2 almond cookies, graham crackers, milk, chips, salsa, cheese, crab, 3 ice cream sandwiches

Man, oh man, what a day this turned out to be. Started out pretty lazy. Up late last night and didn't feel like enduring 261. Getting ready for school I threw a Kleenex into my trash bin while sitting on my bed and it didn't make it so I bent over to pick it up and bingo, I couldn't sit up. Took forever for me to be able to move. Mom thought it was a pinched nerve. Made it to school. Wrote my Shakespeare response in the car. Seriously took me five minutes to get out of the car. Went straight to the USC Student Health Center. I was in so much pain I thought I was going to cry. Got an appointment. Nice doctor. Why could I not be pregnant? I laughed. Lack of sex. He was pretty dry in the sense of humor department, as I continually found out. Ordered to rest for a couple of days. And no heavy lifting. Made it home. Major, major sharp pain. I got a note for my classes. Took a two hour nap after eating and taking my first pain pill. It took me a half-hour to get out of bed and go to the bathroom. Kind of nice to be getting genuine sympathy for once. Dad was all concerned over classes. Watched TV. Why was Friends a repeat I had already seen? That's evil. ER was good as usual. The muscle relaxers – WOW! More please.

January 26, Friday
Still in pretty major pain – talk to Susan, then Donna about Sunday.

Chips, salsa, chicken noodles, 2 egg rolls, 2 almond cookies, teriyaki chicken, olives, Pepsi

Boy I could tell when that muscle relaxer wore off. Bam, it was gone. Kind of moped around the house. Did some Spanish flashcards. Attempted to read Beowulf and Grendel. Couldn't decide if I should prod along in Beowulf or just start Grendel, so instead I snoozed to Sinead. Then went to my room. Read a little from the How to Influence People book then took a nap. What a rough life. By the time I called work Rachel was gone. Susan recommended calling Donna, Isabella was doing inventory. Donna took my Sunday shift. Kind of feel sorry for her because she's going to have to work with Melissa and I know they don't like each other. Susan was totally understanding. I really didn't want to give my shift away though. Rachel wasn't home when I called. Larissa was going to Wok Express, which kind of suckered me into getting some chicken and egg rolls. She got some cookies and offered my some. Yay! If I had asked for them I would have had to pay. The chicken was pretty disappointing. It was really dry compared to the usual fare. Watch Pro World Ice skating. Spent a lot of time thinking about someone and it's starting to bother me. I should just do something about it.

January 27, Saturday
236
Graham crackers and milk, mac and cheese, teriyaki chicken, green beans, olives, finish Pepsi, chocolate mousse pie, finish cheese
Dictionary, bath

I've had some pretty major gas the last couple of days, which is typical of when I eat significant portions of meat. Well, finally after two days I finally took a dump. Major Lincoln Log and relief to have it out of my system, but then I had gut problems. It felt like a bad diarrhea spell coming on. I ended up having a total of four movements. None were actually diarrhea. I was really stopped up. Still felt like a bloated cow afterwards though. My digestive system still isn't with the program. My bowels are probably pissed. I don't eat and then when I do it's all fatty binding crap. Where's the good stuff? Watched more ice skating. Finished the Pros and amateur Europeans. Had Mac and cheese, green beans and chocolate mousse pie along with my chicken. Walking better, but moving while sitting is still pretty rough. Mom went to Yorba Linda for an installation. They kept her pretty late. Kurt and Yuka beat out Brian and Kristi. What a surprise. Paul was really disappointing. Commentary said he became introspective after Sergi died. Went to funeral. Watched most of My Little Chickadee. Mae West is too cool, like perfect, sassy, ballsy woman cool.

January 28, Sunday
237 ¼
Scheduled to work 11-6:30 but gave shift to Donna
2 donuts, milk, finished chocolate mousse pie; Porter's for dinner – 4 slices sausage pizza, salad with blue cheese dressing, bread
Dictionary, Dad had points meeting

    Good Intentions. Heard the REM/U2 inaugural ball version of One. It was very moving. Had thought today would be a good day to start fasting but there was no way. Couldn't avoid the leftover Mac and cheese or my chocolate mousse pie. Then Dad asked me to go with him to the Super Bowl Sunday breakfast which I thought was funny because I just ate and haven't been going anywhere due to my back. Finished looking my words up in the dictionary. Also, had two of the donuts that Dad brought home yesterday. Mom asked me to do brownies. I didn't. She wanted me to "save her from herself." I think they wanted them for the points meeting, but oh well. The kiddies got Kool-Aid. Larissa picked up Porter's. Mom asked me earlier if I would go and I complained about getting dressed. Later she asked me to call Larissa. Man, oh man was it good. I had four slices of sausage pizza, plus a meatball and the salad. Larissa with her bread selection and commenting about the dinner disappearance before I arrived reminded me of how we hoard food in this family. Had to suffer through space crap while eating, but it was worth it. Wondered if I would repeat last year.

January 29, Monday
236 ¾
Only one pain killer today
Reading Grendel, watched American Music Awards

El Rey Taco bean/cheese burrito, slice of toast, olives, grapes, ½ banana, lots of Rice-A-Roni, graham crackers (4)

    The sausage pizza left me having some pretty gnarly dreams. I was surprised with all I packed in yesterday that I actually went down half a pound. Woke up with every intention of fasting. Larissa was at work all day. Mom brought home El Rey Taco then offered me a Bean and Cheese burrito. It would have gone to Larissa if I had declined. She had a chili relleno burrito and a quesadilla. She also had an extra quesadilla. Maybe it would have been mine if Larissa had been home to be offered the bean and cheese. She didn't eat it, it went to the fridge. We covet. I had a slice of toast and salad. Mom eyes my bowl. Later I shared a banana with Larissa. She worked eight hours at the mall and came home with McDonald's. And she talks about losing weight. Not wanting to be her size. Blah, blah, blah! I fixed Rice-A-Roni which was bad. I apparently don't know how to make it. Had grapes while watching the American Music Awards. Garth Brooks didn't accept the Recording Artist of the Year award. He also performed a moving song in tribute to the Oklahoma City bombing. Reba was fighting back tears. I was vegging when I should have been preparing myself for school. Only took one painkiller today. Finished olives.

January 30, Tuesday
237
Shower and school
261 dull, dull, dull
262 loves his voice
430 sympathetic *paper postponed
150 lots of homework to do – quiz and composition on Thursday
Make-up homework, shop at House of Fabric for patterns

    Should have showered last night. Getting up early for it is a drag. 261/2 were both extremely dull. They both love to just ramble on. I swear if I weren't so into this they would totally turn me off of literature altogether. Ferguson was sympathetic to my back thing. New syllabus has our paper postponed by a week. Had to go to parking center for book swap. Came real close to leaving. It was really hard getting myself to go back. But I did. Good thing too. I missed a lot.

There was homework, a commercial, a quiz and composition to be turned in Thursday. Man, I missed a lot between the three days. It's a good thing I didn't push it. Saw smiley guy and Miss Louisiana talk after class. It looked like he got her number. I hate waiting for the tram. Went to House of Fabric to check out patterns. Their measurements run smaller than Victoria Secret's. I bought two. One needs a strapless bra. Went to Sav-On for soda. It's down to $.79. It was a very long day. Watched half of Frasier, then did my taxes. I owe CA $6.27 but the Feds are giving me a refund. Hit the sheets pretty hard and not very hungry.

January 31, Wednesday
233 ¼
Read Lear and worked on Spanish composition homework
2 buttered popcorn, 4 mini quiches, Dove bar, Pepsi

      Why am I in second day slump? Major rain coming down today. Went to school anyway. It was a perfect day for lulling around the house. Mom even left, but I had told myself I need to get to school to study. It's true I don't usually accomplish much here but I don't think I really accomplished much there either. I did some reading. Started my Spanish homework and phrases for my composition. Thought I saw Jason from Spanish 120 walk over to Leavey and I was right. He came up to the fourth floor. Exchanged greetings, which he prompted, when he walked by. My back was to him. I probably never would have known he went by if he didn't say something. I think the commute was a waste and real dangerous in heavy rain. Should exercise better judgement. Don't have to push so hard. Went to Sav-On for more soda. Thought I would pass out or pee in line. Came home and saw Dove bars in the freezer. The pizza was gone. I would have had it, had it still been there. Ended up having four quichey things, plus buttered popcorn after Mom offered a Dove bar. I figured I should go a head and have a little substance first. Law and Order. Up late writing my Spanish composition. Rachel finally called. Movie Saturday/Sunday.

FEBRUARY

February 1, Thursday
230 ½
Much to my surprise, a long day
430 nothing going
150 memorize, turned in homework, Composition quiz ☹
Pepsi

  Even though I ate yesterday I still dropped 2.75 lbs. I need to start exercising again. My back feels okay so it should be safe. Up .75 lbs. for the month. Gained two months in a row. My inches also increased. That's bad. I bet I would be under had I not eaten yesterday. 261 – paper assignment handed out. Talked about it for 35 minutes. 262 – scan test returned. I got a B. I think Courtney got an A. Herma or Henna got an A-. Other chick got a B+. I was a little bummed out about it. I don't want a B. New guy in Shakespeare, Sean, sat next to me today. He's a looker. Paper assignments passed out. They look scary. Of course we can do our own, just as long as we get her approval first. Trying to memorize my Spanish composition all day. I think that went well. Just hope it was what he was looking for. Quiz didn't go so well. And it was out of the workbook. Smiled at some Asian guy while trying to study Spanish in the library and he said hi! Because I was trying to memorize and probably babbling I wonder if he thinks I actually greeted him. No bother. Guy and girl walked in and out of 150 together. Visited Alice. Watched ER.

February 2, Friday
229

Last day to register for Pass/Fail grading, have to earn a C+ to pass
Dove bar, 6 mini quiches
Bath, little reading, laundry – 4 loads
Gene Kelly died. He was 83.
30 minutes treadmill, .7 mile, 43 calories

    Last day to sign up for pass/fail. I really don't want another C on my transcript, however you need a C+ to pass. What happens if I don't get a C+? I don't want to repeat Spanish 150 at all. Besides, there isn't much difference between a C+ and a B- and the B- I would take. I would be mad working my butt off for the C then earn a B but just have a pass on my transcript. Especially after 120. Oh, but what about my fucking GPA!? Oh life! Crept back in the 20's with 229 this morning. Need to get back to the groundbreaking area in the teens though. Mom offered another Dove bar, which blew another second day. She sensed my lack of enthusiasm. Then I followed it with six of those quiche things. Sent me to the bathroom three times. The first was more like two because I was in there so long. The last one really hurt. My stomach and guts were in an absolute uproar. Decided it was time to resume exercising. Did the treadmill. Really took something out of me, but my back felt fine. I tried to read but I ended up just listening to music. Did like four loads of laundry and took a bath. Larissa worked both (starting at Taylor's) jobs today. Walked in yelling she was hungry and tired. We laughed. Total hours = 10 ½. Welcome to the real world.

February 3, Saturday
226
Did calligraphy for Dad, went on cake delivery with Alice, watched Jewel, iced pillars
KFC potatoes, biscuit, 1 piece breast for lunch; Ed Debevic's for dinner with Rachel joining us. Route 66 Burger, fries with cheese and chili, cherry Coke and rice krispy treat
4 BM, felt explosion coming on and had to ask Alice to pull off the freeway somewhere in the hood.
Talk until 1… with Mom?!

    My back was really stiff today from yesterday's exercise. Did calligraphy for Dad's service certificate and got all cutesy to go on the cake delivery with Alice. She and Jewel did KFC before I got there, but she offered some and I caved and ate it. It was the smell that got me. Alice iced, I carried. I did pillars. Not much going on. She asked me if I would go with her to San Diego in March if the job comes through. Of course, I said yes. The Bel-Air Bay Club was nice, but it was really something of a dreary day. Alice says, "These people drive me crazy to the point of driving me bonkers." Drove around Beverly Hills, West Hollywood. Saw Doheny Drive and that one hotel we went to and Planet Hollywood. Pulled in at Ed Debevic's and Rachel was already there. It was louder than I expected and a lot more children. It looked like a major teen scene when we were leaving. Perfect place for Courtney to work. They're expected to sing and dance and act outrageous. One guy performed Wonder Woman. That was funny. Didn't go to the bathroom before leaving and should have. Couldn't make it across town. Felt embarrassed at asking Alice to stop, but it was necessary. Went again soon after arriving home. Talked way too long with Mom. Women nest. Self started. Dare to try vs. every try is a dare. Rice Krispy incident.

February 4, Sunday
230
Work 8-4; markdowns, 2 bags
Heard alarm after my shower
Ruffles, English Toffee piece, cookies, chips, salsa, green quesadilla (had been Larissa's), chocolate cream pie slice, Pepsi

Poured myself into the shower at 6:45 and my alarm was going off when I got out. That hamburger sat like a rock in my stomach. I could feel it almost all day. Rachel had Taco Bell for breakfast and a pretzel for lunch. I scarfed two of those Ruffles bags that the company sent out. Then an English toffee bit. Then some of the English cookies. Not too many left. It's a good thing I took my water bottle. At least I was doing something healthy. We did markdowns. Oh, and the food was free. Talked about whether or not to cut my hair. Rachel thinks I should keep it short. Even said she would give me the $6 for the mall place. I didn't take any greenery from her though. Larissa said the best part about my long hair was the length. The color was dull. Just brown, maybe keep it if I dyed it. Rachel asked me to dinner but I declined. Need to read. Paper due Thursday and writing cycle and ad on Tuesday.

Rachel really has packed on some pounds since the split from Daniel. Went home and after an hour I had some chips and salsa. Not much left. Larissa let me have her other green quesadilla if I'd pay for it. I ate. Think about that pay thing. Thought about Mac/cheese but went straight for pie. Larissa wanted me to call George. She was upset when I declined. Changed to exercise. Decided to read first. Read from about 8:30-9 or basically until I fell asleep. Only remember the first few pages. Never shut off light or kicked off shoes.

February 5, Monday
232
First Shakespeare Paper Due – postponed
Reading Grendel, copy Spanish
Chicken lasagna, 1 slice bread with butter and Bing Cherry
Chocolate cream pie slice, Mountain Dew
30 minutes treadmill, 46 calories, .8 mile; Ab 30-10

Had an odd dream last night. Grandpa Otis was telling me not to stop until I was five. What? My guess is size, but there was no reference, no context to place it in. Didn't even see his face or hear his voice. I just knew the message was from him. Thought today would make a good first day since I seem to have a real problem handling day two. I was wrong. Mom finally baked one of the chicken lasagnas. It didn't really sound good (meat!) or look appetizing but she kept stopping by my room. Ready in a half hour, 10 minutes, I'm eating now. See to lose weight you have to block everything out. Had another slice of Larissa's chocolate cream pie. It tasted real good just knowing she paid for it. Should have had a smaller slice though. Read over 100 pages of Grendel. I am soooo far behind in my reading. Didn't accomplish as much today as I hoped. Definitely should have left the house to avoid the food, but I did get some good time in on reading. Also exercised after Mom left for her meeting. It was nice to do the treadmill with no one here. The half-hour flew by. Larissa came home with McDonald's and went straight to her room. She was eating fries while shitting on the toilet when I went to tell her we didn't know who (someone she works with?) she was pitching Girl Scout cookies for.

February 6, Tuesday
229 ¼
261 Eaters of the Dead
262 Wordsworth
430 Lear
Saw Jason in Doheny (did research) and Christine after Spanish, hit the bookstore, turned in commercial
30 minutes bike, 7.7 miles; Ab 30-10+
Mountain Dew

    Another day in paradise. One great thing about my days at school is the fact that I'm usually so busy and concerned about other things that I don't even think about eating or the fact that I haven't. Talked to Jason in Doheny library. He is definitely younger than I previously thought. Herma complimented my make-up and Dana complimented my green cardigan. I must have done something good. Courtney did the same college try I did, only the years between her first and second attempt were six to my three. Thinks Special is straight out of high school. Spanish was actually okay today considering all of the verbal crap we did. I really need to get in my conversational labs. Went to Doheny to research for my 261 paper. Saw and talked to Christine from 466. She got my number. I said I still had hers, but I'm not really sure if I do. I may have tossed it. Oops! Offered to walk with Dad. He declined. Still got my big old butt on the bike. My back kind of hurts. I think I'm working that sore muscle. I need new underwear. I have four pair that really fit. Everything else just sags which is a serious negative during my period. Some of my bras are becoming ineffective too. Had two waters today!

February 7, Wednesday
227 ½, around 2 it was 226
Fast, Pepsi
Finished reading Grendel, worked on paper
Typing paper past 1 a.m.; diarrhea while typing
Ab 40-10

    Spent all day working on my Grendel paper, or trying to avoid working on it. I don't like it. I don't think it's very developed. Fortunately he looks for progress so even if he doesn't like it if I do well on later assignments that will be reflected in my grade. I copied my notes for that chick in my

262 class. What a hassle. What a nice person I am! Mom ran some errands, got overheated and came home. Made a comment about being so tired she didn't stop at El Rey Taco. I didn't say anything. I bet if I were of the mind I could have gotten some for us. She went out again and bought material for my new reunion dress. Expensive stuff. Larissa came home with an eager eye. Wanted to know our dinner plans. Disappointed at our suggestions of apples, spinach, frozen vegetables. I was having Pepsi. I felt like I needed the sugar. At 2 PM I weighed in again and I was 226 which made me happy. Concerned whether I should have been drinking Pepsi because it was obvious that I wasn't going to be able to exercise. But I drank away anyway. Finished typing around 1:30. My eyes were giving out. I wasn't even remotely interested in what I was doing.

February 8, Thursday
226
Fast, Pepsi
261 Paper Due
Writing Cycle I – Okay, not as prepared
430 – Courtney's oral presentation
30 minutes bike, 7.9 miles; Ab 30-10

Writing Bummer! Weighed in at 226. Really shouldn't have gone for that Pepsi. Did cover sheet before school. Also, had to do photocopy work. In 261 he talked about titles for 40 minutes. I got extra points for clarity. 262 he started randomly calling on people. 430 was same old thing. Other people haven't started their papers either so I don't feel so bad. Because I did the paper yesterday I really didn't prepare for the Spanish Writing Cycle like I should have. I feel real shaky about it, but Mr. Del Villa seems pretty cool. Autumn was absent-missing her oral activity too. That's 50 points. If I could have skipped I would have. I was very tired – no sleep and not prepared. Miss Louisiana wasn't there. Jeremy thought Asian girl was "older, distinguished – 28." She's 22. She's "old" he said. Oh my. Library for Shakespeare research to no avail. Watched ER after exercising. Larissa went to El Rey Taco and Mom had chicken lasagna and graham crackers. She apologized for eating in front of me. Mom asked if we were going to call George. Larissa's trying to push it completely off on me. She acted like I hadn't told her my plan before. Made a comment, "You're usually more prepared." What? I know exactly what I'm doing. Nothing more to prepare for.

February 9, Friday
224 ½
Ab 30-10

  Only down a pound and a half. Exercise, extra water and starved. What's the deal? Mom asked about measurements. She wants to take them for my dress. She suggested after the party for Grandpa. That that would postpone it – give me another ten days. Okay -? I need a strapless bra. Actually, this dress needs it. Seriously thought about going to an English Conference on A Funeral Elegy (Shakespeare) at UCLA, but changed my mind – not my heart. Not really interested in subject. Waste of time travelling, preparing and sitting through it. Not sure if I would get anything out of it. Then I'd have to fight traffic to get home. I wonder.

  Later… My writing prompted me to jump in the shower and go. Shakespeare professor was there. She didn't see me, I don't think. Went to Beverly Hills library afterward. Have to pay for parking so I didn't stay. Drove down Doheny. Kept my eyes open all day. Dad took the family to Guadalajara Inn. Larissa bought a banana cream pie after my suggestion. Sigh, I was doing so well. Should have gone into library. Probably would have missed dinner if I had. Stopped by the bakery. Alice wasn't there. I want to ask her do a cake for Grandpa. Hope she can. It'd be nice to show off. Family shrieked when I said I went to UCLA.

February 10, Saturday
225
Worked on Shakespeare paper
Mom had Melissa's reception, then went to Hope's
Larissa had work incident
Pie, graham crackers and milk, cheese/tomato sandwich, bean/cheese burrito, green quesadilla, +Fig Newtons
30 minutes treadmill, 48 calories, .8 mile; Ab 30-10

	Didn't get any work done on my Shakespeare paper so attending Melissa's reception would have been an abuse of my time. Really kind of wanted to be there. It was a big one. Maybe the biggest one Mom's gonna have, depending on what happens with Holly. I exercised while I was alone, which is always nice. Got some work done on my paper too. Mostly note taking, nothing very cohesive. Woke up deciding this would be a food day. Started right out with graham crackers and milk. So stupid. Just because I blew Friday didn't mean I needed to continue to blow it. Could have jumped right back on. Later I had a tomato and cheese sandwich. Then Fig Newton's. I really did them in. Larissa had a couple, so did Mom. Dad had four. I ODed. Larissa called around 7:30 to find out what we wanted for dinner. She would pick up and order. She went to El Rey Taco. We ordered Mom food too. Mom went to Hope's reception after stopping (dining?) at Mr. Thompson's house. I ate a green quesadilla and a bean and cheese burrito like they were nothing, consoling myself that I had at least exercised. Oh wow. Larissa came home crying. Kayla's sharp tongue set her off. She said she's put a lot of stress on herself this week. First week on the new job and not on next week's schedule at the mall.

February 11, Sunday
229 ¼
Work 10:30-6:30 with Susan and Courtney; Nicole came in
Coke, Taco Bell meximelt and soft taco, red vines, Slice, Wok Express, 2 egg rolls, chicken teriyaki, 2 almond cookies
Shakespeare paper
	Worked all day. Told myself this would be a no eat day, but that didn't last long. Worked with Susan and Courtney. We went to Jack's before opening. I just got a regular Coke. Susan offered her leftover candy from movie night with Arnold. I ate some red vines. Called home and got permission to purchase underwear on Mom's card. Larissa was pushing a hard sell for PJs. Mom and I both thought that was funny since I never wear them. Anyway, made the mistake of asking what the deal with dinner was. We decided Wok Express so when Courtney was going to Taco Bell I went for a taco and meximelt. Nicole came in and we got to talking. She offered a discount for free tickets or something. Mentioned that some

Friday night I should come by. But should I go alone? Courtney got her to open a charge. She was really sick and having roommate problems. Bought size 24 jeans. My black rayon pants are too short. They shrunk and definitely look stupid. Threw them away. Because I came home and ate, my brain was not thinking about Shakespeare. It was really hard to focus. Didn't feel like exercise either. Ended up going to bed early. Courtney's rushing into a relationship. She appears desperate.

February 12, Monday
232
First Shakespeare Paper Due, got up early to work on paper, dropped it off; Talked to Rachel
30 minutes treadmill, 47 calories, .8 mile; AB 30-10
Finished Wok Express noodles and 3 cookies, 7 apricots

    Got up kind of early to work on my paper. Not as early as I wanted to though. Had a hard time deciding if I should finish off the Wok Express so it's gone or let it sit until Friday. Of course, almond cookies sitting on my desk proved to be too much to handle. Had a cookie and a dump before dropping off my paper. Made the drop around 3:15. It was dark and gloomy. A good stay at home and feel sorry for yourself day which is apparently what Rachel did. I ate my noodles and rice and hit the treadmill before calling her. Also had seven dried apricots. Wanted to talk to Alice about a cake for Grandpa but didn't get her. Rachel thinks she'll be able to though. Rachel's having a hard time making a decision about Daniel. She doesn't want to hurt him, but she doesn't want to be with him. She wants the white picket fence and all that goes with it and for some reason she thinks that she could have it with him. She doesn't want to admit to being scared of being alone. She thinks there's still something there or else she wouldn't have a hard time making the choice. Her family gave her a hard time yesterday. She asked for my advice. I wonder whose heart her mind will listen to.

February 13, Tuesday
229 ½
261 papers returned
262 lecture

430 found paper at 11 – thought that was my drop off
Conversation lab
150 turned in homework
30 minutes bike, 7.8 miles; Ab 40-10
Alice doing cake!

 What an awful day. Had a major blow to my self-esteem right off the bat. 261 papers were returned. 4 As, 4 Bs, ? Cs, 1 D, 1 F. I got a C. A fucking C. Unbelievable. I knew I didn't put much time or effort into it, but still. He had a few "wrong word" citing's and lots of unclears. Wants me to talk to him about my writing during office hours. 262 dull – of course. 430 – okay. She heard a noise in the mailbox around 11pm. Her husband found my paper. She thought that I was dropping it off at that time which is annoying because I dropped it off at the appropriate hour. Another blow. Went to a conversation lab for Spanish. Mia didn't acknowledge me. Rude. Another blow. 150 went okay. Miss Annoying Chick told me she was fat. She's gained twenty pounds in the last three months and how awful fat is. I wanted to laugh and I wanted to slap her. Compositions will be returned Thursday. Oral activity due Thursday and a quiz and conversation labs. Talked to Alice. She's going to do an eight inch chocolate cake. Also talked to Jacob for a while. Watched Wings and Frasier before exercising. Thought I'd go to school just to be out there tomorrow, but I don't know. I want to hide and feel sorry for myself. I'm a fat, stupid cow.

February 14, Wednesday
226, kind of 25 ¾ but going high
Fast
Mom and Dad left for Laughlin/B-day weekend
Read Aeneid
30 minutes treadmill, 44 calories, .7 miles; Ab 40-15
Watched TV, work on Spanish

 Mom was anxious to hit the road. Dad, of course, was in typical lackadaisical mode. Mom asked what I was going to get for lunch. It was around 1:30 and she was hungry. Dad offered lunch by the Ontario airport, that place they usually stop at that they like so much. Denny's. Isn't that funny! Tried reading the Aeneid in my room, but kept falling asleep. After they left I read in the family room. It went a little better but I didn't even get close to finishing Shakespeare's stuff, never mind the Canterbury Tales or poetry. Exercised. Slow going. No umph. Larissa called shortly after. Busy time at work. Lots of reports to be handled. She wanted to know if Mom and Dad left so she could park in the driveway. Also wanted to know if I had plans or wanted anything. Mom had asked what we were doing too. Larissa was left to her own defenses. She was even willing to go to the grocery, but she came home. Fixed and ate a whole box of Rice-A-Roni while I took a bath. I watched bad television with her. Knew I wouldn't get through Aeneid. Asked Larissa for help on my Spanish oral activity. She wasn't much. Debated going to school or not. Really feeling down in the dumps. Listened to my stomach gurgle as I waited to fall asleep.

February 15, Thursday
222 ¾
Fast, Pepsi
Skipped 261 - Brianna said only 9 were present
262 paper topics handed out
430 NOBODY read Metamorphoses
150 quiz malo oral shit – no other, 2 conversation labs
Ab 40-15
Major headache

     Skipped my 261 class. Did my other two conversation labs instead. Brianna said only nine people showed. In 262 we got our paper topics. Really should start working on it. I want him to read it first. In 430 we got to the Metamorphoses and NOBODY had done the reading. Like hello! That should be a sign. I'm behind in my responses. Heated discussion about "typical" males/females and ancient gender roles. Quiz in Spanish didn't go so well. I got a 34 on my composition though. He forgot our oral activity. Postponed to next Thursday – so is our other quiz, which means I definitely can't go to the Paramount screening of Black Sheep. Asked questions, didn't know how to respond. Craig said he was the valedictorian of his high school and I automatically asked how many were in his graduating class. He laughed as he answered, "Thirty-eight." And four of the girls were pregnant. Major pot growing. High alcoholism and poverty. Came home with one hell of a headache. Couldn't even imagine getting up and exercising or even doing flashcards. Watched the NBC line up. Larissa came home with McDonald's. She bought me a Filet-o-Fish, if I wanted it. I declined. She had it along with fries (also offered and I declined) and chicken nuggets. She's excited about getting a $660 paycheck. She should be, but her eyes seem to be widening on purchases vs. savings and old debts.

February 16, Friday
220 ¼
Fast, Pepsi
Grandma called, worked on Spanish vocabulary, Larissa's getting sick, Shopped Lerner, picked up cake, paid and talk
20 minutes treadmill, 30 calories, .5 mile; Ab 50-15

    Grandma called and thought she talked to Larissa even though I said it was me. Larissa got home earlier than expected. I hadn't had the opportunity to exercise yet. Worked on Spanish vocabulary cards all day. Larissa's getting sick, slept through her Board Election meeting. She bought fruit salad and offered some to me. Intentionally bought enough for me. I had five bites. Exercised while she slept. Only made it twenty minutes and even that felt like a push. Guess it's to be expected when I'm not eating. My major headache wasn't so bad after I had a BM, but I still felt very sluggish. Showered and got ready to go shopping. Did makeup because I looked sick. Rachel would say something. Had the gray starvation look. At Lerner's bought the two-piece outfit Rachel talked about in red, size Large. Short and snug, especially in the hips, but doable. Amazing. Was going to use certificate, but Larissa bought it for me for my birthday. Work promo offer was blah-blah-blah. Saw Sophia. Talked to Susan. Rachel called in sick. She went to a therapist the day before. Jewel throwing up. Thinks my Monday talk helped her. Maybe talked some sense into her. Pick-up cake. Alice asked if I had a bakery key. I don't. Paid me for the other delivery. Wasn't really expecting that. The San Diego trip is a go. Rachel asked me to write a Dear Daniel letter.

February 17, Saturday
219 ½
Drive to AZ with Larissa and George

2 eggs, 2 slices cheese, 2 slices bread with butter, 6 Oreo's, milk; Prime Rib dinner with potato, green beans, salad & Alice's cake

    Decided to eat early so I'd go to the bathroom at home. Turns out I could have skipped it. George bought gas station food. Had to go to the bathroom as soon as we got there, then again after dinner. That one was nasty. Really enjoyed Alice's cake. Very rich. Had the prime rib dinner. The drive was okay. It was pretty awkward especially since Larissa was in the back and fell asleep. George and I talked briefly. He said something about literature being wasted on youth and I wanted to punch him in the face. Grateful when he started doing some stuff for work, but it also left me feeling self-conscious about cranking the tunes. So I didn't. It was just an annoying situation and easily the most boring road trip of my life. Grandpa looked pretty good. A little thinner than I remember. He said the same thing about me. Grandma was definitely thinner, but not as much as I expected considering the sizes of the sweaters she sent us. Watched some videos of the boys. Brandon was in an 8th grade variety choral show. Received a Golden State exam recognition for Algebra (One in three at his school). At graduation he performed a song. You could actually hear him. Also wore a medallion for some scholastic acknowledgement. Tyler was in a play, Miner Bob, about the gold rush. A lot of gushing going on for people who didn't even care enough to show up. Grandma's stories and recollections have become increasingly negative. Missed the point of them but did take note that she made precisely no comments about my transformation. None. Apparently, not even to Mom who later told me not to take it personally. "Your Grandmother can be… jealous. She's not one to share the spotlight."

February 18, Sunday
217 ½ in AZ
½ grapefruit; Red Lobster – fried shrimp, coke, drive home, Pepsi; Porter's Pizza – 4 slices and salad with blue cheese dressing; cornbread; 10 Oreo's, milk
30 minutes treadmill, 46 calories, .8 miles; Ab 30-10

    They overbought on their breakfast supplies especially for people who don't usually eat in the morning. Went to Red Lobster for lunch. Had the fried shrimp. Also had one of

Mom's stuffed lobster mushrooms. It was all right. Wore my new red dress. A little uncomfortable since it is so short and I'm not used to short dresses. It was especially awkward getting in and out of the car. At home I noticed the back has a tendency to creep up. Mom, Dad, Grandpa and Larissa all said something. Think George was just there. But hello Grandma. She was self-absorbed. We all took note of her size 18-20 loose blouse. She wants an open house party for her 80th. Drove home in 5-5 ½ hrs. George used my nasty bathroom. We ordered Porter's for delivery. Chowed on four slices plus had cornbread and ten Oreo's with milk. Got on the treadmill for my 30 minutes too. Dad really pissed me off. Kimberly and the boys could have and should have been there. But weren't. Dad said I was being greedy and jealous. Excuse me! Greedy? How? Jealous? Of what? Boy Scouts? Hello, I WAS a Girl Scout and I thought family was more important than Scouts. Mom was even quick to point out that Larissa and I have attended Graham stuff and we aren't their grandkids. It took Mom and Dad eight hours to get home. Four stops. Mom wasn't too happy about that. Dad's such a road wimp. Two of the breaks were one hour food breaks. Mom and I are going to shoot Dad and Larissa for feeling sorry for themselves to the point of driving us nuts.

February 19, Monday
226 ½
Frustrating day. Slept in, rainy, lots to do but didn't
2 slices bread with butter, mac & cheese and a slice of cheese
USC student films on PBS
30 minutes bike, 7.7 miles

     Man, oh man, did I sleep in. Realized yesterday that some of the chores I wanted to do today I wouldn't be able to do because it's a holiday. Another good feel sorry for yourself Monday. Put off eating. Really could have started fasting today. Mom wanted pizza. They almost ordered from Porter's, but they're closed on Mondays. Called our local pizzeria instead. Knew all the smells would get to me. Almost went to El Rey Taco, but fixed Mac & cheese instead. Plus had two slices of buttered toast and an extra slice of cheese. Then I had to exercise to live with myself. Figured that would help me maintain or even go down considering I was eating fairly healthy. There was a PBS special with student films. Two were from USC. One – Gun Society by Kafka and the other No Humans Involved, by a female. Wished I remembered her name. Didn't get any reading done and didn't even really study for my Spanish midterm. I know I fell asleep. What an awful day. Called Rachel. She said she almost gave Daniel the axe last night, but he has Jewel so it's going to wait until Friday. He makes no attempt to be a father to that child. I haven't done the letter and I have no time to baby-sit.

February 20, Tuesday
228 ½
Shakespeare quiz postponed, Spanish midterm
Studied in Leavey for midterm, went okay; Sav-on's
Finished mac and cheese, 24 Oreo's and soda, El Rey Taco small nachos and taco, 1 Ex-Lax before bed
30 minutes bike, 7.7 miles

Really shocked that I went up 2 pounds. Although the bulk is going in without anything coming out. Skipped 261, 262 and 430. 261 midterm is in a week, but I doubt I missed anything. Need to ask for a revision though. 262 – didn't even start reading and didn't want to sit there feeling stupid. Same for 430. In fact, I am behind in my reading responses for 430. Missing may have been bad. She might have returned our papers to us. I kind of hope not. Anyway, tried to study in Leavey Library. I'm much too easily distracted. Should have studied vocabulary more intently. Part of my problem is what I didn't learn in the first semester. Think Hannah thinks I tried to cheat off of her during the listening part. That bothers me. Allison was asking questions. That was truly annoying. Louisiana came in very late. She was the only one left when I left. Craig dyed his hair. Went to Sav-On for soda and Oreo's. After the morning shock I finished the Mac & cheese and decided to go for the Fat Tuesday. Went to El Rey Taco and got small nachos and a taco. Wanted soft but forgot to say it. Had milk and twenty-four Oreo's. Surprised it all went down. Exercised and ended my day with an Ex-Lax. Dad asked me to do GC.

February 21, Wednesday
227 ½

Fast
BM before weigh in
Persuasion, Spanish workbook and vocabulary cards, dumped some clothes, Metamorphoses
30 minutes bike, 7.8 miles; Ab 50-15

  Felt a pain and a rumble in my gut. That's what finally got me out of bed around 10 AM. Sat for a while. Kept thinking I felt something but man did I have to push for it. It was big. No diarrhea associated with it at all. The floating factor bothered me though. After ODing on El Rey Taco and Oreo's I managed to go down a pound. Of course, I can only imagine what joy I would be in had I not Oded. Having a headache day. Is it the ponytail or lack of food? Hard to tell. I never feel like I accomplish as much as I should be able to. Fell asleep. Oh Larissa was put on salary yesterday. She said per month her money went up about $150-160. Still unsure if she'll be around after primaries. Read some of Persuasion and Metamorphoses. Didn't really get far enough with either one. Went through Spanish workbook so maybe if he uses it for our quiz I'll know what to do. Also, made my flashcards for chapter 10. It was hard getting myself motivated to get on the bike but I did and I'm glad. Also, got my butt on the floor to do the AB isolator. Thought I might read after my shower, but it was late enough I said forget it. Not looking forward to going to school. Worked on Dear Daniel.

February 22, Thursday
224 ¾
Fast
What a bummer day - 261 and 262 were dullsville; Behind in 430 responses, paper returned without a grade, rewrite advised; 150 Oral Activity, stress
Sav-on for soda, worked on Dear Daniel, Lou Reed on David
30 minutes bike, 7.6 miles; Ab 50-15

  It's like I woke up knowing today would be a crappy day. Barely got to 261 on time. Wrote a Dear Daniel letter. Midterm next Tuesday. Need a blue book. 262 he gave a narrative lecture. Had to take notes to stay awake. Asked voice questions I didn't get. Courtney's a little strange. Missed a few 430 responses. Only turned in two today. She returned papers at the end of class. Said there were people who asked for rewrites, which we can do, just have to talk to her first. She didn't even put a grade on my paper. Unthinkable: textual analysis missing. Talk about blowing my day. Then I had an oral activity in Spanish, which I just hate. At least I volunteered as second and got it over with. Another quiz. Doubt I did very well. Didn't go to the film for extra credit, but Don Juan is still playing two more weekends. I just wanted to go home. Shared Rachel's problems with Christy, then Hannah (with Peter present.) Oh I hate life. Definitely feeling very sorry for myself when I just need to get off the duff and do it. Why am I erecting my own barriers? 430 rewrite before spring break. Talked to 261 about a rewrite but that so isn't happening. His "wrong word" notations are because I'm writing at too high a reading level. He advised me that if I wanted to be published I needed to use words with fewer syllables and simple sentence structures. Ummm, this was a paper for an upper division lit class. What the fuck?! But if I want a better grade I need to dumb down my paper for him. I told him that I didn't think that was in my best interest and he said it was if I cared about my grade. What an ass. And then there's Rachel. And work. And bills. And the bank. Exercised. Kennedy on Conan. She's really annoying.

February 23, Friday
221 ½
Reading Persuasion, worked on Daniel letter some more, felt limp/weak, gut pain until release
El Rey Taco small nachos, green quesadilla, 12 Strawberry Newtons
30 minutes bike, 7.3 miles; Ab 50-10

Really hard to get motivated today. Worked on the Dear Daniel for Rachel even though I was really dreading the idea of her calling me for it. Decided that I wouldn't call her, after all, she was asking for my help. Read some more of Persuasion, but didn't finish it. I was feeling really weak, kind of limp and useless when Mom asked if Friday meant El Rey Taco day. I really didn't feel like getting it, but it sounded good. Larissa came home and she ended up going and I went with her. Got nachos and a quesadilla. Ate all of both. Felt nauseous afterwards. Almost wanted beef burrito but didn't go for it. Really kind of proud of myself about that. Then I scarfed down a dozen Strawberry Newton's. Still felt pretty bad, but did feel better after taking a long awaited dump. Surprised that Rachel never called. Ended up feeling kind of bad that I didn't call her with my letter. Had a really hard time sleeping. Kept thinking about Rachel and Daniel and the whole situation makes me worry about Jewel. Watched The Lion King. Liked it a lot more than I thought I would. Exercised – felt sluggish, but I did it.

February 24, Saturday
222
Work 9:30-3:30
Pretzel from Target, Dark Milky Way, deli ½ plate Mixed cheese and potato wedges, 3 Strawberry Newtons, slice banana cream pie
30 minutes treadmill, 48 calories, .8 mile

    Had to get up early to go to work which was no thrill for me. Walked down to Target and got a Dark Milky Way and a pretzel. Susan was making me hungry. The candy bar was satisfying a dark chocolate craving. Actually a dark chocolate truffle from See's would have meant more. Called Larissa from work to find out if there was a plan for dinner. Didn't want to eat at work if I wasn't eating at home. She picked up from the deli, and I picked up a banana cream pie. With the pie special going on financially I won that deal. Had a mixed cheese sandwich and a large slice of pie. Saved it for after my exercising though. Mom and Dad were at the theater. The potato wedges came back in one nasty belch. I haven't had something like that happen to me in a long time. I had the whole sandwich. I just kept piling it up. Had major gas too. Wonder if it was the cheese or the wedges. Larissa talked about needing to exercise, but never did anything about it and lord knows she could have. When shopping at the work promo she told me to get a dress she likes, that way she could inherit it when she works her way down to where I am. But I see no change in her behavior.

February 25, Sunday
225 ½

A cheese horn Danish, 7 Strawberry Newtons, 8 oz. milk, 2 slices toast, ½ waffle, 2 slices cheese, 2 slices banana cream pie, 2 egg rolls, pint of noodles, Mac and cheese, hot chocolate
Eaters of the Dead DONE!!!
30 minutes bike, 7.6 miles; Ab 30-10

    Relieved I didn't have to work today. I started and finished Eaters of the Dead. It was actually pretty good. I stayed up pretty late trying to finish it too. I started my day eating away, with a cheese horn and I'm not even into that Danish crap. I also finished off all of the Strawberry Newton's. Of the pack I think Larissa had two. Then I had toast and cheese and half of a waffle. I also had two slices of the damn pie. Why was that my idea? Why did I do this to myself? Why can't I be more firm and focused and self-centered? Larissa called from work. She was going to Wok Express before coming home. Asked me if I wanted anything even though I was grumbling at it and meat the other day. She bought me two egg rolls and a pint of noodles. She was going on about the economics of a meal vs. a pint after coming home. She observed that the lady gave Dad's tray extra meat. She's so centered on food. I exercised. Still was suffering from major gas. Sometimes my lower gut felt bloated and uncomfortable. Later asked Larissa if she wanted Mac & cheese. She didn't, but I had been wanting it for a while so I made it anyway. Although it was late. 97.1 played REM B-sides. I taped them.

February 26, Monday
228 - Oh my God!
Fast, Dr. Slice approximately 1 liter
Beowulf, Spanish homework – did real bad, three responses for 430
30 minutes treadmill, 46 calories, .8 mile; Ab 50-15

    Really surprised by the jump up in my weight though I really should not have been. I did eat late and had pastas, but I also dumped. Oh well. Decided today would be a good day to start fresh and focus. Did my Spanish homework. Did a very poor job too. Reading Beowulf. It's easier to read now that I've been through Grendel and Eater, which are roughly the same stories. Got my butt on the treadmill. Someone had used it briefly since the time that I last did. I wonder who? I have no idea when or who would have. My guess is Mom. She would have the most opportunity, but would she? I did three responses for my 430 class. Two focused on women. Dido in the Underworld and the nymph of Jove rape's in Arcadia. I never did finish Beowulf. When I was reading the neighbor's child decided to yap non-stop for forty-five minutes. I thought I was going to lose my mind. I really wanted to open the back door and yell, but then I thought how foolish that would look. That would probably provoke laughter rather than produce results. I didn't even touch Canterbury Tales and I know that's going to hurt me since he's really into that Middle English shit.

February 27, Tuesday
224
Fast, Dr. Slice
261 Midterm - two passages were right on ? others, Brianna not there. Skip 262, so did Courtney. Hamlet, turn in four responses
Raining, Know me in LL, Spanish 6 week grade
30 minutes bike, 7.7 miles; Ab 50-15

      I just wanted to die after the midterm. I know I nailed two. He didn't provide the seven choices that he promised. There were only six. Beowulf I miss placed where it happened so the significance is also wrong. Canterbury Tales M1 misplaced what was being said. Canterbury Tales 2 didn't know who was talking to who but I think the rest is right. Oh my God! What is wrong with me? I was supposed to nail this semester. Brianna wasn't there. Guy to the right of me hates him. I'm right there with him. Skipped 262 and so did Courtney. That was funny. Hadn't finished Persuasion so I figured why bother. It was raining. A perfect day to go home. 430 glasses girl wanted class to be cancelled. Troy needed to use his jacket as a cover to zip his fly. Turned in four responses. Wrote about Ophelia in Hamlet. Really wanted to skip Spanish because of the rain, the subject and my general mood. We had homework due though and those are the types of points I can't afford to give away. We got our six week grade I'm at 80% which is a B. Watched TV for an hour and a half before exercising. Really needed to get some work done on my paper for 262, but didn't do a damn thing.

February 28, Wednesday
221 ½
Fast
Up late working on 262 paper, Mom got a perm, Grammy night, typed up rough draft - too short, finished at 4 a.m.
30 minutes treadmill, 45 calories, .8 miles; Ab 50-15

    I got up really late and for no real good reason. Started working on my 262 paper. Mom seemed really annoyed with me. She left and I exercised. I was still working on my paper at the same spot when she came back. She got a perm. It looked good. The exercising session kind of dragged. Grammy night. We taped them for me. Larissa and Mom went over to the mall for promo shopping. Typed an extremely rough draft around seven. The draft was definitely too short. It didn't even hit page five and this paper is supposed to be 5-7 pages long and I knew there was a lot of stuff to dump or alter, which of course would make the paper even shorter. Sitting at my desk might have helped. I went back to the text for line by line analysis. I probably don't have enough though. All said and done the paper turned out to barely hit the fifth page. There was more personal analysis than I originally thought there would be. I wonder if my broad intro and conclusion will be marked down. Also curious about my thesis, if it is provocative enough. I think I answered it. Actually, I ended up liking the paper overall. Finished typing around 3:30-4 a.m., but still had problems falling asleep.

February 29, Thursday
220
Fast
262 Paper Due, Shakespeare take-home quiz NOT passed out
Skipped 261 and Mom asked if I dropped a class (ugh!), 430 talked to her after class, Spanish quiz
15 minutes bike, 3.9 miles; Ab 55-15

    Had a very difficult time getting out of bed. Larissa made a comment about my still being here when she left for work. That really pissed me off. Mom asked if I was okay. Said yes. She never actually saw me. Skipped 261. Didn't exactly feel bad. Doubt he had the midterms done. And even if he did I don't think I want to know just yet. 262 dragged. Hell my whole day dragged. I just wanted to go back to bed.

Talked to Ferguson after class. I think she expected me to go to her office today, but I didn't want to. I wasn't ready to. Will talk again on Tuesday after I can get some work done. 150 wasn't so bad. We had readings to go over so there wasn't a lot of being called on stuff going on. I like that. The quiz was okay too. I looked at Christy's a couple of times, but that was mostly for self-assurance that I was doing the right thing. It was from the workbook again. I remembered having done it. Watched NBC. ER was a repeat, but new to me. I rode the bike, but my energy is totally shot from not eating anything. I only made it for 15 minutes. Guess that's better than nothing. Watched two hours of the Grammy's. Bed at 1:30. 430 quiz not passed out.

MARCH

March 1, Friday
217 ¾ - YES
Went to LBCC – request transcript, graduation application (last day), Sergi skate, big load
8 oz. milk, 5 pancakes, 2 quesadillas and ½ bean/cheese burrito, 1 chocolate muffin, 12 oz. milk
30 minutes bike, 7.3 miles; Ab 55-15

    Came this close to not going to LBCC today, but it's a real good thing I did. Today was the deadline for registering to walk for graduation. They had a line for getting a retrograde diploma, which I marked off. Also, requested a new transcript be sent to USC. Went to Cal Fed and deposited Alice's check. Came home and Mom was out. Decided the lightheadedness needed to go. Ate the five pancakes left in the kitchen with milk. My stomach was in pain before and after. That's the joy of fasting. You never feel good no matter what you do. Until you see the results on the scale, that is. Mom went to Sam's Club. Brought home muffins. Boy did they look good. Mom asked if Friday meant El Rey Taco day again. What can I say? I'm weak. I buckled. El Rey Taco - I would be insane to turn it down and I'm not insane so I had two green quesadillas and half of a bean and cheese burrito. It was more than I could hold, but I made it fit anyway. No wonder my stomach hates me. Later I had more milk and a chocolate muffin. Boy was it good. Got on the bike. Weak from days of not eating and loaded down with a heavy meal I felt sluggish. Watched the Sergi-Celebration of a Life Ice Skating special. It was very moving. Finally had a dump. It was long overdue. Hard coming out, but it finally did. Took a long time. Hit the sheets around 1 a.m. again.

March 2, Saturday
220 ½
Work 12-7:30 with Rachel and Susan and Yajaira
Pepsi, 2 pancakes, 1 blueberry muffin, 2 slices cheese, 3 slices peaches, Rice-A-Roni, green beans
Asked out – no go
30 minutes treadmill, 47 calories, .8 miles; Ab 55-15

  The idea of getting up was miserable. Had to be at work at 12 noon though. Rachel asked what I would be doing tonight. She made plans to go out with a pretty unfamiliar customer and didn't want to have to go it alone. But I was a no go. Jacob said he would meet them at the Safari Bar, but he can be really unreliable. Rachel got her review. Rated as a four. No pay raise. Allison stipulated the same for Melissa and Susan as well. What a Bitch! There's zero activity in this little mini-wanna-be-mall that is under 50% occupied, but Allison's taking it out on Rachel. The associates... Sophia and I are the only pay raises at being rated as 3's. Almost everyone is a five. The rating system sucks. They aren't rating people, they are blindly rating numbers. Tell me you can't afford to increase my pay, but don't tell me I don't do my job. Mia's pregnant and her Dad is kicking her out of the house. Poor girl. Letty's Bridal Shower is on the 10th at Alice's. Made a purchase after all. Pants and sweater. That's it. No one home. Exercised. Kayla stole one of Larissa's sales. Made Larissa cry to Margaret. Larissa never mentioned it to me. Had a blueberry muffin before exercising. Wondered about Mom and Dad's whereabouts. Larissa and I had Rice-a-Roni and green beans watching Angels in the Outfield with Mom and Dad. Also grabbed two slices of cheese. Bed around 1:30 – no 2 AM

March 3, Sunday
222
Fast
Work 2:30-6:30
Shakespeare paper
30 minutes treadmill, 48 calories, .8 miles
Larissa offered Wok Express, egg roll and cookies - had neither

I need to stop this early morning to bed routine. It's no wonder I can't get up in the morning. Started period. No wonder my face has been looking like an attack was upon it. Took advantage of an early morning empty house and hopped on the treadmill. It felt real good. Then had to shower and get ready for work. It was a nice way to start my day. Worked with Susan. We had pretty steady business that will really help my figures. I keep arguing with myself over this food thing. Rachel pissed me off yesterday when she said fasting works, after I said diets don't. Fasting is a diet. It's an extreme diet and look at her. She's really packed on some pounds. She obviously has some food issues that fasting didn't handle. Anyway, I've told myself no food until 210. Larissa went to Wok Express. Thought she would. She didn't have money for everyone so only bought us egg rolls and cookies. I think Dad had my egg roll. I'm surprised she didn't call, but the money thing answered that. I'm glad she didn't call, it was hard not taking that egg roll. Even harder telling my grossly obese father that he could have it because I wouldn't. There in lies the cruelty of change. Blocking out things and especially people you love. Did I hurt him by allowing him to eat it?

March 4, Monday
221
Rewriting 430 paper, called Grace and Amanda, Linda called
Egg roll, almond cookie, deli mixed cheese sandwich, potato wedges (3 total cookies)
30 minutes treadmill, 49 calories, .8 mile

So much for all that. Hard time getting up again. Saw that egg roll and cookie were still in the kitchen. Thought I would let it pass. Weighed in at 221. Respectable, but another starve day would make me happy. Yeah, well that didn't happen. Ate both the egg roll and the cookie. Had a craving for a deli sandwich that skyrocketed after Mom came home with Subway. Exercising felt great. I was really pumping it. Called Grace. Talked to her for maybe like forty-five minutes. They're putting our reunion books together on the 24th. She invited me to join them. Called Amanda. She said she would call Grace tomorrow. Wasn't going to go if I wasn't going. Just as baffled as me as what to write in our letter. Then Linda from 262 called. I hadn't even studied for my midterm in that class. I spent all day pulling information out of Richard II for my Shakespeare rewrite. In fact, I worked all day on that paper and only produced an introductory paragraph that I wasn't even sure if I liked. Drove Larissa to the deli. She got out and I waited in the car. Got extra cookies too. I ate the whole half plate order with potato wedges. Going to bed I was really regretting it. It weighed me down. I felt sick, like I needed to puke.

March 5, Tuesday
223 ¾
261 Midterm returned – not good, 262 Midterm went great, Shakespeare quiz due (no midterm), Skip 150
½ banana, graham cracker, milk, OJ, 2 eggs, cheese, raised glazed, 2 dozen circus animal cookies
Got pretzel, Letty's gift, strapless bra
30 minutes treadmill, 46 calories, .8 miles; Ab 55-15

  Jumped nearly three pounds. I definitely shouldn't order half plates anymore. Got my midterm back in 261. Bad. Real bad. Bastard down graded me for sure because I would not play his little "wrong word" rewrite game. Seriously considering filing an official complaint. Problem is the fucker is tenured. He'd probably only manage to make my life even more miserable. I'm just pissed because he's fucking with my GPA and I care about my GPA. Damn it! If I could drop the class I would, but I don't know if I can afford to. My 262 midterm went by really well. Not nearly as bad as it could have been. Talked to Courtney more than Linda. I hope she doesn't feel snubbed. She just seems to be picking my brain anyway. Talked to Ferguson about intro paragraph. Conversation went well. Don't necessarily have to have a done paper Thursday. I can go with a rough draft. Yeah! Skipped 150. Nothing due, no quiz, no readings. Went to the mall. Allison was in our store. I really wanted to talk to Rachel. Bought Letty's shower gift and books at Target. Then I went to Victoria's Secret for my strapless bra. They had a Buy 1 Get 1 Free promo going on so it ended up costing me $40. Damn! Got home and just started eating. Mom was on her way to a meeting so I got to do the treadmill alone. Then Larissa and Dad had to come home – the bums. Bought Circus Animal cookies at Target and just shoveled them in. After exercising I had eggs, cheese, OJ, even the doughnuts Mom offered and I don't even like doughnuts. What's the deal?

March 6, Wednesday
225
Shakespeare paper
3 eggs, 2 slices of cheese, 2 slices of toast, OJ, apple
3 ¼ dozen animal cookies, bowl of bean soup, toast
30 minutes treadmill, 49 calories, .8 mile; Ab 55-15

Hitting 225 kind of bothered me. I don't want to surpass that, but I started my day with one heck of a hearty meal. Three eggs, two slices of cheese and buttered toast, OJ, and an apple. Figured I needed to fuel up to sustain myself for my paper writing. Davis always instructed his students to eat healthy. Give the brain proper fuel. Spent yet another entire day working on that damn Shakespeare paper. Exercised on the treadmill. Again I was pumping it. Funny how it fluctuates. Larissa came home and took over the living room. I was working on my paper and she just pops on the TV to watch the comedy awards. She thought I wanted to see them too, which I did, but I couldn't afford the time. It really pissed me off that she didn't say anything before turning it on. Then when I protested it was like, who was I? She didn't even apologize for it. I didn't want to send her out of the room or anything, but she should have informed me of what she wanted or at least what she was going to do, but no. I was up late typing then reworked the stuff I had typed, but I was too tired to type up the next draft before bed. Damn, I wish I had a computer!

March 7, Thursday
224 ¼
Skip 261, miss 262, talk to Ferguson about paper after class, skip 150
Graham crackers and milk, PB sandwich, apple, grill cheese and fries, salad with blue cheese dressing and 6 mozzarella sticks, 3 chocolates
30 minutes bike, 7.9 miles; Ab 55-15

Real happy my weight actually went down. I guess healthy eating and exercise can pay off! Also had a BM yesterday. First one in a while. It bothers me that I'm so irregular. Maybe healthy eating – fruits/vegetables – will change that. I hope. Spent the morning typing my 430 paper. Skipped 261. I really hate that class. I so want to drop it. Missed 262. My watch stopped and by the time I went up class was well in session. Went to 430 office hours. Saw Wagner in the hall. Felt kind a bad. Skipped 150 and I hadn't planned to. In fact, I wanted to go for the reading review. Oh well. Fooled around instead. Had a food craving so Larissa and I went to Denny's. Had grill cheese, mozzarella sticks and salad. The dressing and service was disappointing. Larissa is really annoying. She had two sticks. Her approach to food just bugs me. We talked about school and the possibility of my dropping 261. Hit See's. Came home and hit the bike. Looked up what requirements I still need to fulfill. According to classes I could drop 261, but then I looked up my unit requirement. Keeping all of the classes I'm in I'll still need four more units next year. That has me contemplating summer school, which just kills me. But do I want to do five classes, six classes? Ouch!

March 8, Friday
225
Finished reading The Rules, made 2 batches of caramels, really hard
El Rey Taco small nachos, green quesadilla, PB sandwich, 3 chocolates
30 minutes treadmill, 46 calories, .8 mile; Ab 55-15

Finished reading The Rules today. Just bought it Tuesday. I'm going to give it to Rachel. She really needs to follow some of those rules. She moved too fast and makes the move first. Most of the book was common sense. It was also pretty old fashioned. But what's wrong with that? I guess. Sometimes. Actually, it was pretty cheesy. I made two batches of caramels for the breakfast on Sunday. They turned out super hard. More like sugar daddies. I had to use the electric knife to get any squares cut and still it took forever and majorly strained my right hand. Mom sent me to El Rey Taco again. This is like the third Friday in a row. I'm not complaining about free food, but man, what am I doing to myself? What happened to the girl that wanted to fit into that checkered skirt and suede shorts? What happened to my determination, my desire to be thin? Huh? I did manage to get my butt on the treadmill. Mom and Dad left for dinner and groceries. I think Larissa came home while or just after I was exercising. She wanted to go see The Birdcage. I want to see it too, but I was all-gross, plus long day tomorrow, no money and well, why should I make myself so available to her?

March 9, Saturday
225 ¾
Bakery at 9, shopping in the downtown Flower Mart, Beverly Hilton
OJ, Egg McMuffin minus the ham, hash brown; Acapulco veggie fajitas, veggie dishes

    I was at the bakery at 9 a.m. like a good girl. Alice went to McDonalds and bought us breakfast. Took out the ham. Delivered a birthday cake at the Beverly Hilton. Mary's dog lady had ordered it. Isabella and I were really disappointed that we didn't get to deliver it to the polo room. We wanted to go inside, but no. We went to Party On! A party supply store in Beverly Hills close to the Beverly Center. We also went to the Flower Mart in downtown LA, close to school. Reminded me of My Fair Lady. Went to Target so Isabella and Alice could purchase Letty's gifts. Then we went to Acapulco. I had the veggie fajitas. It was more than I could eat. At Alice's we got out dishes to clean them. I dropped a casserole dish. Tamarra came over. I am amazed at what she puts up with. Jacob talked on the phone for a very long time. Christina, the Italian bracelet – oh I'm pregnant – girl called. Got Jacob in a bit of trouble, but not much, which to me means none at all. Jacob's car was hit and the idiot didn't have insurance. Now he's going to be paying for it. New car, but couldn't afford the insurance. Missed not exercising. Jewel was actually pretty well behaved. Slept in Rachel's room since she was out.

March 10, Sunday
Letty's Bridal Shower 6:30
Vacuum and set-up
Won candle in legs/corsage game
Donuts, Subway, veggie, Key Lime pie, brownies, punch
Food, food, food!

    Having McDonalds, Acapulco, and Dominos really wreaked havoc on my lower digestive tract. I'm talking major gas. I can't handle all that grease. I vacuumed the stairs and just generally helped Rachel set-up. Put the cheese mixture in the celery sticks. Alice noted that it's always the same people that help with these kinds of things. Had a veggie sub for lunch. Munched all day. There was so much food. I actually wrapped Letty's gift. It wasn't very good, but trying from me is a gift. I think the cheese/broccoli sandwiches also had ham chunks. Tried one beef skewer. Had a couple of brownies, key lime pie and plenty of champagne punch. Almost won cucumber game. Between me and Donna. Could see for the pin the macho on the man contest so nailed it. Admitted to being able to see so Sheri got the prize. Called bingo. Wrote the word scramble. Won the corsage/cross your legs game. Like – totally nailed it. I was all over it. Almost obnoxiously so. Courtney was annoying as usual. She tried to tell Sophia something about her daughter. It was really immature and inappropriate. Sophia handled it well, I, as usual, got some good slams in. Rachel went to bed before I left. She was also a bit baffled at my ability to participate in the shower and work on my Shakespeare paper at the same time. But a girl's gotta do what a girl's gotta do. Took lunch for tomorrow. Alice works too much.

March 11, Monday
228 ½
Jury Duty for Spring Break – SUCKS! Day 7, one panel called, not on it (4:15), worked on book writing twenty pages
Party leftovers, hard caramels, noodle dish
10 minutes treadmill, .2 mile, 14 calories; 30 minutes bike, 7.7 miles; Ab 55-15

Another dull day of Jury Duty. I was glad that I decided to take all of the goodies that I had packed. The chocolate éclair in the morning hit the spot. Spent the whole day just dumping my brain onto pages. Wrote about twenty pages. Considering the amount of time I spent it felt like it should have been more. But it is a start. Came home and Mom was still being – distant, I guess. She was going to a visitation. Asked me if I wanted to go too. I said no. She didn't want to drive alone. Oh well. Larissa came home all high and mighty. She said something about my putting out the trash, like yeah right. What a bitch! Started to exercise on the treadmill then Dad came home and ran up the volume of the TV. He's allowed to rule his TV and his living room, but come on. He could have at least said something first. When I decided to leave the room he said he missed me this weekend. Yeah, whatever. When I'm here he doesn't really notice. Then he said he missed watching this stuff. Well then, I guess his tape was more important, especially since he never came back to talk to me at all. Spent the rest of the night in my room. With shit like that I think it just might be easy to reject them and get back to losing weight again.

March 12, Tuesday

Jury Duty all day yesterday and only one panel called. I wasn't on it. Sat through another day and no panels were called at all. It was awful. I spent some quality time working on my Shakespeare paper. Some lady, after I went back to writing in my notebook, asked if I was writing a book. She noticed me going at it and that I never seemed to stop. Well, of course, I said yes. Although it was the answer she seemed to expect she still seemed to be a bit surprised. I think I also surprised myself. I really am writing a book. I really am working on something in the hope and preparation of putting it out there. I've got to a point where I just might be willing to share myself to a mass audience. Of course, I'll always be selective in what I share, but it's there. It is coming. I am really breaking out all over my face and head. It's super gross. Skipped washing my face for two days. I'm sure that has a lot do with it especially since I still exercised. Watched TV and typed up a new rough draft of my paper. Dad saw the heart doctor. He has shin splints or something. Should bike, not walk. Asked if he wanted me to swap the equipment. I got a "are you willing?" As if I wouldn't.

March 12, Tuesday (separate entry)
225 ¼
30 minutes treadmill, 44 calories, .7 mile; Ab 55-15

Yesterday was definitely a positive day for me. In jury duty I was able to get twenty pages written about weight loss. I just opened the flood gates and let it start pouring. It was mentally exhausting, but great. I think all of these thoughts have been building up for too long; they needed out and I need to release them. There is a certain permanency in putting them in ink. I always edit but there is still something permanent about letting go of your thoughts and putting them out there for reshaping and review. I think it helped me realize why I haven't been losing any weight lately. How increased physical activity relieves stress – something that was helping me lose weight and how being smaller I think I have more offers to do stuff where I can't avoid food without it being noticed. I think Rachel's break up with Daniel has affected me too. She's packed on some pounds. But what really gets me is the increased amount of time spent with her. She wants someone to do stuff with all the time and frequently that someone is me. Unfortunately, our doing something together usually ends up with food getting involved. I am very proud that for the past three months I have at least maintained my weight. I know that that is an accomplishment especially considering how much I have shed. But now if I am going to go down again I must retreat and isolate myself. I know I can. I've done it before. Retreating from my family is a pleasure. When Larissa came home yesterday I just felt disgusted. She annoys me so much I find it funny that she's only had this job for a short time period, but she's really acting cocky. Then Dad comes home. Flips on the TV and blasts it beyond belief while I'm exercising. He didn't even say anything first. "I'm about to do this" would have been polite. I left the room and went for the bike. He said he missed me this weekend but he also missed the tape. So, gee, I wonder, which did he miss more? Well, the tape won his attention, so… I should have stayed away longer. It's no wonder I can isolate myself from these people. That's one reason to go back to fasting. I know I can reject them. Mom was going out to a meeting and asked me if I wanted to go. She didn't want to go alone. She seemed annoyed that I wasn't interested in going with her. Oh well. She also seemed annoyed when I came home Sunday. Like, was anyone listening when I said they wouldn't see me all weekend? I really wonder because I get the feeling from both Mom and Dad that they're annoyed by my being gone or not telling them where I was or something which is just crap because I did. I hate them. They are so annoying and forgetful.

March 13, Wednesday
223 ¾
Fast, bits of caramel
Ninth Day of Jury Duty. Let go before lunch 11:30, 430 paper, watch/dump Anthropology tape
30 minutes treadmill, 45 calories, .7 mile; Ab 55-15

    Although I swapped the treadmill for the bike yesterday evening Mom just noticed it this morning. I wonder if Dad will even use the bike, or was this just a step up and eventual excuse. It's not like he asked me for the swap, like someone who actually wanted it would. Oh Saturday I got a letter from LBCC. On the Dean's List – Great Distinction, which means I got an A in English 2. Kind of thought I would, but hadn't checked. Feel kind of bad that I didn't go back to pick up my final because I said I would. Also kind of wish I had that work. Oh well. Let out of Jury Duty early, around 11:30. Came home. Didn't get much work done on my paper. Tidied up my room a bit, then decided to watch and dump one of my tapes. It was all Anthropology stuff. A couple episodes I hadn't seen before. Ate a couple of bits of caramel. Also exercised. Watched Law and Order. It was good. Yesterday Mom asked me if I wanted to go to her club meeting with her. I said no. She made some comment about my not having school this week and I pretty much said so what. Hello. That doesn't mean I want to go hang out with a bunch of old, I mean older, ladies. Looked up community colleges. I might have to take a couple more classes and I want as many options as possible. Larissa asked what Lerner I wanted to go to Friday. Even when she's nice she manages to annoy me.

March 14, Thursday
218 ¾
Fast, bits of caramel
Hips at 4?. Got to keep this up.
20 minutes treadmill, 30 calories, .5 mile

    Felt real good weighing in since I went down another five pounds. That is an amazing ten pounds in two days. If only it was all real and not mostly water weight that I'll regain as soon as I eat something. Had to do some more work on my Shakespeare paper. After typing it I decided to rework a paragraph. Dropped it off late afternoon. I was worried about seeing Ferguson since I didn't shower – looked and probably smelled really bad. Nobody home though, I was safe. Called work. Rachel wasn't there. She called in sick or something. But then I called the house and nobody was there. Thought about doing the La Brea Tar Pits, Pink's Picnic and Library thing. Sort of glad she wasn't home. It ended up being a real rainy yucky day for a picnic. I watched some TV. Lord only knows why I wasted my time on the crap that's on TV. I should have done some reading. I did get my butt on the treadmill but I didn't even get a full thirty minutes on it. I ended up stopping after twenty. I felt weary. The combination of not eating and exercise is unwise, but the results are nice. Skipped doing the AB isolator. Went to bed kind of early. Just didn't feel like being up. Also, probably feeling relief about having finally finished my Shakespeare paper.

March 15, Friday
217 ½
Apple, 8 oz. 1% milk, 8 powdered donuts, mac and cheese, cornbread; El Rey Taco – green quesadilla and bean/cheese burrito, chips and salsa
Ashley called, I called Melissa, Lerner shopping
30 minutes treadmill, 47 calories, .8mile; Ab 55-15

Very happy about weighing in at 217 ½, but know what the weekend has in store. I knew that I should eat something so that I don't have problems in San Diego. That would be very embarrassing. Oh, Melissa thinks I'm very funny. I had her rolling at Letty's shower. I had an apple, then went for the powdered donuts, then fixed some Mac and cheese. Rachel called about this weekend. To get someone to work my Sunday (that I took from Amanda). Ashley called inviting me over on the 24th to do reunion stuff. I still haven't written my letter yet. Called Melissa but got an answering machine. Ashley was on her way to Solvang. Larissa called while I was exercising (Mom and Dad were having dinner so didn't answer the phone) so she left a message to remind me about our shopping plans. As if I would forget. We spent quite a while shopping. Larissa made me try things on. She paid a $60 difference from my gift certificate. Wow! What a present, huh! Plus the red dress from February and the ring! While checking out I realized that one of the outfits had pink in it. Rachel has warped me. She is evil. This and the museum thing is too much. Went to El Rey Taco before home for To Wong Fong, Love Julie Newmar and While You Were Sleeping. Bed at 11:30.

March 16, Saturday
220 ½
San Diego cake delivery, Set-up, Tony Roma's, Stay at Hyatt Islandia
Mac and cheese – other ½, Sammy's California Woodfired pizza

    Staying up so late was not wise when I had to be at the bakery at 8 AM, setting off for a very busy day. Got to the bakery a little late. Had the other half of the Mac and cheese for breakfast. Went up three pounds. Oh, how quickly it comes back, but at least I did the shit thing yesterday. Alice doesn't plan well and sometimes not at all. They didn't know where to meet in San Diego. Turns out they vacation there every year for a week at a time. Okay! Setting up the cake was something of an ordeal. Went to Sammy's California Woodfired Pizza across from the Pavilion. It looked real trendy. We had a cheese pizza (no tomato sauce) and Fettuccini Alfredo. It was good. While waiting for the set up we saw the entrance part. I felt nauseated. I think it was the food, the excitement of the event and the nervousness of what I had to do. Party members were very nice. Checked into the Hyatt by Sea World. Alice went for a suite. Met Rachel at Sea World entrance. That was an ordeal. Jewel was still pleading for her pink kitty, which Rachel promised her. They go all out for that kid. Too out. Went to Tony Roma's and had a slab of ribs. Intimidated/pressured into it. (Sort of) but still. Then hit Ralph's. Jewel had a bath before bed.

March 17, Sunday
Stay over in San Diego, beach walk, Sirens lunch, Seaport Village, Soup Plantation, Drive home, No exercise (except the walking around while shopping)

    Set the alarm, but never heard it go off. Jewel and Rachel went walking out by the boats while Alice and I got ready. Alice thinks it's probably a good thing that I haven't been losing weight lately and that I've been maintaining. Thinks I should stabilize for a while before trying to lose more.

We agreed that Jewel's thrown bunny should be taken away. Maybe even thrown away. Don't indulge temper tantrums. Went to the beach, just for a little while to let Jewel play in the sand. Went to Sirens for lunch. It was good. Mexican. Went to Seaport Village to do some shopping. Didn't really do much purchasing, just looking. Munched our way through. It was a mental strain. Between Alice and Jewel it was an experience. Jewel, Rachel and I went on the carousel. I told Rachel if she told anyone that I would deny it. I was also wearing my new outfit that has pink on it. The shorts are a little shorter than I'm used to. A few pounds should take care of that though. Couldn't believe we were doing dinner before coming back. I was so stuffed. Went to the Soup Plantation. Could barely choke anything down. The drive home was nice. Less than two hours. Not much faster than Rachel, but I still lost her. Thought I would exercise, even wanted to but then to be nice I started talking to Mom. Ended up talking for quite a while. Like after two hours I just decided to go to bed instead.

March 18, Monday
226
Fast, cornbread chunk
Slept in really late, read two pages, tidied up room, took a nap, talk to Larissa
30 minutes bike, 7.6 miles

Wow! What a weekend. Up to 226. Slept in until after 12 PM. I guess the weekend took more out of my mental charge than I thought. Then when I tried to read Dickens I got through maybe two pages before my mind started to drift. Decided to tidy my room. It really needed it, especially after having left for the weekend. Ended up taking a nap too. Man, what a lazy day. I just couldn't get motivated to do anything and yet there was a lot I wanted to do to be prepared for school. Like my oral presentation for Spanish. I knew I should have done it at Letty's shower. I didn't even get my reunion letter done. Or really do any reading for any of my classes. Looks like I'm going to have to do summer school just to rake up some units so I can graduate when I want to. Larissa was all like, it wouldn't be disgraceful to take an extra semester. Hello $12K. Plus my agreement with Mom and Dad was two years. Sure they said last year I could take three, but that was last year.

Plus, I want it done. Exercised on the bike. That felt good. Had a little of the cornbread that was leftover from Mom and Dad's Friday night dinner. Asked Larissa for help on my Spanish presentation. I don't know what to say about my favorite holiday. I hate holidays. Thought about birthdays, but I don't even like those all that much.

March 19, Tuesday
223 ½
Fast
261/262/got papers and midterm back. Grades, all good. ☺
In library for 150

Went to 261. He said he would hand out the paper topics Thursday. Class is cancelled on the 28th because he'll be in Texas. Oh, of course, we could still show up and discuss literature. Wrote 430 response during break. 262 got papers and midterms back. Said papers indicated good thoughts from unheard voices. I got an A-. Surprised by the midterm. Did a bit better than I thought. Thought I misunderstood parts that I apparently got. Courtney got a B, which was a surprise. It surprised her too. Got my 430 paper back with a note about it being well done and a serious revision. I wonder if my grade would have been any better had this draft been my original submission. All in all I was pretty happy. Felt a certain redemption. Knew I wouldn't be able to prepare for Spanish presentation so I worked on my Table Manners presentation. Checked out a book. Was in the east for GC night. Got introduced and into the minutes. Talked to Sandra and Robert for a long time. Sandra has packed on some pounds. Robert likes USC's foreign travel/study program. Rates the schools foreign study as the best in the US. He went to some of those films during the Spanish festival. We joked about his tutoring me. Talked at home – could feel a major cold coming on. Drank some OJ and took vitamins.

March 20, Wednesday
221 ½
Dentist 9:30, Shakespeare paper, Linda called, Rachel called, went to Daniels, AAA, Norm's
A few graham crackers in milk, Jack in the Box chocolate shake, potato wedges

30 minutes bike, 7.5 miles

    Getting up early just to go to the dentist for a filling was an awful way to start my day. Then he spotted another and took care of it since I couldn't come back next week. So both sides were shot up and numb. Wanted to take a nap, but couldn't for some reason. I get drowsy reading, but never writing. Went to Jack in the Box. This was definitely a shake day. Mom bought. Yay! Working on next Shakespeare paper. Will it ever end? Linda called to find out what happened Tuesday. Won't be there Thursday either. She's graduating and going on job interviews. Going to Michigan. I wished her luck. Rachel called asking for a friend. Picking up Jewel and stuff tonight. Needs help. Doesn't want to go alone. She told Daniel she was filing for divorce. They were arguing over Jewel. Daniel won't return Alice's camcorder without some kind of pay off. He says it's Rachel's fault because she's not being civil. He is so mental. He left a sex anonymous number on her pager. Probably can't prove it was him, but who else would? He's psychologically abusing Jewel yelling, "Mommy doesn't love me" and "Mommy doesn't love you" at her. He's sick. The pick up was tense, but successful. Got clothes. Jewel locked keys in car. Went to Norms. Rachel and Alice going to lawyer tomorrow. She second guessed it for a second. Needs a hand to hold. Worried about money. Alice thanked me.

March 21, Thursday
225 ½
El Rey Taco small nachos with chips, Pepsi, blueberry sls
261 paper topic handed out, 262 nobody in class, 430 – 150- missed oral presentation bad quiz stem changing verb

    Getting home so late didn't make getting up to go to school easy. But I need that paper topic so I got it together. Hair in tight ponytail. Looking pretty bad. 262 we started with seven people. I pitched in when Michael was called on. Five people walked in late. Courtney missed class. I told her I probably wouldn't be here Tuesday. Christy gave me a Wow! when I walked through the door. Hannah shared catalogues. Told her I might not be here Tuesday. She wished me a good birthday. Thought about preparing the oral presentation just in case, but then didn't. Should have because I would have been able to do it. We went over readings and superlatives. Quiz on stem changing verbs straight out of workbook, but I bombed. Totally clueless. Came home tired and hungry. World's figure skating men's and pairs were on TV. Mom sent me to El Rey Taco. She paid of course. Right on! Had nachos and the stupid assholes put sour cream on it. Larissa benefited from their mistake. Oh Shakespeare Ferguson is definitely a democrat. Dad pisses me off. So what's new? They did a lot of Rudy hype and Dad said, "All of that build up, and for what – a queer." He didn't even watch his performance, which was simply beautiful. Dad was annoyed with the way Mom was voting. "He's just mad because I'm not letting him vote my ballot."

March 22, Friday
225
Green quesadilla, Parmesan pasta, 2 liter Pepsi, slice of cheese, graham crackers in milk
30 minutes treadmill, .7 mile, 43 calories

  Major laundry day sorting and dumping some of the stuff Rachel gave me. Of course I had to make room for all of the stuff I was keeping which meant dumping some of my larger and worn stuff. I had my leftover green quesadilla with Mom (she had one too) for lunch. It wasn't enough so I made Parmesan pasta, which we shared. I drank a whole 2-liter bottle of Pepsi today. Later snacked on a slice of cheese. Dinner was graham crackers in milk. Got it together and on the treadmill although it was a slow going session. I also had a letter for my reunion to write and two school papers – Shakespeare and 261. Instead I avoided my real responsibilities and played house. I rearranged where things were. I had to make decisions about what to keep, what to dump. But that was time better spent working on other tasks. I still don't know what I'm going to do about summer school and a possible vacation. I think I'd really like to get away. But at least this time I won't be running.

March 23, Saturday
226
Work 9:30-3:30 with Rachel
Daniel phone calls, called Grace, Safari Bar
Pretzel, Pepsi, El Rey Taco bean/cheese burrito, green quesadilla, rice, 3 midori sours, 2 rum and Cokes

30 minutes treadmill, 43 calories, .7 mile

    Had to be at work in the AM. Opened with Rachel who was having some Daniel problems like usual. It was phone call day. He pages – she calls. He threatens to kill himself to get to her back. He seems to think she'll rush back to save him. He just doesn't get it. He had her crying in her office – AGAIN! I'm doing what I can to be a good friend and to be there for her which is sometimes trying because I'm not good in certain situations. People crying makes me uncomfortable and I'm having a hard time understanding why she listens to anything that asshole says. At least he gave back Alice's camcorder. Had a pretzel from Target. Instead of working on my paper I worked out after work. Called Grace about my work in progress letter. Had a large El Rey Taco dinner before meeting Rachel to go to the Safari Bar. Wanted plenty down there to absorb the alcohol I knew I would be drinking. Jacob went with his friends Joe and Freddy. I think the guy's name was Freddy but I kept calling him Robert. Jacob disappeared for a while. I told him he was a dog. He said he just gives good massages. Danced with two guys. Joshua – 3X's – creepy and Mr. Smiley. Rachel had her fill. She definitely needed to get away – go out and have fun.

March 24, Sunday
226 ¼
Ashley's book party – everyone was late
Grace, Melissa and Denise left around 5
Chinese chicken salad, rosemary muffin, wine, strawberry, chicken, mac/cheese, green beans, taffy cookies, 2 donuts

    It was so hard getting up to go to Ashley's for the pre-reunion luncheon. I was worried about being late and I was by almost an hour, but I was also the first to arrive. Considering I never knew Ashley that well during our year I'm glad I wasn't early. Melissa, Grace and Denise joined us. Melissa is marrying Matthew in October. They asked me about men. I'm the only one among them that's free. That was a little odd. Joshua (Ashley's husband) is quite the cook. We had a Chinese chicken salad and rosemary muffins that he had prepared. When I got home it made me feel very restless. I don't want to live at home anymore. I want to go somewhere that's mine. It also reminded me of a time when I had money. I want money again. I'm miserable being poor. It really doesn't suit my personality. I miss having a full-time job. Odd because Denise complained about hers. They all want to be (eventually) full-time moms. I want a real job. I don't want kids, but a man might be nice. I am definitely missing some kind of human connection. Weird. They want what I have and I don't know what I want.

March 25, Monday
230 ¾
Shakespeare paper due *postponed*, Sizzler with Rachel
2 toast with jam, deli mixed cheese sandwich with potato wedges, Sizzler – salad and fruit, chocolate mouse

    Rachel's B-Day. We were supposed to go to lunch. She didn't tell me yesterday when I called that her schedule changed. At 2 PM I went to the deli for Mom and me. I spent almost all day on stand-by for Rachel. Larissa sent a card with me, which contained a $500 check. Rachel couldn't accept it. It surprised me a little, but not really. Mom's credit card paid for our Sizzler dinner. I did the salad bar. I actually ate more than I expected to. Came home and watched the end of the Oscars. Ended up finishing the rest of my deli sandwich. There was no ambition on my part to work on anything associated with school – even after the Oscars were over. I guess because I knew that I would be missing school the next day, but that was stupid because I was just postponing the pile up. I should have at least done my reunion letter so I could fax it from Alice's tomorrow, but NO I didn't even manage to get that done. Sometimes I wonder if I'm setting myself up for failure or have my priorities shifted? Do I need to become more selfish and less concerned about the people around me? I spent a lot of time today at someone else's beck and call. I didn't like it.

March 26, Tuesday
230
Shakespeare Oral Presentation "Table Manner" *postponed*
Lunch with Mom at Guadalajara Inn, cake delivery at Diana Ross', Spanish, Alice's

    Felt great sleeping in on a school day. And no bitching out of Mom. Wow! Alice called while I was showering.

Returned her call and then talked to Rachel. I'm a planner. They aren't. They both sounded like they were pointing at each other saying, "isn't she going with you?" I went to Diana Ross' house alone with the cake in my trunk. I should have moved my car after checking in but didn't. It was major heavy to carry the distance I had to go with it. Then I was invited to stay for the party. Like, Oh my God, Yes! Thank you! Only I couldn't. Even though Alice and Rachel had left me to do this delivery all by myself, on my birthday, we were still planning on getting together for dinner. And I couldn't be a no show for my friend. Well, I'm stronger and kinder than I thought or realized. I was supposed to be having an adventure – lunch at Pink's, shopping at the Beverly Center. I could have had an adventure partying with Diana Ross on our shared birthday. But instead, my adventurous birthday was reduced to a job. A mission to accomplish and walk away from. The lunch Mom and I had at Guadalajara Inn turned out to be my only meal of the day. (We tried to go to a roped off Bicycle Club.) Dad started my day with a cow miniature and Mom bought a blue bunny ice cream cake at Baskin-Robins. After delivery I got Spanish help from Susan. Went to Alice's under the ploy that Rachel, Alice and I were going to go out to dinner. But that didn't happen. Why? Daniel threatened to file first. Rachel spent the day in hysterics over it and was napping when I arrived. When she finally got up she was super cranky. Larissa never paged us for the political party. Alice paid me for San Diego. Tamarra called and I told her Jacob was a dog. It so wasn't my place to say, but I was in a foul mood after my birthday was twice fucked that I lashed out. He says he doesn't blame me. Mostly because I didn't tell Tamarra anything that wasn't true. I just didn't have to say anything. Received a promise that we would celebrate later. Sure.

March 27, Wednesday
227 ½
Chips and cheese, blue bunny ice cream cake, olives
Shakespeare presentation, Spanish presentation

    Went to the store for Velveeta cheese and chips. Mom and I dug into the blue bunny. Told her that the highlight of my day was our lunch out. I wanted to cry. She and Dad were the only two that didn't crap on my day. She doesn't think I should feel at all bad about the Jacob thing. She showed concern about my getting too involved. Hope it isn't or doesn't interfere with my career. I skipped school – an important day – to have an adventure, but was reduced to employee and loud mouth informant. Even Rachel tried to cover her brother's ass. For someone who claims her life is an open book, hers is not. She definitely didn't want me saying anything about Saturday to Alice. I have involved myself too much. It has affected my schoolwork. Maybe I wanted the interference. Maybe I didn't really want to work on something, but I made a choice. I can't afford to go back, nor do I want to. We finished the cheese and the blue bunny. I spent all day working on my oral presentations for Shakespeare and Spanish. Didn't actually finish Shakespeare thing, but I should be ready.

March 28, Thursday
227 ¼
Shakespeare Oral Presentation
261 cancelled, 262 Jane Eyre – Linda got a job offer, 430 presentation went well, 150 quiz presentation postponed

Alexander scheduled to be in Texas so I didn't have my morning class. Finished off my Shakespeare presentation. I wonder if it's long enough. Oh well. Went to 262. Paper topics passed out Tuesday. Seemed annoyed by those of us who were absent. Courtney missed Tuesday. Started talking to Linda so sat next to her, which turned out to be a mistake. She's doing a pass/fail, which he hates. Apparently, went off on her the other day about not reading. Well for the second day of discussion on Jane Eyre I hadn't even cracked the book open. He was annoyed by the lack of discussion. Linda got a Michigan job offer with Nabisco – entry level, $40K. She wants to stay in the LA area though. Oral Presentation went well. It was at the end of class – I hate the waiting. Had a Spanish quiz that went okay. Was supposed to do my presentation. Allison wasn't ready. Zed left it in the dorm. Summer was absent and Jose and Travis had to leave early. Allison acted inappropriately. Argued with our student teacher. She wanted to do it, just not at the top of the hour. During the quiz she said, "Those who can't do, teach." There was an audible gasp and I swear all the oxygen left the room. Got lots done today. Wrote/typed my letter. Oh, and Mr. Spanish took my late homework.

March 29, Friday
223 ½
Shakespeare paper due, worked on paper all day, faxed letter to Grace
Chips, toast, Wok Express chicken, 2 egg rolls, 4 almond cookies
30 minutes treadmill, .7 mil, 41 calories; AB 30

    My Shakespeare paper was due today. I worked on it all day, but it just wasn't going to happen. Larissa agreed to do my fax at Farr's. Had to call Grace for the number. She called back when Larissa was gone and her hours are usually 7-3 or 3:30. Whatever, I ended up doing it myself. Had to pay a couple bucks, but it was better than going to Alice's and getting into conversation and wasting time that I didn't really have. Ended up eating Wok Express, which was just stupid. I know I gave in because I remember it tasting good to me at one time, but it doesn't' anymore. It's just so fatty and gross. Why did I allow myself to get suckered in again? The almond cookies are still good though. I got on the treadmill. Needed to get the blood moving. It was a lackluster performance but I at least did it. I spent my whole day working on my Ophelia Shakespeare paper. Then had to stress over when and where I would leave it. I started singing Cecilia – only changing the words to fit a Hamlet theme. I'd ask for extra credit for it, but she'd probably make me perform it for the class. A computer really would have eased my load today.

March 30, Saturday
225
Letty's Wedding, start of convention, reunion dinner at Hansa House, 430 paper
Leftover Wok Express, toast, reunion dinner

    Had leftover Wok Express and toast for breakfast. Larissa and Dad left to go to the opening sessions. Mom left on Thursday. Kimberly Thompson called her on Friday. I worked on my paper until leaving for Letty's wedding. I thought I was late arriving at 2:50. Music and the kneeling pads weren't even set-up. They started nearly an hour late at 3:25.

William hardly ever looked at Letty and in the fourth row I could barely hear a word out of either of them. They really didn't look all that happy. She had a billion people around her though. And she was beautiful. The ceremony was a combination of English/Spanish. No my classes did not help me here. Having witnessed weddings did. Went to Hansa House for my reunion dinner. Oh! Rachel filed on Thursday. Daniel will be served on April Fool's Day! Worked on paper until Grace arrived. Helped set-up. Everyone that talked to me, which was just about everybody, said I looked great. Amy is working on her English Literature Masters. Nicole and Stacy are single Moms. Abigail is totally veggie and Samantha is an actress. Really – not much changes. Olivia broke her arm. Kimberly is an RN. Nancy's proud of me.

March 31, Sunday
226
Appointments, 430 paper, Baker's Square
El Rey Taco nachos, green quesadilla, salad
(Holly won sweeps)

After getting home last night Amanda called. Her mother paid for her to be at the reunion, but she just didn't feel like coming. So I was on the phone when I should have been working on my paper. More work for today. Not done when I had to leave to meet Amanda. She kept me waiting twenty minutes and then had to change. I was actually starting to wonder if she would show or if she was going to back out on me. Her Mom gave her money for parking and food, which she spent so she came with nothing. Met up with Melissa. The plan was to go to Baker's Square. Melissa drove us. It was actually awkward having Amanda there. She doesn't seem willing to cultivate these old friendships. Since I had an El Rey Taco lunch I had a salad for dinner which hit the spot. Mom had a lot of good news and winners to celebrate. My two girls are both from the south. After getting home I still had more work to do on my paper. I finished around 2:30 AM.

APRIL

April 1, Monday
226 ¼
Chicken/eggs, 8 slices of pizza

    No sleep for procrastinators. Up at 6:01. I was beating it to school to shove my paper under Ferguson's door so that she hopefully wouldn't know how late it was. Nobody is on campus at 6:45 a.m. Okay – a few athletes. Came home and took a nap that was real hard to shake out of. Went for my first escort. Charlotte had to introduce us. Grace arrived about five minutes too late. Stayed to hear the speech for Amanda's girl. Amanda used me and my paper as an excuse to leave. She even falsely claimed she might come back, even though she knew that wasn't gonna happen. What a liar! She wouldn't even go to our reunion dinner, like she would go back for the circle walk. Got home and vegged out. Eventually started working on my paper for 261 which oops! is due tomorrow. Ordered from our local pizzeria. Hungry, didn't want to cook and it sounded sooo good. I spent way too much money and oh my god ended up eating eight, yes eight, slices of pizza. Larissa had the other two. I was up typing my paper into the wee small hours. Ran out of typing ribbon. Had to finish printing the last paragraph. Bed around 2 a.m. – sleep, what's that???

April 2, Tuesday
230 ½
Fast
261 Paper due, up typing, visitor in 430, 150 presentation

Got info out of Mom, up late!
Some fries, apricots, popcorn, Pepsi

Nobody finished the reading for 261. Why was Alexander even surprised? He also did the title review thing again. I don't like how Linda talks to me during class. Then she left early. I get the feeling that Wagner is getting annoyed with me because of the association. He mentioned giving us a quiz on Thursday. We had a visitor in 430. Seemed to make Ferguson a bit nervous. She pretty much was the same, just a bit more – alert. I had my oral presentation in Spanish which went okay, I guess. I lived through it anyway. Came home – Mom was unwinding after all her hoopla this past week. We talked about her girls. She was upset that one of her 'nuns' lost their habit and Mrs. Moore had the sewing team make a new one. Plus the girls went to a high school to perform, leaving the convention – a big No! No! Especially since a chaperone was their escort. She's annoyed that Emily's saying stuff that she shouldn't and shouldn't even know about. Who knows what two years can bring? By the way Mom described her girl out of Buena Park she'll be great in her office. Mom didn't really realize that the things she said about her would peg her for it, which given Mom's nerves, is probably a good thing. What that conversation prevented though is now weighing on her mind.

April 3, Wednesday
225 ½
Worked on room, talk to Mom, Spanish Comp Toast, rice krispie, Helen Grace chocolate bunny, El Rey Taco bean/cheese burrito and 2 green quesadillas
30 minutes treadmill, 44 calories, .7 mile

Slept in real late. Guess I was making up for everything I missed. In 262 I was taking notes and my eyes started to close. Yes, while the hand was moving. I was tired. I ate the Helen Grace chocolate bunny that Larissa gave me. Had some major clean up to do in my room after neglecting it for papers and reunions and such. We did the El Rey Taco thing. Mom only had $3 and Larissa had $5. She threw up in my face that she would have more if I paid her back for Wok Express. It amazes me. I know she owed me money for extended time periods and I would casually remind her after a while… back when I was the one working full-time. Now that she is, it's like, "Oh my god, can I have my two bucks?!" in your face. Arrows point – she owes me, she owes me. I worked on my Spanish Composition and started thinking about my 262 paper. I also got back to my treadmill, which I had been neglecting. It felt good to get back to it. I can't believe the reunion is really over. I feel a certain sense of emptiness in that regard. Like, I didn't take it all in, didn't say and see and do all that I wanted to. Or maybe I just miss all of those close friendships that have kind of faded away and yet are so intense.

April 4, Thursday
225 ½
261 paper returned, 430 paper returned ☹, 262 quiz ☺, 150 composition OK, Persuasion paper
Major headache
PB & J sandwich, cup of soup, apple

  Yucky – blah day. Got my 261 paper back. He said we need to talk again. Bite me. More "wrong word" bullshit. I really don't want to talk to this guy, but I especially don't want to drop and repeat the course. In 262 he gave a two question (off-the-wall) quiz that I clearly failed. I had read the two poems too. That, I do believe is the scariest part. Okay, skimmed more than read, but still. He is just going to hate me. I wonder what this is going to do to my grade, especially with a paper being turned in Tuesday. Ferguson handed out graded papers which really surprised me because last time she took a while. She wrote between Ophelia and my last revision I'm currently in A minus/B+ territory. That truly brightened my day, but I still gotta pull it up. Spanish went okay. Composition went well I think. Went to bed with wet hair last night which caused a full return of the not quite gone cold. Major headache all day too. Went by bakery to drop papers off. Saw Rachel's car, no van, no lights. Came home. Decided to eat. That really didn't seem to help my headache though. I just felt wiped out. Worked on my Persuasion paper even while I watched ER with the rest of the family. Had a hard time falling asleep.

April 5, Friday
223 ½

M & M's, Pepsi 2 liters, KFC dinner – slaw, 2 biscuits, 3 pieces of chicken, BBQ beans
Worked on Persuasion paper, diary entries
30 minutes treadmill, 46 calories, .8 mile

    Slept in. For some reason Dad didn't go to work today. He and Mom went to the grocery. My cold is still hanging around. Thought that and not eating was what had me so miserable yesterday, but this morning proved it to be the start of a killer monthly cycle. Maybe a case of eating healthy proving not to be such a wonderful thing. Anyway, I spent the morning buckled over in pain. Thank God I didn't have to be anywhere. I spent a lot of time on my Persuasion paper. I'm really nervous over it, especially after the disastrous quiz thing. Got on the treadmill. That felt good. Had hints of something good for dinner. Dad ended up going to KFC. I battled with myself, but decided to join in. I ended up having three pieces of chicken. Mom asked me about lard ass cupcakes. She really wants some for Easter. They are at Ralph's, I told her. Having that chicken was a huge blow to this day. It gave me this gnarly dream. I was eating at a bird and maggot type creature popped up. I freaked out. It scurried back to the bird and I threw up three times, red and white. When I told Mom about it she said "See, you're even a problem solver in your dreams."

April 6, Saturday
224
Work 4-7:30 with Rachel. She invited me over tonight and Easter, I declined both
2 slices toast, two plates of chips/cheese/olives, 2 lard ass cupcakes

    That dream bothered me all day. When contemplating the chemicals/hormone's they pump into poultry/cattle Mom and Dad said I have been reading propaganda. Maybe they should review those FDA regulations again. Mom and Larissa went shopping, Dad went to a meeting and I worked on my Persuasion paper. Had to go to work after. Wore the dress that I bought last summer. Closed with Rachel. She and Susan are going to Orchard's after work. I was invited to go along, but declined. Rachel also asked what I was doing for Easter. Her family is doing a barbecue in the park. Daniel was served Thursday, instead of Monday. He's making her life hell. Calls constantly whenever she's home. Now he's complaining about his rights as a father. Rachel requested a restraining order. What rights does he have? I keep hearing how he dumps Jewel on Tracy or goes back and forth with Rachel on when he can watch her. He doesn't want her but he doesn't want Rachel to have her either. Tracy said that she called him to pick Jewel up the weekend of Letty's wedding (think the 29th) but he didn't want to. He wanted to wait until the next day. Tracy pushed the issue. Daniel showed up "wigged out." They think he's back to doing speed. I can't believe that he is allowed to see Jewel at all. I wouldn't allow it.

April 7, Sunday
227 ½
Mountain Dew, 2 lard ass cupcakes, ½ PB & J sandwich, boiled dinner, chips and cheese
Slept in, Persuasion paper, Spanish Writing Cycle

  Easter Sunday. Losing an hour is always such a drag. Even though this was a pretty relaxed day I could have used that hour. Spent a lot of time typing. Complained to Mom and Dad about not having a computer or even a word processor. Hello! I'm a writer. Chisel and stone anyone? Mom fixed the English style boiled dinner. I enjoyed it along with the rest of the family. Asked Mom if it was a no nightmare recipe. She really wasn't amused. Did some reading for my paper while they played cards. I also started to prepare for my Spanish writing cycle, which I'm actually pretty worried about. Had to explain to Dad why I might be doing summer school. I also wrote to Debbie and Melissa. I was actually pretty proud of myself for getting off the dime and doing it. Had a very difficult time going to bed. In fact, I should have gotten back up and got something on, but didn't. I've had a real hard time shutting off lately. My sleep cycle is all confused. Just can't seem to get it back on track. Mom gawked at my having a plate of cheese and chips - then she ate some.

April 8, Monday
227 ¾
Fast
Finished Mountain Dew

Worked on Persuasion paper all day, Typing until 2:40 a.m., Evelyn called for Mom who was at Glory of Easter

With all that I ate yesterday I was a bit surprised that I only went up a quarter of a pound. Spent all day working on my Persuasion paper. It's really annoying having to type and retype. I went from ten pages to eight to five. I just hope that I made it enough of a correlation between Anne and Mr. Elliott and that Dr. Wagner gets it. At least the paper took my mind off of my stomach. It made it pretty easy to avoid food. Also the fact that I ate so much this weekend helped. Evelyn Ellis called after Mom had already gone to the Glory of Easter thing with her district. Evelyn wanted to talk to her for a bit. Pretty dull day. Called a few JC's. Cerritos' schedule comes out mid-April. Long Beach had theirs come out today. ELAC has an April application due date. What to do, what to do. I really need to talk to a counselor about taking Spanish this summer. That will help in my arranging my schedule for fall. I cleaned my bathroom, even my tub and shower. It really needed it. Also gave it some Drano. Did some laundry. My hamper was starting to over fill. Checked out some recipes yesterday. It would be so easy to go totally veggie. Typed until 2:40 a.m. then couldn't sleep.

April 9, Tuesday
225 ½
Fast
262 Paper due, Writing Cycle II, skipped 261, turned in paper, 430 cancelled
Talked to Lisa, Started Cleopatra paper, Avoided Spanish WC
Mom and Dad both had meeting (Dad hosting and Mom at Buena Park – trouble related to the phone call from Evelyn Ellis)

Paper for 262 due today. Missed 261 and read in library instead. Did the reading for 262, but was still a little lost by Wagner's questions. He's so bizarre, like a little troll man. Courtney and Linda were both absent. So was Dana. 430 was cancelled, sign posted on door. Talked to Lisa. We were both surprised that Ferguson would cancel a class. Lisa has Alexander for a 42? Class. She hates him too. Started working on my next Shakespeare paper. Think I'll do Antony & Cleopatra. Wanted to do anything to avoid the Writing Cycle for Spanish. It went okay I guess. Not as well as I would have liked, but about the same as the last one. Dad had the board watching a tape when I got home. Didn't know Mrs. Hill is back on the board. She said Mrs. Peterson asked her if she wanted her job. I almost lost it. Mrs. Hill is either delusional, lying or Mrs. Peterson is desperate to let go of the reins. The board is having problems with Trisha. Mom had to go to Buena Park. Thompson, Miller and Johnson are causing problems. Kimberly wrote to Mrs. Ellis. Basically don't know how Alexis got her appointment and they want it taken away. They want to blame and bitch "how did this happen?!" because they (not that 'they' were all there doing the recommendation and scoring) only wanted her to be a representative. They never thought she would be appointed to a 'higher' office than Melissa. How narrow and selfish. Put Mom through hell. And to think of what could have been.

April 10, Wednesday
220 ½
Fast
Up late, Mom called Evelyn, more talk, Started reading, work on 430 paper, did addresses, took a bubble bath
Headachey, lack of energy

Couldn't breathe when I woke up. If this is a cold, why is it lasting so long? Mom suggested that I'm really just allergic to SC. She called Evelyn to give her the scoop. Buena Park adults are very small-minded. Started to do some reading. Mom left to do errands. She stopped at Subway before coming home. She ate a foot-long sandwich while I copied addresses from my reunion into my book. Need to buy stamps & pick up LBCC Summer Schedule. No energy to do a damn thing. Mom asked me if I wanted to go to Sam's Club. Gave her a half ass yes. Fell asleep for quite a while and I have no idea if she went or not. Having a hard time concentrating. Worked a bit on my next 430 paper. Figured why not? Hip measurements were low so I decided to try on my size 18 jeans again. I didn't have to lie down to zip them up. They're still pretty tight though. Soon. Wasn't looking forward to standing up for a shower so decided to go for a bubble bath. It was so relaxing. I think it really did me some good. Larissa ended up working at the mall tonight. They must have her office work number. Wondering whether or not I'll go to 261 or 262 tomorrow. I don't want to go to either. I don't want to talk to Alexander, though I know I probably should.

April 11, Thursday
217 ¾
Fast
Coke, cranberry cocktail, crumb of crust
Skipped 261/262, Ferguson' grandpa ill, 150 quiz
Headachy

Had a rough start. Felt very disoriented this morning. Went to LBCC to get a schedule of classes. Need a returning student form, but got a continuing. Oops! Went to Santa Monica College and the bookstore was closed. The whole freaking school looked closed. Maybe it was their Spring Break. Went to WLAC. It took some time to find. No schedules yet. Bought a Coke. Don't think I'll even try there again. Courtney went to 262. Said the correlation between Conrad and Arnold was actually kind of interesting. Ferguson' grandpa is ill, but hanging on. Jordon's doing a swim-a-thon on Saturday. Helped him raise funds by soliciting from everyone in class. He'd asked me when we were alone and after a group of students I just kind of announced it like, hey he's doing this so sign his sheet with your pledge. I don't think he was going to ask everyone in class and I know he didn't expect me to, but I also know it's a lot easier to ask for donations when you're doing it for someone else vs. yourself. I didn't even think twice about doing it but he made a point of thanking me for the help. The quiz was from homework we just did. Should have been easy, but I didn't review it after getting it back. Mom went to Sam's Club today to get stuff together for her reunion thing. I watched Friends in my room. Mom bought an apple pie and it looked really good. I took a touch of crust. Kind of kicking myself about it too because I already had a bottle of Coke and a can of cranberry cocktail – that Hannah didn't like. Watched the repeat season finale (last years) of ER with the family.

April 12, Friday
216 ¼ - Yes! Finally a NEW breakthrough
Fast

Turned down a quesadilla, work on Antony and Cleopatra, read Heart of Darkness, school schedule planning, mailed letters

    Even though I drank calories yesterday I still pushed through to a new breakthrough. Knew today would be hard. Haven't had a day five in a long time. Mom went out during the day to run errands. I took a nap. She came home and offered me a quesadilla, but I turned her down. She sounded surprised. I stayed in my room after that. I really didn't want to smell her stuff. Saw the quesadilla in the refrigerator later with the apple pie. It would be so easy to slip. But I didn't. Did more work on my Antony & Cleopatra paper. Started to read Heart of Darkness. My mind kept drifting. Checked out the school schedules. If I take Spanish and Music this summer I still need an extra unit, but when should I take that unit? And what should I take? More decisions to make. Don't even really know for sure what exactly I'll be doing and I hate being in the state of flux. I need to get some of this stuff nailed down. Went out to buy soda and stamps and get my letters in the mail. A petitioner tried to stop me. Said my residence was in Santa Clara. No idea where that came from. When drifting during Heart of Darkness it hit me how late it was and maybe I should just go to bed. Hello!

April 13, Saturday
214 ¼ - YES!!! YES!!! YES!!!
Work 1-7:30
Chocolate bar, salad, Pepsi, ½ avocado and egg salad sandwich, nachos (homemade), slice of apple pie

    I wore my short black skirt to work today. I looked good. Felt pretty weak though. I had a killer headache. Hen offered me something but I knew it would not do any good. Rachel's selling candy bars for Jewel's school. Wonder if Daniel is too? Anyway, she's going out to dinner with Angela tonight. Sounds like Jacob's going to be terminated. Think Rachel thinks Tamarra has something to do with it. Tamarra broke up with him again on Easter. Big blow up apparently. Working 6.5 hours, I buckled. Chowed on one of Rachel's candy bars. I wolfed it down. Then ordered a salad and sandwich from the mall's sub place. Hit the bathroom before the real food got there. Went again after eating. Couldn't finish the sandwich. The rest went in the fridge. Larissa and I had nachos after she got home from work. I did the cheese. They turned out okay. Since I was already blowing it I went for a slice of apple pie. Mom bought a peach pie. I don't know what this thing with pie is but it could really stop. Yes, I hit the bathroom again. A total of four times. It was not pleasant in the least.

April 14, Sunday
215 ¼
Work 10:30-6:30
Sbarro's garlic bread and cheese pizza, nachos, 2 Pepsi, apple pie
30 minutes treadmill, 42 calories, .7 miles

Surprised (and grateful!) with all that I ate I only went up a pound. Guess I shouldn't be because I also majorly flushed my system of crap and built up fluids. Worked yet another day with Melissa and Courtney. I was so well behaved. Didn't pick on Courtney nearly as much as I could have and usually do. Larissa called me at work about doing nachos again for dinner. I agreed to it then had a Sbarro's lunch with Melissa. They've changed their style of garlic bread. I didn't like it nearly as much. Of course, I went for the cheese pizza. Got home and Larissa was in the middle of preparing the cheese for our chips. I even had a slice of apple pie finishing it off. After that I felt like the bloated cow that I was. Mom and Dad were off at some meeting thing. Got my butt on the treadmill. It had been a while. I need to get back to exercising. Since I did it rather late I knew I wouldn't be able to fall asleep for a while so I wrote some letters, ones I have been meaning to – like to Sandy and Tricia. Wondered how Rachel's dinner went with Angela, but didn't really want to call and be nosy. I'm sure they had a great time. Alice and Jewel went to see James & the Giant Peach last night. Nicole came in to make a payment.

April 15, Monday
218
Bite size Baby Ruth, 2 Reese's eggs, 3 Musketeers, finish Saturday's sandwich, potatoes, stuffing, beets, OJ
Wrote letters, Heart of Darkness
30 minutes bike, 7.5 miles

Thought today would be a no eat day but that didn't last long. I put the Easter chocolates in the fridge and offered to Larissa and Mom. Naturally Mom didn't touch but Larissa raided. Of course, she took the good stuff. Anyway, I finished what was left telling myself that I deserved to and kicking myself for even having taken it in the first place. I think I didn't want Larissa to finished eating it so I pounced. Also, finished the egg salad and avocado sandwich from Saturday. Amazingly it was still good. Wrote my letters. Dropping notes to Grace and Ashley. Did some reading for Heart of Darkness. It's okay – yet another travel/adventure story though. Mom went to Yorba Linda tonight. Got on the bike. I was last to use it. How disappointing. Fixed stuffing. Larissa did mashed potatoes, added beets for quite a dinner feast. Mom's girl Julie was accepted at Princeton with a $2,000 year scholarship. She was also offered a full scholarship to USC. She asked Mom if USC was a good school. This girl has some thinking to do. Mom gave Holly an angel pen for her sweeps win. The Thompsons were there and cheering, but also avoiding Mom.

April 16, Tuesday
220 ½
261 paper topics handed out, 262 called on papers not returned, 430 topics on Thursday, Skipped 150
Raining, bookstore, counsel – Doris, Lane Bryant payment, talk
     Ouch! Even though I exercised yesterday I went up 2 ½ pounds. Noticed I haven't had a BM since Saturday's foursome. Glad I went to 261 since he handed out paper topics. I think this time it's best that I go for the creative writing exercise. Wagner said he had our papers graded, but not recorded. Called on me today. I felt a blush. Hope it didn't show, but I'm sure it did. I amazingly was able to answer the question even though I hadn't finished the reading. 430 Ferguson said we would get our paper topics on Thursday and discuss party plans. Decided to skip 150. No real good reason, until I realized it was raining. I was wearing a T-shirt and didn't want to walk around getting soaked. Like I never just wear a t-shirt, so when I do it rains. Went to the bookstore, then the English department to clear my thing for registration. Picked up a coarse description write up. Went to Lane Bryant to make my payment. Baby barf stain on my T-shirt (from Rachel.)

Saturday and today Rachel asked if I noticed her weight loss. I'm really bad at noticing these things in others and it kind of bugs me when people ask for attention or praise. I guess she's happy. She does look healthier than I've seen her, but I think that has more to do with being happy than her weight. Larissa and I went to the deli to pick up dinner. Watched TV and talked. Mom had her Buena Park meeting tonight.

April 17, Wednesday
222 ¾
Worked on Fall schedule, Winter's Tale
2 eggs, OJ, cheese, toast, potato wedges, leftover sandwich, lemon/cheese muffin
30 minutes treadmill, 42 calories, .7 mile

    Read through the course description list. The Middle Ages really isn't looking so bad. Had a hell of a time trying to figure out what I want to take and the time lines. Wish 472 was offered in the morning instead of afternoon. I don't think I want to stick around a couple of hours and then get out at 3:15. That was a problem with that other tutoring job. And man do I want to change jobs. Cut up some potato wedges in eggs and it was good. Later I finished my sandwich. And the wedges. Had a craving for cookies but didn't want to go to the store, especially not just for that. Larissa gave me a lemon cheese muffin that was filling but not satisfying. Did some reading on the Winter's Tale. It's funny. I think I like Perdita. Had to really coax myself to get back on that treadmill but I did it. Read some of the cliff notes for A Portrait of the Artist As A Young Man. I think I might actually have the capacity to like this novel. I should. The stream-of-consciousness is something that previously appealed to me so maybe this time I'll read it in a new light. With all that I've eaten – still no movement!

April 18, Thursday
224 ¾
Potatoes with cheese, pizza, more potatoes, 3 circus animal cookies
Skipped 261, Persuasion paper = straight up A, paper topics in 430, Courtney & Derek in 420 next semester, Spanish 150 Conversation Labs due – Oops!, Register tomorrow

Slept in an hour and I did not even mean to. Had potatoes with cheese. Did the overalls cute thing. Missed 261. Went to Leavey, read The Winter's Tale, but I didn't get my response done in time. Got our papers back in 262. Noticed Courtney got an A, so did I. Yeah! Courtney and Derek both said they'd be in 420 next semester. Courtney said she might change her 263 (so did Dana) to take mine. Spanish Conversation Labs were due today, but he extended it to Tuesday. Wonder if I'll even bother to do it. Went to the grocery before coming home. Bought two Four Cheese pizzas, extra cheese and the Circus Animal cookies I have been craving. Had more potatoes and one of my pizzas. It was good. Vetoed watching TV, but didn't have the energy to exercise. Mom said I got an afternoon/evening phone call – young female. It's a mystery. Told Mom I had a good day at school. Did she ask any questions? NO! She started going off about her reunion this weekend. Whatever. Worked on my school schedule again. Thought about dropping Romantic Age for Modern Novel but I want to be able to tutor in the afternoon. Thought about 472, but that conflicts with my Ethics class. I hate this process – the indecision!

April 19, Friday
222 ¾
Cleaned out middle desk drawer, watched Oscars
Pizza with cheese, pretzel, 7 circus animal cookies, Pepsi, noodles, avocado

Didn't eat much Wednesday, but went up two pounds. Ate quite a bit yesterday and dropped the two pounds. Exercised Wednesday, but not Thursday. Cleaned out my desk drawer and blue file folder holder thingy. Finished watching the part of the Oscar's that I missed. Larissa was really annoying me. Finally got off the dime and went to LBCC. Paid my graduation fees and also filled out the application and received my telephone appointment for registration. Went to Lakewood Mall - Robinson's-May for Clinique stuff, then to Express for tights. No tall – only medium. Bought them anyway. Went to Bath & Body Works and bought shampoo. Fine looking man behind the counter. Bought a pretzel on my way out. I want to quit my job, but I want money. Alice hasn't paid me for the Ross delivery. Came home and ate my other pizza. Also enjoyed my avocado. Larissa had to go to work so I had the house to myself for a while. Thought I might sit down to the piano for a while, but it never happened. I did enjoy listening to music though. Rachel called. I let the machine get it and then called her back later. She doesn't need to know everything. Going to the Viper Room tomorrow. She's a club girl now and can get the code.

April 20, Saturday
224 ¾
El Rey Taco small nachos, green quesadilla, Pepsi, Guadalajara Inn with Larissa – cheese enchiladas, Tommy's
Checked out recipes, Roxbury with Rachel, Jacob and Susan, home at 4:30 a.m.

     Thought Rachel would have me off the schedule considering tonight's plan, but no I work at 9 a.m. tomorrow. Big promo changes. That sent me to El Rey Taco. Decided to console myself with nachos. Larissa had to work all day. I didn't accomplish anything at all. When Larissa got home I vented my frustrations to her. She suggested standing Rachel up. I don't have go out dress up clothes. The purple silk blouse I wore I got from Rachel and ended up being uncomfortable. Daniel's not coming to Jewel's birthday party. The Viper Room wasn't doing a code thing tonight because Vic Lightning & Stray Cats guy were going to be there. Susan was late. Jacob also joined us. We went to the Roxbury instead. $12 cover and $6 drinks. I can't afford this kind of thing very often, not if I'm traveling this summer. And neither can they really. Melissa and her friend Sandra met us there but they bailed early. It was 70's night, which was no great thrill for me. Noticed a guy sitting in the corner table. After my brief stint on the dance floor he was gone. Kind of weird. Rachel claims she drank too much. We went to Tommy's after. Yet another experience in getting directions from a drunk, but at least he was right. Freddy paged Jacob around 2:30 a.m. He gave Rachel a really nasty rash. Great to know. Think Jacob was dozing off during the ride home. Bed at 4:30 a.m.

April 21, Sunday
226 ½
Work 9-3:30

Pepsi, Cheez Its, Sbarro's cheese pizza slice, potatoes with butter
Nap, made caramels that turned out runny

      Hating life and my alarm clock. Last night was supposed to be some great night but was very anti-climatic for me. Just reminded me of things I want to change. Thought I would skip eating today, but one slice of cheese pizza was a good excuse to leave the store and take a break. Then I chowed on Melissa's Cheez-its. Managed to make it through the day. Melissa is dreadfully annoying. Kept wanting to talk through the work. Went to the grocery and got the fixings for caramels so I could make them for my class party celebrating Shakespeare's birthday. Took a nap. Right when I was about to drift off Larissa called just to say she didn't want to go anywhere for dinner. I hung up. Woke up around 8 p.m. when she arrived home. Think Mom and Dad were annoyed with the messy kitchen and my sleeping. I did my caramels while Larissa fixed potatoes. She of course left me when her stupid little space show came on. Think I stopped cooking the caramel just a little too soon. Thought it was kind of runny. Mom didn't think so. Went to bed around 11:30 p.m. and I could hear her starting to clean dishes. She was up for quite a while.

April 22, Monday
226 ½
The Tempest, watched Brett Butler on Oprah, cut caramels
El Rey Taco green quesadilla, bean/cheese burrito, chips/salsa, Pepsi, Root Beer

      When to start, when to start? Why do I keep putting it off? This is what I want. No matter the ridicule, no matter the tease, no matter the isolation, alienation and destitution of thoughts. I am alone. I am different. Should continue to use that. Why let them open me up when that isn't something I want for myself. Watched Brett Butler on Oprah. She's quite a woman. She echoes some of my sentiments, but hers were in relation to alcohol. Started reading The Tempest. Two and a half hours to cut and wrap caramels, but at least they were easy to cut this time. Didn't even need the boiling pot of water. Asked Mom about dinner. Offered to go to El Rey Taco. She was cool with it as long as we went cheap. Hell, for free-to-me, I can handle that. So I also had some chips and salsa. Didn't finish the reading for Shakespeare but was mentally drained anyway so tried to go to bed at a reasonable hour. I hate it when I don't really do anything all day and yet I'm all tired. Hell, I didn't even exercise today and I had told myself to. I haven't been exercising much lately, which is starting to bother me.

April 23, Tuesday
225 ½
Frosted Flakes, caramels, 1 cookie, Dr. Pepper, 2 plates of cheese and chips, celery, cheese on cheese crackers
430 only drained

    Figuring I would eat during 430 at our little party I started my day with Frosted Flakes. Think Mom was annoyed by how late I was leaving. Went to Leavey Library. Did Tempest reading. Didn't feel like concentrating much though. Wrote my response for the Tempest then finished the one for Winter's Tale. Might have been able to go to 262, but just didn't feel like it. Might be called on and I didn't do anything to prepare for class. Shakespeare was less festive than I thought it would be. Had two interesting Sean moments though. Well, actually three I guess. Might have a meeting next Tuesday to make up for the one we missed. Sandra chopped her hair and looks like she gained a few. Missed the evaluation for Wagner – damn! Courtney tried to register for my 263. We'll see. Spent three and a half hours in Doheny Library researching Shakespeare. Think I'll write about Antony and Cleopatra. Viet was in the section when I got there. I had no intention of actually staying there that long, but I wasn't wearing a watch. Had two plates of nachos when I got home. Plus lots of celery. Man was I hungry. Why? I don't know.

April 24, Wednesday
227 ¼
Fast
Worked on 261 paper, stayed in room most of the day, done with paper around 12:30 a.m.

    Woke up really early today, but did (again!) the lazy thing and lolled around in bed for hours. And I have a paper due tomorrow. I should be stressed about it. I need a really good grade on it. This is the class that I hate. That's probably why I've given up. But that's so wimpy. I just feel like I'm beating my head against a wall. Like I could spend days on this paper, but Alexander's already decided how I'm going to do. Like Swift could write my paper for me and Alexander would give it a C- saying it wasn't in Swift's style. STP canceled their free shows in LA, NY and Chicago because lead singer, Brandon, is back on drugs and under medical care. Guys sounded shaken, but had the integrity to make the announcement themselves. Amongst the angst youth rockers April is quite a month. They all seem to be in love with dying. You never know just how you look through other people's eyes. Hum. Pepper. Spent almost the whole day in my room working on this stupid paper. And for what? This guy wants me to use little words. Stoop to the lowest level of readers. Fuck him. I threw in as many lengthy words as I could. Even cracked the thesaurus to fuck with him. I can sacrifice a grade, but never my artistic or personal integrity.

April 25, Thursday
224 ¼
261 Paper due - Yes! Last Day!, still passed on 150, 430 meeting Tuesday
Chips/salsa, quesadilla, bean burrito from Taco Bell, brownies (my doing)

Didn't eat yesterday. Surprised I only dropped three pounds. Anyway, this is my last school day. Yeah! Had to suffer through 261 since our papers were due today. 262 also dragged. We talked about Yeats which was okay, but we all just wanted to get the hell out of there. 430 was kind of funny. It was obvious not everyone (self included) had finished the reading. Thought briefly about going to Spanish. I mean it is the last class meeting and all, but no. Gave it the old veto. Had some chips and salsa when I got home. That was as close to Spanish as I wanted to get. Larissa called from work asking about dinner. She offered to go through Taco Bell. Watched Friends while Dad played with his new toy – the Power Book. I went to Sav-ons for soda and brownie mix. Larissa and I arrived home at the same time. I downed that Taco Bell. Fixed the brownies in time to enjoy a couple during ER. I was satisfying a major craving. The plan to fast after Sir Willie's birthday was kind of blown out of the water, but oh well. Still did the veggie routine with Taco Bell. Yeah!

April 26, Friday
223 ½
Slice of toast, 2 slices of cheese, chips/salsa, Lipton noodles, 1 lard ass cupcake
Watched Patriot Games, start Utopia, Antony and Cleopatra paper

    Surprised that brownies at 10:30 p.m. didn't have an effect. I actually went down a pound. I guess my day was strenuous enough the calories were put to use. Started reading Utopia. I hate professors that require reading the intro. Introductions are rarely useful. They usually say nothing, except how pompous the non-writer translator is. Also started working on my Shakespeare paper. Had checked out books on Tuesday so I was going through those. Decided to do Antony and Cleopatra – gender relations and the structure of love. A little ironic considering everything going on in my life. Mom bought lard ass cupcakes and yes, of course I couldn't turn them down. That would just be wrong. Watched Patriot Games with the family. It was good. Had only seen the end before. Mom commented, "Why the family scene at the beginning for this action thriller?" I had the answer. Sometimes it's nice to know. Dad had to share about the technology stuff. I tuned out. "Oh, we've had such things around for so long, but nobody believes it until it's written and translated to film" or whatever – blah, blah, blah! He obviously admires Clancey or Wolfe or whomever wrote it. Hippy yeah.

April 27, Saturday
225
Frosted Flakes, chips/salsa, Shepard's Pie, pecan pie 1/6
Picked recipes, framed Jewel's present
30 minutes treadmill, 43 calories, .7 mile

    Got up and had my Frosted Flakes. I must like to cook when I get stressed out. I did it in October and again now. Two crucial papers I wanted to avoid. The first and the last of the year. Pressure. Anyway, I picked out recipes for today and tomorrow. Dad even gave money to Mom to give me to go to the store. If I was cooking he was willing to pay which sounded even better to me. I even exercised to avoid doing my reading or working on my paper. It felt good though. And it had been quite a while since I exercised. I noticed that lately I've really been slacking off in that department. Made a vegetarian shepherd's pie. It was really good. Could have used a little more time in the oven. Also made a pecan pie. It was a little runny. Too many nuts I think. It was all good though. Framed the bunny picture I cross-stitched for Jewel. Mom recommended splitting a baggie to cover the front. I know she's done that in the past to help protect the work, but I think it looks cheap so I passed. Besides I hope they don't notice the tiny stain that's already on it and that way by the time they do they might not think it was there when originally given.

April 28, Sunday
226 ½
Jewel's party at 1:30 in Parnell Park
Avocado (2), slice of pecan pie (2), chips/salsa, macaroni salad, Cheez Its, strawberries, fettuccini soufflé, strawberry shortcake

Planned to work on my paper before going to the park for Jewel's birthday party, but I didn't. Tamarra was there. What a stupid girl. Oh, but she isn't Jacob's girlfriend, they're just really good friends that happen to hang all over each other. Okay. Sophia and Monica came for a while. Monica maybe going to a new dance school. Her old one fired her when they heard she was thinking about applying to the new school. Her wrongful termination prompted her and Michelle to quit. Something the teacher didn't expect, but deserved. Donna, Larry and Erika came after all. Never really talked to Larry before. I like him. Daniel said he wasn't going to show. Left Loose Ho on Rachel's pager and then had the nerve to show. Left, came back. Left again, came back again – calling Rachel over and in spite everyone telling her not to go she did. It's the co-dependency sick thing. She loves the attention. Later she had an upset stomach. She allows him too much influence over her. She really shouldn't care. Friday she saw him watching her from across the street. I could barely muster up any sympathy for her – sorry to say. Made Fettuccini Soufflé and strawberry shortcake when I got home. Larissa didn't finish her dinner, but had desert – PISSED ME OFF!

April 29, Monday
227 ¾
Fast
Classes end, Shakespeare paper – worked on paper all day, typing until 3, still no final draft

    Thank god Ferguson gave us an extra day to do our papers because I spent all day working on it and still didn't produce a final draft. I spent so much time in the kitchen that should have gone to reading for my finals or working on this paper. But I didn't want to deal with the stress. Besides, there's something methodical about cooking and a great sense of achievement when you're done. I really felt good about myself for having done it. I was hoping that that good feeling would help produce a great paper. I did a couple of drafts. The first was way too long and I was like – what exactly do I want to say about these two great characters and their awesome love affair. What can I say about love? What do I know? What am I seeing? And yet through it all I was producing a very sensitive reading of an idyllic romance. Just the opposite of what could be expected to come out of all the crap I've been going through. Maybe because in a play it can happen that way. But what about life? Finished typing at 3 a.m. But I know I have to do another draft before turning it in. Ouch. Made it through the day fasting!

April 30, Tuesday
221 ¾
Finish paper, attended class, major heat wave, Utopia
7 p.m. weigh in 219 ½, feeling weak, disoriented
Popcorn, nachos with Larissa, tangerine, mint chip ice cream, toast

    Had to get up at a decent hour just to finish my paper, which I finished about ten minutes after one. Got to class early enough to do a proof reading, but Lisa (I think) showed up and we actually got to talking. Sean was out of his normal work wear and in sweats and a tank top looking mighty fine. Before I left home Mom got a phone call and ordered an emergency board meeting. She also had to call Mrs. Ellis. Came home really tired. It was so damn hot today. Took a nap. When I woke up Mom was gone and Larissa was walking through the door. She had the fixings for nachos and I buckled. She also had ice cream, which I practically begged for. When I woke up around 7 p.m. I was totally disoriented. I felt extremely weak, like I would keel over any minute. Lost 8.25 pounds in 36 hours. Guess that's too fast. Later I even made a bowl of popcorn. Mom had to wind down after her meeting. The girl in the east was kicked out. Two others resigned. All because of a note and gossip and outside activities that really should have been left alone but someone made a stink. I don't think Mom and I were exactly on the same page with how it all was handled but girls ultimately gotta make decisions for themselves. Dad had the nerve to ask me if I was sure about Mom being at a meeting. I wanted to scream. Started to read Utopia before going to bed.

MAY

May 1, Wednesday
220 ½
Finished Utopia, review Sir Gawain, 1 ½ hour of sleep
Peanut butter sandwich, tangelo, 2 slices of cheese, buttered popcorn

      Shocked that I actually went down after all of the junk I ended up eating yesterday, especially since I was eating so late in the day. Finished reading Utopia. It was a little drier than I thought it would be. Like a report that's worded in politically correct terms. All in all it was pretty good though. It's probably a better reference book than a piece of great literature. I think Brianna said that at the beginning of the semester now that I think about it. Ended up eating today. I was kind of hoping I wouldn't. At least I was eating healthy stuff. Reviewed Sir Gawain. Actually I pretty much was going through the notes. Although I started by doing it side by side. But then I realized how late it was so I thought I should pick up the pace. I tried to go to sleep at a decent hour, but I couldn't sleep so I got up again to continue reading. That lasted a little while, but my body was giving up. Unfortunately, my mind wasn't. I kept watching the clock. I think I only got an hour and a half of sleep before having to get ready for school.

May 2, Thursday
220 ¾
English 261 Final 8-10 a.m., Spanish 150 Final 4:30-6:30 p.m., 261 went very well, talk to Nicole, clean out overhead

El Rey Taco nachos, green quesadilla, slice of cheese, pasta, pecan pie slice

Yuck! First final at 8 a.m. That wouldn't be so bad except I've never had to go to school so damn early. Plus I didn't have any sleep. But actually that was probably okay – I was so wired. The final went very well. I think I can relax about my grade. Got my paper back. He graded me better than I expected given how the semester has gone, but I still hate him. I know it deserved an even better grade, but he hates that I won't play his game. At least I stuck to my academic principles. Came home. Thought I would take a nap, but I couldn't. Started to review vocabulary for Spanish. Just when I was getting drowsy it was time to go to El Rey Taco. Mom paid. I ate. All hyped up I went to school. Talked to Nicole for a while – as well as others. She'll be working through the summer. I should stop by and visit her. She's a nice girl and I think she's a good person. Well, the final went way better than I anticipated. Wow! It felt too easy. Got the fixings for another pecan pie. Had pasta for dinner and pie during ER. I think this time it had too much time. It was still good though. Also watched Friends. Everyone else was going to bed and I was still wired. I cleaned out the overhead of my closet. Didn't even touch the sheets until after 1:30 a.m. Wow! What energy.

May 3, Friday
223 ¾
Slept until 10:30, Rachel received bullshit write-up, registered for Summer School, laundry, notes
Donuts (3 total), avocado with salt, pecan pie (2 slices), cheese noodle dish

Well, I knew I was eating far too well for it not to show up on the scale, but it finally did. Ouch! Three pounds. I majorly slept in. Larissa coming home with doughnuts was the only thing that got me out of bed. Usually they don't sound too appealing, but man was I primed and ready for a big old lard ass raised glazed. And did I ever have it. Called Rachel just to be sure that she kept me off of the schedule. She did. She also had other bad news. She got the restraining orders against Daniel, but he still calls. (Oh, before Jewel's birthday party Rachel had a meeting that marshals had to escort her out of because of the way he was acting.) Jessica visited Tuesday.

Rachel had to cut her vacation short, put in all kinds of crazy hours. Melissa's calling in sick a lot and Allison – this morning – dropped out of UPN for sales. Rachel is certain that she's out of a job. I never heard of anyone getting fired over sales. Considering the state of the mall it's not even something we can even really control. Allison's a bitch. Rachel doesn't suck up so Allison's getting rid of her. Registered for summer school, did laundry and copied notes.

May 4, Saturday
225 ¾
Heart of Darkness, Betelgeuse, Couldn't sleep
Pecan pie slice, potato wedges, mixed cheese sandwich, cookie, strawberries, Foster's sundae

    Picked up reading Heart of Darkness where I felt off. It took me forever to get into it. My mind kept wandering. Mom and Dad went to a meeting together. They were having an initiation. Mom was running the practice because Brittany's in Hawaii. Larissa had to go to her store to do some shopping. I asked if she would bring home some deli then and she did. Dad made some comment about us wasting our money and it would be easier if I would pick up my insurance. I have no time or money so let's throw some guilt. He's just jealous because Larissa didn't buy him dinner but does he forget that rule he and Mom implemented about us buying our own food. So, if we're wasting our money on dinner does that mean he actually wants us to not eat? At all. I don't think so. That pissed me off. He was annoyed about my book bill too. Mom apologized to me about Dad and the power book (which he won't let me use, even for school) and tried to explain why he's being protective (meaning covetous) of it and how it's battery operated – whatever. Then she was mad at me because I wasn't even surprised that he hasn't let anyone play with his new toy. Watched Betelgeuse and fixed my strawberries. Funny time check. Mom asked, Larissa answered. Dad asked "Are you sure?" I lost it. I totally went off. Mom and Larissa were laughing. I was funny. But Dad, "Are you having a problem little girl?" Always has to find a way to be demeaning. I wanted to shove my shoe up his ass after that one. And he thinks he's not a jerk. Had a Foster's sundae and finished my strawberries.

May 5, Sunday
228 ¾
Finish strawberries, slice of toast, Italian cheese pasta, corn, bean/cheese burrito, green quesadilla, 3 brownies
Called Rachel, copy notes, gas, Heart – Part II and III

    I can't believe what a freakin' yo-yo I am. Up eight pounds in three days. It's what I get for eating like a fucking pig though. Had some Italian cheese pasta by Lipton. It was really good. Getting frustrated with my notes. I decided to call Rachel. Angela was in the store at the time. She was also written up for sales. Larissa brought home El Rey Taco. Rachel got a cell phone between Friday and Sunday. I really don't think she needs it. She says she's worried about Daniel. She probably wouldn't be able to get to it in time to call even if he did attack. Finished reading Heart of Darkness. It felt like such a major let down. I kept thinking something was going to happen. I made my dark chocolate fudge brownies. Gave one to Mom. They were really good. Had a very hard time falling asleep. Although I don't have anything tomorrow I'm still stressing with major anxiety over what's to come. Went out to the kitchen after Larissa's light was out. I noticed a brownie was gone. I had offered to Mom. Thought she said maybe later – tomorrow. Checked Larissa's food diary. If she ate it she didn't log it... yet. My money is on her though because Mom isn't the one known for sneaking food.

May 6, Monday
227 ¾
3 brownies and milk, chicken/broccoli rice dish, corn on the cob, Frosted Flakes, chips/salsa
Portrait of the Artist, copy notes, notes in Anthology

    Finished off the brownies. Think I ate practically the whole pan myself. And why not? I bought and baked them and damn they were good. Still going through a major food fest. Made a Lipton rice dish and finished it. Also had corn on the cob and Frosted Flakes, then chips and salsa. Will I ever stop? Had three movements today. That's probably a good thing. I've lost my regularity. Copying notes is a drag. Put my notes in my anthology for my 262 final. Not looking forward to it. Dr. Wagner asks such bizarre questions there is no way to study for it. Read notes on Portrait of the Artist through the fourth chapter before giving up. Put some of the notes into my book and started praying for a question about Stephen's relationships with women. Rachel got off the phone with me yesterday saying she would call me later. She never did. Sunday is her big night at Bobby McGee's. Guess she forgot about me today. I don't like one-sided things. I don't want to try so hard when time shared ends up just frustrating me anyway. Oh how I need distance.

May 7, Tuesday
230 ¼
English 262 Final 11-1 p.m., copy notes until 2
Frosted Flakes, personal pizza with extra cheese, cheese in salsa/chips, potatoes with cheese, 1 lb. strawberries with sugar, Pepsi

Final three is on its way. Had to go to the bookstore to purchase blue books first. Saw Courtney outside and we talked. He asked about the moral crisis in Heart of Darkness and my first thought was – where the hell was I? Scary, right, but I took a second, processed it and was clear to proceed. Until I read the Portrait question. Decided to roll with it instead. Used notes. Skipped My Last Duchess. We discussed it in class and I didn't want the midterm experience for my final. Courtney said something as I was leaving, but I wasn't sure as to what. Went to Lucky's before coming home. They're having a special sale on soda. Saw Ruth LeFranz in produce. She didn't recognize me at first. She looked at me real funny. Got shredded cheese and a frozen pizza. I really felt like treating myself. I also bought a pound of strawberries, which I proceeded to eat all of while I was up until 2 a.m. copying notes for my Shakespeare class. She said all of the passages would be ones we discussed in class. Felt really good about my 262 final. It was such a relief to get through. He didn't offer as many questions to choose from as he implied there might be. Hermina walked in an hour and a half late.

May 8, Wednesday
231 ½
Copy notes
2 cinnamon rolls, mashed potatoes with extra butter, Pepsi

Thought that with everything I ate yesterday that I could easily get through the day without eating. Such was not the case. Mom made a stop at Sam's Club, which turns out to be a diet pratfall. Not only does she usually buy something tasty, she has to buy it in bulk so it's just sitting there waiting for you to nab it. This time it was cinnamon rolls with major glaze action. After having one I figured I might as well eat something real so I had some of the mashed potatoes. Unfortunately I had to add a little extra butter. Then I figured I might as well drink the Pepsi I had to buy since Lucky's was out of Diet. The rolls were so tempting I ended up having a second. All of this in between my going over Shakespeare notes. There was just no way I would be able to reread all of those plays – so why try at this point. I started to worry that I would confuse The Aeneid and Troilus and Cressida though. In any case I spent the entire day reading and reviewing. Had some cramps and started my period. It's about time too. All in all it was a draining day.

May 9, Thursday
229
English 430 Final 2-4 p.m.
3 eggs, 2 slices cheese?, 2 slices toast ← Tuesday
Mashed potatoes, mini Mexican frittas (3), Nilla Wafers, Pepsi

Slept in and had breakfast before heading off to school. It was really eerie. Very calm. Plus there were a ton of white chairs planted everywhere across campus in prep for graduation. I felt it upon me. I was over a half hour early for the final, but I just wanted to get it over with. The flowers around VKC smell like Mrs. Manning. I felt very young and very old. The final went beyond well. Talking beforehand made me feel like we were all in the same boat. She asked us if we wanted clues while we were taking the test. Plus four people are doing it take home because of a time misunderstanding. I don't think it's worth much. That is to say, I think our grades are for the most part decided via all the work we've already done and this test was something of a formality that she didn't want us to freak out or stress about. It was reassuring. Came home and was suddenly anxious and very hungry. Went to the grocery with Mom's money. Got ingredients for Mini Mexican Frittas and some Nilla Wafers. I just needed something sweet and cakey but not too sweet. Making a new recipe made me feel good too. Watched the NBC line up. After my 430 final I picked up my 262 final. I got a B, which is fine but I thought that I did better and I don't like it when expectations and reality don't meet. Got an A on my Antony and Cleopatra paper. She said it was a great paper. We suffered through graduation rehearsals during the end of our final. Odd endings.

May 10, Friday
228 ½
2 mini Mexican frittas, cottage cheese, Nilla Wafers, grilled cheese, ½ honeydew
Called Alice, Rachel called, Scrapbooks, Financial Aid
30 minutes treadmill, 44 calories, .7 miles

      Yesterday Larissa asked to have some of my frittas. I said yes – then without asking she took extra shredded cheese to top hers with. I wanted to hurt her. I finished the critters today and didn't have to add any cheese – that bitch! That fat bitch! Making off with my shredded cheese. Finished off the Nilla Wafers too. They went fast. Fixed a grilled cheese and had the other half of our honeydew. It wasn't entirely ripe. Rachel's phone call is what got me up. Wanted to know if I could work Sunday. I said sure that I was done with finals. She thought Mother's Day would be a problem. I laughed. Called Alice about doing crystallized rose petals. Sophia was picking up a cake at the time. Took care of the financial aid stuff so hopefully I'll get a better deal this year. Worked on my scrapbooks. Just starting to sort and dump which is very time consuming. Man was I dumping a lot of stuff. Finally got off my butt again to exercise. I've gotten out of the routine. It really felt good though. Rachel only scheduled me for Sunday. That's kind of annoying since I told her I was done with finals and available. Oh well.

May 11, Saturday
228 ½
Donuts and milk, spinach lasagna, cherry cheesecake
Up early, cooked all day, sort scrapbook stuff

      I was a very good daughter today. I got up real early (for me on a Saturday.) Mom was asleep on the couch. I showered, hit the ATM and hit the grocery. I bought a ton of shit for this weekend's meals. Spent over $50. Now I'm feeling really annoyed that Mom asked me to cook and even more annoyed that I decided to do two days, but hey, that's on me. I started with the cheesecake, then did the Spinach Lasagna. Mom and Dad only ate a little of the lasagna before they went to some club party at someone's home. Larissa went to the mall to do some shopping and stopped at See's to get some chocolate for Mom. Dad thought she went to work so she jumped on all of us, "Why do you all think I was going to work? That wasn't the case at all." I came out to sit down and Dad went to the kitchen to do some cleaning. Mom said he went out to be with me, but I was in the family room when he left. While they were gone I did some sorting of my scrapbook stuff. Larissa was annoying me – big time. She wouldn't touch the kitchen, but she kept talking about our trip. So I dropped that we might not go – or go in August. She got all huffy. She got even huffier when I said no to church on Mother's Day.

May 12, Sunday
230 ½
Work 10:30-6:30
4 donuts, lasagna, Sbarro's pizza, bread, pasta salad, garlic bread, olives, apple pie
Rachel called

When I got up to take my shower I heard Mom and Larissa leave for church. When I went to weigh in I noticed my donuts were practically gone. I checked Larissa's food log. She ate them last night not even for breakfast this morning with Mom. I was disgusted and angry. I knew I should have taken them to my room, but that too is just sick. Then I was upset about being upset. But hey, that was my lunch that I paid for AND she didn't ask NOR did she tell me about it and she totally had the opportunity to. I went to work pissed and hungry and then had to work with Melissa and Courtney. Left a message for Rachel and Alice. When I got home the fat cows were playing poker. I went to the kitchen to start dicing. Dad spooked me on the bread so it ended up not getting enough time. I took a stab at Larissa about eating my lunch. She didn't get it. Mom cleaned the kitchen this morning. Larissa even said, "Why should I clean the kitchen, I'm not the one that messed it up?" However true, she certainly did eat. The food she didn't prepare OR pay for. That really pissed me off. Then she acted all high and mighty. I wanted to slap her. If I were ten I would have. She picked the cheese out of my pasta dish too. Rachel called from her cell phone and I made my first apple pie.

May 13, Monday
233
Work 1-5 (Rachel called in sick)
Leftover mania – apple pie, pasta, cheese, lasagna, cheesecake, olives, garlic bread
35 minutes treadmill, 45 calories, .7 mile

Rachel called in sick so I got a phone call from Courtney around 10 a.m. Yes it was getting my fat ass out of bed. I said I could be there at one. When I got there the new sale wasn't even set up. Susan hadn't changed the banner and the back counter was covered with signs. When I asked – where to start she directed me to pick up the four-ways Courtney hadn't finished. Courtney wasn't even setting the sale. Hello!? I asked if she wanted me to finish promos first. She was flustered, needed a breather. I got to work. I didn't expect this from Susan. When I got home I went to town on the leftovers. We pretty much had a little of everything left. The bread when properly heated was very good. I finished off the cheesecake that (in this house) was starting to look like it had been abandoned. I had anticipated that this might be a start day, but hell I made all this shit, I should enjoy it to the fullest extent right? Plus I decided that if I exercise, which I did, I shouldn't be too hard on myself for enjoying a little nourishment. Of course, the donuts also reveal that I still to a degree, covet. But seriously, Larissa really should have asked.

May 14, Tuesday
233 ¼
Fast
Started Lord of the Flies, sort through scrapbook stuff, cleaned toilet, dumped trash
30 minutes, treadmill, .7 miles, 40 calories

What to do? What to do? So many things I want to accomplish that sometimes it's real hard to figure out where I should start. And that can be tragically frustrating. Decided that with summer some 'summer reading' should come in handy. On The Road did something for me last year. Anyway, I picked out Lord of the Flies. I got through the first chapter, but I think it might be a little too intense for me right now. Although I did have this odd dream. A senate lock-in. Only a few females. What would happen to politicians if they were left to their own defenses amongst each other – to live. Might they start seeing eye to eye? I imagined one of the females would become a slut and the ruler. Is that a variation of the mother whore archetypes? She'd have their attention anyway. That's why I picked Flies. Then I decided to turn to Erma Bombeck. I need something with a little more wit and heart right now, but I'm definitely going back to Flies. Did more sorting through my scrapbook stuff. I can't believe all of these pictures and tickets and flyers and random stuff I saved. I had so many bags it's amazing. I got my butt back on the treadmill again. I earned a star in every color. How long has it been since that happened?

May 15, Wednesday
227 ¼
Work 9:30-1:30, talked to Amanda until 2:15
Alice visit until 6
Lunch with Alice, Jewel, Jacob – grill cheese, key lime pie, lemon cake, 4 frittas, Pepsi

     Picked up Courtney's hours for today since she is covering for Sophia. Opened with Melissa. Her boyfriend Alfo dropped her off. I think she tried to scam the store out of $10, but didn't realize that I saw her double check the change at the bank. I turned my back and two five's suddenly appeared in the bag. Susan was late by like an hour and a half. Talked to Amanda for forty-five minutes after my shift. She always makes me feel good about myself. She thinks I should teach in Europe. She feels blessed for having known me, that I'm a rare person to meet. Decided to visit Alice. While I was there Rachel and Jacob showed up. We did Polly's Pies. Didn't really want to eat, but didn't have an excuse nor did I want to make one up. It was a very nice lunch. Rachel started to freak out about her watch being missing. She needs a root canal. I stayed to talk to Mom when Rachel and Jacob left. Alice is bothered by Rachel's activity and lack of responsibility toward Jewel. Can't blame her. She's been put in a bad position. Rachel's been incredibly inconsiderate. She thanked me. She's grateful Rachel had the opportunity to get to know someone like me. She's saying things Alice never thought she would. It was odd. Like Alice felt the growing distance.

May 16, Thursday
227 ¼
Fast
Worked on scrapbooks, gloomy day
30 minutes treadmill, 4 calories, .7 miles

  Spent most of the day getting some major work done on my scrapbooks. Sorry I finished off the key lime pie and lemon cake because I had a real sweet tooth all day. Instead I was a very good girl. I drank my water and exercised my butt, although it was slow going I did it. And I didn't eat all day. Actually it was a very gloomy day. Yesterday was the day I had envisioned a reunion. Odd I ended up doing lunch. I looked good too. I really could have gone to the library. That would have saved me from eating and making the frittas that I had to clean up after. I imagined that the gloominess of the day was fashioned after the lost bloom in my heart. It's just that I'm not ready to start anything in the state I'm in. I know I'm not finished yet. I don't really know if I ever will be, but I haven't accomplished enough despite what Amanda thinks. I just don't like the comments I have to endure. I think it was most satisfying when no one knew my suffering, when no one recognized my change. Now they're all on Patrol and I have to ignore them all. Watched Friends and ER – season finales.

May 17, Friday
223 ¾
4 Mexican Frittas, graham crackers in milk, apple pie
Sunny day, Pepsi
Bombeck's Family, desk/papers
30 minutes treadmill, 44 calories, .7 miles

  Had a pretty big case of the lazies. At least today was a bright and shiny day, so much better than yesterday. I tried to avoid the kitchen and food all day, but it was pointless. I really didn't want someone else to eat my frittas because I'm still a fat covetous cow and annoyed about having to do the cleaning. Then I decided to have some graham crackers in milk. Later I thought about all of my apples so decided to try another pie. This one was even runnier. Mom said something about the apples. Then she said something when I was rolling crust, but she got the idea I was annoyed so left me alone. It's not like she had to have any. Used too much cinnamon. She ended up having a slice. Did some reading from Erma Bombeck's Family Ties. It's funny. I should do that – just my way. And I do believe I will. Cleared the papers off of my desk finally. They were really bugging me. And I even managed to exercise again. I was able to pick up a little speed too, which is nice. Watched Guarding Tess and Cutthroat Island.

May 18, Saturday
224
Work 11-4
Pepsi, 4 Mexican Frittas, apple pie III
30 minutes treadmill, 43 calories, .7 miles

Agreed Wednesday to coming in to work today. We got extra hours for a one day sale. I think I worked more this week than I did in the last two months. I bought my graduation dress. Amanda recommends that I take up the hem. I agree. Susan had bad cramps. I helped her with her IA p-pack. It was extensive. Yajirda is a hell of a sales hog. She eats everything! Snapped at Rachel. She was kind of annoying me. She has to one up people. She also asks for a lot of praise, which as a concept bothers me. She needed new jeans to party and "kick it" in. She asked if I had any plans. I hate how she asks at the last minute. I don't really like to operate that way. I told her about how I'm getting a computer lesson. She seemed minutely disappointed that I wouldn't be able to join her and her brother for a night of drinking, dancing and acting stupid. Instead I went home. Hit the treadmill feeling very proud of myself. I also put together my gift to Angela. Found a flowery two side frame thing that looked very much like something she'd own. Went through scanning and dumping more magazines until the eyes just didn't want to stay open any more.

May 19, Sunday
225 ¼

Work 10:30-6
Angela's "Surprise" B-day party

    Exercised and the scale still jumped forward. Really didn't feel like getting up to go to work. I was a bit late. Susan, for once, beat me to the store. She skipped going out last night. Rachel called to thank her for inviting Courtney, who actually did more to invite herself. Now I'm really glad I didn't go. Linda (the new girl) also went AND got drunk. I can't see that as being a good thing. Did transfers until I ran out of sheets. Talked to Amanda about Rachel. She tried to say she hasn't lost respect but does expect better from Rachel. Doesn't like this going out thing, general sluttiness and leaving Alice to parent (vs. grandparent) Jewel. I couldn't agree more. We met at Acapulco. She invited me to Bobby McGee's afterward. She left early to pick Emily up, so I took the opportunity to ditch her. Andrew didn't pick Angela up so we had to call her. So much for the surprise. Andrew showed up late. Ava will be teaching first grade next year at Don Julian in Puente Hills. Met Sue and Kris. They seem like a fun pair. Probably a bit more loose than I like, but fun. My being quiet was commented on a few times. Yeah, that opened me up.

May 20, Monday
227 ½
Fast
Finished two scrapbooks, updated diary, read Erma
30 minutes treadmill, 44 calories, .7 mile; Weights

    Feeling major relief that I didn't have to go into work today. I really don't enjoy going to work and even being there with Rachel doesn't brighten it up. She's been on such a party binge and I hate being asked, "What are you doing tonight?" Made it through the day without eating which was actually pretty impressive. Worked a lot in the family room on scrapbooks. Surprised Mom never got to me. In the scrapbooks department this was a very big day. I finished two. Neither are much to get excited about because I really didn't do that much during the time period they cover, but hey, they're done. In fact the books might be getting some school stuff added later because there was some empty space but I'll decide that for sure later. Read more from Erma Bombeck. She was really funny. She recently died. I imagine she's a little older than Mom but I think they're roughly the same age. Same generation anyway. Got my butt going on the treadmill and even did some weights afterward. This was a highly motivated day. I wish I could report that I had more of them.

May 21, Tuesday
224 ¾, hip measurement 44 ¾
Fast
Work 9:30-1:30
Pick up cap and gown, Macy's Clinique, Rockwell ATM, nap
30 minutes treadmill, 45 calories, .7 mile

    Another motivated day. I had to work in the morning, which was no great thrill. I hate having to drive Melissa to the bank. I don't understand how she can let some parolee she's known for maybe a couple of weeks just take her car. He may never come back. I don't like being totally dependent. Had the lowest hip measurement I think I've ever had in my adult life at 44 ¾. Of course, I realize I was sucking it in, but I need that kind of motivation right now so I'm running with it. After work I went down to LBCC to pick up my Cap and Gown. The sizes were really strange but I think what I got was okay. I now have my gold tassels though and that is what is important to me. Also went to Macy's because I needed Clinique stuff – then doh! - left the card for a free something at home. Went to Rockwell and visited the ATM. I was all over the place, but I think I was doing it just so that I wouldn't be home staring at the walls wondering what I could eat. I need a new something to get passionate about – that is what I need. Made it through another day though and I even exercised. Had to totally motivate myself to do it, but I did!

May 22, Wednesday
221 ¼
Finish scrapbook, grocery
Deli ¼ cheese with wedges, Strawberry shortcake
30 minutes treadmill, 44 calories, .7 mile

    Okay, so not every day is as good as the last. I still accomplished today and that means a whole heck of a lot – to me anyway. And hey! I'm the most important person in this relationship so there! I finished another scrapbook – for now. I'm sure when, if ever Larissa gets to hers she'll dump stuff that

I can add, but from all of the tons of shit I have it is a done deal. Had deli sandwich with Mom. Went in to pick it up looking like crap and a USC Alumni noticed the shirt. Brief, polite conversation. Had to wait a long time considering I called in the order, but a free small drink smoothed my irritation. Hit the grocery for strawberry shortcake fixings. Those strawberries, man, are pretty freakin' good. And healthy. Even though the food was weighing me down I made it on the treadmill. I should give myself something for every time I do that. Also, eating made me have three movements. I really hate that because your guts get into such an up roar and then your butt's sore. It's miserable, but I felt better after dropping a load. Four days between the last. I needed it.

May 23, Thursday
222 ¾
Strawberry shortcake, more strawberries, small nachos, green quesadilla
30 minutes treadmill, 46 calories, .8 mile

    Wow! That deli sandwich and potato wedges had me go up a pound and a half even though I exercised. Wonder how bad it would have been had I not done the treadmill. Started my day with a shortcake and of course had to add some strawberries on top of that. Ended up doing El Rey Taco which in and of itself is bad, but I did nachos and a quesadilla. I swear I wish they would just go out of business. They make fasting or dieting in any form beyond difficult for me. It's just too hard to turn down anything from them. Plus I had to do a double whammy. Couldn't just stop with the nachos. I felt my stomach stretching, returning to an old but not forgotten shape. I don't really want to be able to carry that much food. It makes me tired and sluggish. I had to really force myself to exercise but I think the fact that I did chow down helped motivate me to push myself while I walked because my numbers were slightly better than usual. It's Lauren Morris' birthday today. I sent a card. Grace's not sure if she moved or what. No word from her, but no returned mail either. I hope to hear from her.

May 24, Friday
223
Work 1-4:10

Graham crackers in milk, pasta salad, garlic bread, dark chocolate brownies II
Recipes book, sort papers

Rachel pretty much woke me up this morning with a phone call to come into work. She's having a really bad morning. Susan doesn't feel well and ten minutes after she told her she could go home sick Melissa's mother called to say that Melissa wouldn't be able to come in today because of her reported migraines. Rachel hates getting these phone calls from other people – and rightfully so. It isn't her mother's responsibility. Anyway, she needs help so I went. She's going to have to work a stretch after an already long week. Did some sorting and dumping of my papers in the blue folder. It was getting obnoxiously thick. After work I stopped off at the grocery store for pasta fixings. Of course, when I saw a mix for dark chocolate brownies it made its way into my cart as well. They are just too good. I think I like them better than fudge brownies. Worked on my recipe book while watching Homicide with the family. It's actually a pretty good show – well written. I just got the pages in the book. Don't know what I'll actually keep. It's not organized at all.

May 25, Saturday
226
Work 4:30-7:30
Breakfast, finish pasta salad, brownies III, small nachos
30 minutes treadmill, 46 calories, .8 mile

Ouch! I went up three pounds. I realize I didn't exercise and I certainly ate, but for the most part I ate healthy shit. Guess I'm going to have to get back on the mill. Continued and finished sorting papers. Went through my tax envelopes from the past couple years. I finished off both the salad and the brownies. I definitely need to exercise. Had to work 4:30-7:30 p.m. Was asked again, "What are you doing tonight?" I said I was going to San Diego for a friend's birthday. I shouldn't have to say. That really annoys me. I guess it's just friendly curiosity but I feel like it's probing intrusion because I know if I said I was going home to veg it would lead to an offer that is then hard to politely wriggle out of. Went home and those fat cows had gone to El Rey Taco and didn't get anything for me. Felt stupid but I got right back in the car and got myself some nachos and ate them in front of them. Still managed to exercise which is a real good thing considering all the stuff I chowed down on. It was Lara's birthday yesterday. Sent a card and wrote something. Really missed seeing her at the reunion. Amanda's birthday is today. She also got a card. Yeah! I'm proud of myself for keeping up!

May 26, Sunday
227 ½
Graham crackers in milk, Taco Bell – 3 chicken and cheese quesadilla, Water, Carrow's, prime rib, fruit salad, fries, g. bread, apple, caramel sundae
Leave at 11:05

    Oh yay! Going to the desert for a visitation. Larissa had a stick up her butt. Mom was concerned about the noise of my car. Thinks I need a wheel alignment. Stopped at Taco Bell before the event. Mom and Larissa didn't want to go in. Wore my choir dress that's only ten years old. It's a lot looser than it was then. I probably shouldn't have worn it. Mom needs to take it in. Compliments from many – Debbie, the Robertson clan, Peggy, etc. Apparently the officers are now responsible for the making of their own conference attire. Debbie's working on her Master's. Unsure of work for next year. She took the CBEST and didn't need to take the GRE. Lucky girl! My new MD has a real sucky predecessor. No dress bag, travel bag or nothing. Jenny asked me to do a sweatshirt/cardigan thing. I said yes, but I hope she didn't want me to give it to her before she travels because she leaves on the 8th, but hello! I leave on the first. Olivia and Mr. Anderson were also present. Pulled out of a parking lot so Mom wouldn't have to eat with Buena Park. We went on to Carrow's. I had prime rib. The earth moved. Also had desert. When Mom's banana cream pie was sent back to the kitchen due to rotting 'naners I felt bad.

May 27, Monday
229 ¼
Work 9:30-6:30
Rice-A-Roni, 2 slices of toast, Circus Animal cookies, pretzel, avocado, strawberries, Pepsi

Slept in for as long as I could which wasn't very long since I had to go to work. Walked down to Target first to get a drink and to look at cookies. Picked up a bag of Circus Animal cookies. No joke. That bag was gone within an hour. Melissa and Yajirda like them too, but I was the real scarfer this time. I just kept popping them into my fat face. Then as if that weren't enough I had a pretzel. The mall was unbelievably dead. We had zip customers. Anyone that was even coming to the mall seemed to make a beeline to the theater. Larissa canceled going shopping with me to Wherehouse in order to do yard work. That really pissed me off. She knows I hate to shop especially alone and she dumped me for the yard. She's not even going to work on her room. Wonder if she's taking my threat about not taking her on vacation seriously. I am. Went to Wherehouse anyway. Had an avocado and strawberries for dinner. Larissa asked if I was mad. Like, duh! Later that evening we actually talked a little bit. She got the car rental in line and was inquiring about insurance coverage. She's been doing and not telling.

May 28, Tuesday
229
Work 9:30-2:3
Toast, Olive Garden – bread sticks, Alfredo sauce on fettuccini, watermelon

Worked this morning with Susan. Rachel called in to say she would be late. When she finally did make it she was ready for lunch and wanted Olive Garden so she wasn't there very long. I got some breadsticks. Ended up taking them home with me because they never really gave me a chance to eat them there. Rachel had a thing hanging down from her hair. She, her Mom, Jewel and Jacob went to the Disneyland Hotel for the weekend to get away. I was surprised Alice went until I heard she paid. She also paid for everyone to get these hair things. It reminded me of the girls my year who got braids at Venice Beach. Carlos was bugging her to see her. Sorry to say it but when she walked in she really looked trampish to me. Her skirt was shorter than I think she even realized. Then she proceeded to bitch and moan about her job. She didn't feel well. Said she shouldn't be there and she was going to leave. I really didn't know if she was going to make me stay or what.

And it seemed to me she just didn't want to be there and all the fun she's having outside of work is making it difficult for her to keep her shit together at work. She used to be focused and serious about her job and lately she just doesn't seem to care. Turns out she did leave early and called Amanda in early. Boiled up leftover fettuccini and added the Alfredo sauce to it for dinner. Mom finished it for me. Had watermelon.

May 29, Wednesday
229
Work 5:30-9:30
Graduation practice, Sam's Club
Avocado, 2 chocolate chip muffins, 2 Celeste pizzas with extra cheese, milk

Had Graduation practice in the morning. It was so freaking dull. Felt very awkward in those little chairs. My butt is still a bit too large. Of course, the fact that I didn't shower before going didn't help my state of comfort. Went with Mom and Larissa to Sam's Club. My graduation gift is a boom box with a CD player. The price for the one I wanted was a little steeper than Mom expected so she recommended checking out Circuit City. That killed me. They are overpriced and out to sell. I hate going to Circuit City. So many temptations at Sam's Club but we were actually pretty good. Got a carrot cake for tomorrow. Rachel scheduled me to work tonight with her. Not so sure if she realized how I wouldn't appreciate working the night before graduation. Then she asked if I wanted to go to the movies with her after work. Guess she got over whatever was ailing her yesterday. Got a sick pleasure from saying no. She informed me that she was seeing Mission Impossible with Alice and Jacob in a feeble attempt to get me to change my mind. But hello! Bed. I need sleep before graduation. Besides I'm going to see it Friday at Paramount Studios. She forgot. Then she turned her attention onto Christina and tried to push the wife and mother of three into abandoning her responsibilities. Nice. Real nice. Christina was having precisely no part of it.

May 30, Thursday
230 ¾
Graduation

Strawberries, El Torito - Enchiladas Rancheros, 2 raspberry margaritas, chips/salsa, carrot cake, cherries

It was really a calm peaceful morning. I ate a pound of strawberries for breakfast. Same speeches as last year's ceremonies. Kind of avoided Dr. Stone. I didn't really want to talk to him at the occasion. Mom went camera happy and they even had me stand next to the Dean's board. Dad pointed. It was so embarrassing. Definitely a step into Geekdom that I didn't want to take. Had El Torito for lunch and snoozed the afternoon away. Larissa's gift is a perm. We were going to go after she went to the DMV. She left late and then stopped at AAA which I'm glad she did because I didn't want to and I'm not sure if I would have. We had carrot cake and cherries. It was too late to get a perm. Thought about doing it Friday before work but Saturday sounded better to me. Didn't want to stink out the people at Larissa's work. She agreed. Mom asked me if I felt smarter today. I said no. They seemed pleased. Said I felt smarter when I aced my genetics test. Like hello! Or when I set the curve in three classes in one semester. Or when Dr. Black wanted to use my report as the example of what to do. Or when USC accepted me.

May 31, Friday
231 ¼
2 slices of carrot cake, then a third, small nachos, Green quesadilla

Really didn't feel like getting up today, especially since a portion of my day would be spent hanging out, keeping myself busy at Larissa's work. She didn't exactly tell me what time she wanted to leave which is just annoying because she expects me to be ready on time. She drives through a lot of little side streets to get to work. Her car is very scary. I felt like it was going to fall apart any second. I started to do some writing but felt strange because I was kind of waiting for someone to ask what I was writing and I didn't want that so I decided to read. I took Lord of the Flies. I didn't get very far before it was making me drowsy. Wearing a snug blouse didn't make me feel very comfortable either. Met the people Larissa works with. Melinda is really stupid. She, Jonathan and Taylor had a belly button piercing/sex conversation that I wanted to interrupt (because they didn't know what they were talking about) but didn't. Larissa doesn't talk to these people. She never seems to have anything to add, but that isn't true. She is so repressed it's annoying. Mission Impossible was pretty good though. Walked down to the trophy booth. Stopped at Sav-on's before coming home.

JUNE

June 1, Saturday
228 ½
Perm at Mary's, pick-up car, Lane Bryant, Sam Goody
ROAD TRIP WITH LARISSA!!!
Skipping town at 7:10 p.m. and 17,000 miles
Green quesadilla before leaving home, Denny's tuna melt, coke and 4 mozzarella sticks
She eats French fries with a fork and then belches. I have eighteen more days of this. Mom gave us a gift. Dad said, "Don't do anything stupid." If not now, when? Grilled chicken or cheese. Josh has to pay the bill. Denny's $10. Bad Girls → Mission Impossible → The Cranberries. Las Vegas for three hours – lost $8.85. Arizona welcome center at 4:30 a.m. and watched the sun rise as Larissa snored.

June 2, Sunday
Burger King – 2 French Toast, hash browns, OJ, Large fries, 4 chicken tenders, chocolate shake
7:00 and we're up and moving. Went to neighboring Burger King. Bought too much. My eyes were burning from lack of sleep and over use and I cried deeply within a laugh. We decided to go up to Salt Lake City but we never saw the lake. Stopped at a viewpoint, there was a cyclist, got two royalty rocks for Rachel. Stopped for a bite at another Burger King. Should have skipped the chicken for Little America. It's a hotel city. Time warp signs. Went quite a ways before stopping again. Naked baa baas. Had a T-bone steak at the Iron Skillet – damn it was good. Need to push more fluids. Laramie.

Stopped at Cheyenne, Wyoming to sleep. Very clean rest stop. Real cold. Larissa's knee was bothering her. Evil orange slice.

June 3, Monday
Buffet at the Cookery – chicken/salad, eggs/vegs/ham, pancakes, spearfish
SD rest
Larissa complained about her back. Already. And the smell. And yesterday she said she wants to move out of California. Mentioned (sort of jokingly, that she could be a trucker. A change in plans had us heading to Mt. Rushmore. At the rest stop there was a man and his dog from Dena, California. Decided to hit Devil's Tower along the way. After Larissa cried for more sleep. On the way to Devil's Tower. A rain storm of bugs. Trees grow out of rocks. The cow grunts. We walked along the trail. The voices we hear from behind. Panting. It was dark when we left. Tried to use gift shop phone. Bought a beautiful hair clip. Ditzy new cashier opened someone's beer. Sentenced to the vacuum. Flashes in the sky. Fire. Smoke screen. Natural phenomena or Indian Ceremony. Lightning storm avoided. Pushed on through to Spearfish. Major meal served at Perkin's Family Restaurant. Texas women. We always stop at this! Called Rachel – no money exchanged, he still has to sign. Called home – told we were going into bad weather. Waiter sucks up while we eat. Larissa quickly seeks the bathroom. The untranslatable oral tradition. Slept hard and long. Did most of the driving today – 400+ miles to Larissa's 200.

June 4, Tuesday
Larissa woke up around five she says. I was quiet for her but she chatted away for me. Nice rest stop. Friendly employees. Leaving around 11:15. The bugs on our hood are attracting flies. Larissa changed our plans to include a stop at Deadwood and the Black Hills Cave. Deadwood was quaint until a woman with an alleged niece in Sturges approached us in the travel center parking lot. She wanted to know if we'd give them a ride. Um, NO, I don't think so. I like living, Thank you. Wild Bill was shot here. A saloon of 117 years of drinking and carousing was getting a face lift. The oyster bar had its own version of Uncle Sam. Hair, vest, hat and all. Wife in

Wyoming. Jenny arcades. All the trains so far have been cargo. Larissa paid for my tour of the Black Caves. It was cold until we started hiking up. Only place in the world with logomite. Paul took our names and asked where from. Amy started what Otis finished. Sensory deprivation. My legs were really feeling the hike as Larissa's chest heaved. Coming out I had to wait for her. Then she just had to tell all the employees about Otis's geology student theory of what killed the flow something. Paul said it was hands. Otis reminded me of fuzzy face. I wonder how he is doing in Illinois. Dead cave, live cave, uncool, coal. Made our way to Keystone and ate Buffalo Burgers at Rawhead (or was it Railhead) Restaurant. The museum was closing and we passed paying for the tour. Stopped at Homemade Fudge. Way good divinity and turtles. Picked up a Travel Book that had a coupon for a Mt. Rushmore picture. The stairs looked evil. Would have liked to have dared a trail. But I didn't have enough energy for both of us. Moved on to Crazy Horse. Beautiful painting on the wall. The collection of books made me wish I had more time and money. Took a picture for other travelers. Nice film slide show. Great story. When legends die dreams disappear, when dreams disappear there will be no more greatness. Someone was hella bent to see buffalo and so we circled around. Eventually found them. A real wild western plain. Those are some ugly mothers, but gentle. Drove well over 50 miles of winding road. My arm felt like it would drop off. We pushed on to Cheyenne. Debated whether or not to stop in Denver at all, but seeing how we were going to get so close it would be kind of dumb to miss it. Made it to Cheyenne. Tell me if this makes sense. Larissa wanted to drive because if she didn't she would fall asleep. Hello. She was driving and still had a hard time keeping her eyes from glazing over. Even mine felt like they were burning. We at least made it to Cheyenne. I had the front seat and wasn't looking forward to it.

70 miles in 2nd
Going straight to hell
Black Hills homes no fences
Glittering in the air
I took a dump on the President
LA Ferguson in the gift shop
Trees grow in water

June 5, Wednesday
Pork chops and eggs, meatloaf
Only five hours of sleep but the sun rules all when on the road. It's a difficult thing to avoid. Larissa went to the restroom at the rest stop and took almost an hour. My god. We left when she got back to the car. I didn't even feel like getting out of the car, cleaning up or waiting for anything. I just wanted to get back on the road. Larissa left her sunglasses in the trunk and was having a hard time seeing. She made it through Denver though. Never saw a place to eat. Even got past Aurora to Hank's Truck Stop. Sometime right before Denver I felt a pressure or pain in the right side of my chest. Finally asked Larissa what she thought. She said heartburn which sounded strange to me. I moved positions and rubbed, but it didn't really help. She gave me less attention than I gave her stupid splinter that is in the crack of her finger and this was chest pains for Christ sake. The truck stop was a regular little Cheers. Even Larissa noted it. Marsha came in talking about her son Mike not passing a class. He was the youngest in his class. He's been struggling. Might as well hold him back. When we first came in a man was talking about lying politicians and how they should at least do some truth telling. Waitress used to live in Cody, Montana. Whole conversation on Montana. Jean did yard work and a girl traveling in a truck with two guys attracted quite a bit of attention. Goofy grins and sarcasm. These people know a thing or two. Twelve earrings, a belly ring. I saw a couple of tattoos on her back. Thought of Christy. I appreciated her freedom of expression and I'm glad she feels comfortable enough or secure enough to do it, but I don't think she realizes that it just makes her look cheap in the eyes of those who will judge her. Bottled water discussion. Marsha's concerned about the attentiveness of her son's teachers. Got a $.37 coke in Kansas. They also offered meat snacks in alligator, buffalo, venison, kangaroo. The guy at the counter strained to see my driver's license. He looked so young or maybe I'm getting old. We finally stopped for dinner at Country Kitchen in Junction City. Tessa M. was our waitress with an attitude. Overheard a conversation over the salad bar after Larissa pissed me off and had me going to the bar by myself. When we left a cop was making the circuit. Not long after we got on the freeway the weather built up. Glowing

windshield guts disappeared. We had to pull over for over an hour. Tornado warnings and flash floods. Larissa drove through it all. She said she was ready to die, but I didn't believe her. We didn't stop for the night until we reached Odessa, Missouri. There we had a heck of a time trying to sleep through gusty winds and constant rain. But we did.
Lightning branches

June 6, Thursday
Day after the rains. Everything felt so still and calm, quite a stark contrast to the night before. Getting moving wasn't made any easier by the heavy humidity. Air shouldn't be so thick. Hair was still managing to look decent. Our first stop was Columbia to visit the state university. Craig mentioned that it was a beautiful place to visit and I'm glad he did. Visited the Museum of Art and Archaeology for quite a while. A lady monitored us from a distance. After Larissa put in a donation for us she mentioned a new exhibit to open next week. Misty weather, but Larissa with her ever ready camera got a few shots. The Anthropology museum seemed a little weak. We rushed through it to get to the bookstore. Larissa was going to town. Kansas U is apparently their big rival. Bought Missouri Tiger cow print boxer shorts. Too cute! There was a Future Homemakers of America convention going on. Woman in the bathroom with her rolling pantyhose. Discovered Larissa is just as bad at navigating as driving. Trying to get back to the car she had us trooping all over the school. Then she lied. She said she saw the car when well never mind. Stopped at Gasper's and Ozarkland. Ate fried catfish (Channel) and blackberry cobbler. Don't think our waitress thought I would go for the twenty-five minute wait or wanted me to. It's prepared differently but tastes the same. Ummm... I'll take it the way I ordered it and see for myself. I got the time. A woman and her father caught up on TV, gossip and the kids. Then Pop dropped some sort of card. Watched a new girl walk through her first training steps. The Ozark lady was nice. Didn't ask for our IDs although a posted sign said she could have. Still more misty air and slight sprinkles.

Moved on to the Arch. It was a bugger to get to and almost decided to pass, but had to go back. Shared the ride up with a man from San Diego and two native young lovebirds.

He was proud and it was cute enough to make me want to puke. A foursome from East Texas found ways to amuse themselves and had Larissa laughing in the meantime. Walked around staring down at the city. Shared the ride down with the same lovebirds and they asked, "why St. Louis?" Asked about Florida after being surprised about the cross-country haul. Larissa had a problem just after stepping into the museum shop. I swear everything on her is falling apart and is the cause of complaint. It was bull. We watched a film about the making of the Arch. It was a lot cooler than I thought it would be.

From there we decided to make some time to Illinois. Stopped at a Steaks 'N' Shakes (Frisco burger and cheddar fries) just before they were hit with a high school stampede. Waitress and West Point encounter. Intimidation and same 'ol shit everywhere. Making room and who visits with whom. Bathroom call said the time had come which wasn't really a pleasant feeling. Didn't buy anything though. Stopped at a rest stop south of Pontiac, IL not too long after and so was able to take care of the situation. Black father and son coming out together with me. They had serious money. Son went over to take notice of our plates which he verbalized. My trusty companion was oblivious to it all. In fact she was snoring in minutes. Just after chattering at me. She never says anything until you don't have the patience to listen. I had to hit her to wake her up to stop her from snoring. The repositioning helped though sleep seemed to be such a labor. She was unaware of her physicality. I drifted off after a while.

June 7, Friday
2 Zingers, J.B. Winnberry restaurant - scallop and shrimp patties
Decided to head for Northwestern University first since it was the most northern destination in the Chicago area that I wanted to visit. We had to drive through much of the city to get there. People roam streets a bit much, it was bothering my companion. The constant sprinkles didn't help me. A smiley black teen taught us a new trick for cleaning the windows without leaving lines. But it was raining and our windows didn't need the cleaning. Evanston was a small quaint community. There was obviously money floating by Lake Michigan. The campus looked like homes. We ended up not

getting out of the car. There wasn't any parking available in the one lot we found and Larissa didn't want to risk a ticket. Our morning started late enough thanks to Larissa's need for a million hours of sleep and I was hungry, frustrated and tired of fighting traffic that I didn't really feel like fighting her too. We moved on to Oak Park. We made it just in time to go to the Ernest Hemingway Museum. It's only open Friday – Sunday for a few hours in a church. It was at once cool and scary. He lived there the first twenty years of his life. They had stuff from his childhood that reminded me of all of the papers I've been re-encountering among my own stuff. Some of the similarities in our personal histories were spooky. I'm afraid it means I'm meant for something. There is some potential I must fulfill. I am capable of so much that I must do much in my brief existence to explore, develop and share that experience. My life and talents are not meant for me alone. To keep them to myself would be selfish and wrong. I just hope my elementary ghost story doesn't come back to haunt me. The lady was much more friendly than the man. I think they both donate their time. She was a total Hemingway fan and enjoyed sharing it. Ate down the street from the church and bought chocolate from Fannie Mae. Saw some downtown night life. There was a Bull's game going on – the tickets were sold out. Larissa got her picture of Wrigley Field. I think what she really wanted was to stand in the middle of the field while cheers of fans filled her ears. Maybe someday. We hopped back on the freeway. It was getting late and we wanted to find cheap lodging. Ended up at Shore Lodge Inn. It was for sale. Looked like an establishment with a long history. Elderly man left his wife at the kitchen table watching the Bull's game to help a college age girl check us in a room. Watched 20/20 while Larissa showered. A sad AIDS story was on – it was very moving and disconcerting though not very surprising. Not sure which is worse. The story itself or the fact that it didn't surprise me. There was also an expose about the Equinox guy. One woman was very generous in her humiliation, I felt for her. Taking a shower after a long week of time and travel felt great. Erasing a week of dead skin and peeling away the days left a renewed feeling for the future. Trying to figure out what we'd do tomorrow was difficult. I had to map it all out. Didn't feel as if I could trust Larissa to do it plus she's been taking all kinds of notes that she has to catch up on that if I had to wait for her we'd never get anywhere.

June 8, Saturday
Wanted to get up early to pack a lot into today, but Larissa never changed her watch so I ended up thinking it was 5:20 when it was 7:20 and went back to bed. We both took showers again after she got up. I still didn't really feel like getting out of bed but this was one of my days. Stopped by the Chicago campus of Northwestern and even found the bookstore. Laughed at their Rose Bowl sweatshirts. No catalogues available which I personally thought was strange. They don't call it the windy city for nothing. Larissa was taking my lead. Walked through a law school building. She mentioned something about being a lawyer that I found amusing. It was freezing especially for June, but I loved it anyway. From there we went to the University of Chicago and crashed their graduation. It was great. Squirrels roamed the campus and the smell of champagne permeated the air. The gothic buildings were too cool. Walked by the Alumni Relations Center – Robie House. Frank Lloyd Wright prairie style house. The Oriental Institute was closed for renovation and graduation. Heard wealthy New England accents and saw a royal Jamaican family and then there was us – on this day representing white trash. Sure we might be several generations removed but in this crowd on this day in our cut-off jeans and baggy sweatshirts you'd never know it. Walked up the wrong way in the bookstore. From there we found our Italian eatery at Oggi. We went for the Oggi Special (pizza). It was huge as were the chunks of toppings that they had spread over the top. From there we made our way to Ohio. We stopped at a travel center in Indiana. They had South Bend Chocolate Factory stuff that we didn't buy. Almost got a Notre Dame thing but decided that I couldn't, I just… couldn't. Larissa got a shot glass for her Bull's fan friend. The checkout girl looked beat by life. If she breaks out of the life she has she could probably make it. Drove to the other side of Cleveland. Planning on going back to the Hall of Fame, but I wasn't certain if we had time. Larissa convinced me that I would be upset with myself later if I didn't. And she was right. Noticed Cuyahoga Falls not too far south

out of Cleveland and although that sounded very tempting I knew we definitely didn't have the time for it. Another time.

June 9, Sunday
Cleveland on a Sunday morning is very still. Of course there was also plenty of humidity to keep everything in place. The Hall of Fame is close to the shopping center and Lake Erie. Passed the big Free stamp. That was way cool. Larissa loves her skylines. She takes a picture of every single one. The Hall of Fame was not to be missed. We started at the top and worked our way down. Surprised by how much U2 stuff there was. There wasn't really much R.E.M. The Wall from Pink Floyd was way cool especially the burden of insight quote. The costumes appeared so incredibly small. Surprised how much Patti Smith stuff was there. Not much Go-Gos or Bangles. Lots of Nirvana. We kill our rock 'n' roll idols. We kill our social commentators. Music's influence was felt. Made our way up the hill to the mall and the Great Steak Fry Co. The sandwich was more than I should have eaten but I managed. We decided to go to Niagara Falls. Even decided to get a room and check it out in the morning. Larissa was interested in the $50 3-4 hour tour. I wasn't. I just wanted to go see it on our own. Didn't feel like we needed to spend money on a tour. End result, we didn't see the falls at all. I had a hard time dealing with that one. She was being a total baby. If she couldn't have it her way we weren't going to do it at all and she made that decision for us and since she was driving at the time there was nothing I could do about it. She just decided without really talking it out with me first. Is this really my vacation or am I a temporary tour guide? In Cleveland I had to tell her how to carry a purse. I don't know if I felt like a mother or big sister. I guess a sister because she still has a way of completely ignoring me. Definitely reached a point where I was tired of sharing my car space with her but I had no choice.
Syracuse, NY at 2 a.m.

June 10, Monday
Up/leaving 10:30. Had to wait on Miss Thing to get up and instead of using the rest stop facilities we decided to wait until breakfast. Had a late breakfast at Sam's Lakeside Italian. It was a total family restaurant. A party of about a dozen came in for

a set up buffet. There was a couple in the wall section who talked about the work grind. A wife of the man works sixteen hour days – gets four hours of sleep a night so has to make up for it on the weekends – then up starts her week again. They never get to get away. They sound like they're barely living. We decided to skip Canada. I didn't have my passport and we really didn't feel like fighting customs so that meant an unscheduled detour through Vermont and New Hampshire to get to Maine. That also meant that we didn't have rest stops or other info available. Stopped at a Vermont rest stop. They had a ton of brochures but most of it was along the other side of the state. Shriner's were saving aluminum can tabs. Ended up having pot roast for dinner at the P & H Truck Stop. The Vermont maple cream pie was to die for. A woman with her two sons sat behind us. One son learned that oxygen becomes thinner in higher altitudes and since the brain needs oxygen to function properly shorter people, breathing denser air were therefore smarter. Okay. One also started making comments about freshmen that caught the waitress' attention. They were total locals. We all have to be dorks sometime. A woman with her daughter was talking to a man. Couldn't tell what his relation was. Sounds like she's been housing a Harvard boy. I stayed to listen while Larissa paid the bill. The fresh chicken people had already left. Lisa and Sophia were on the job. The gas guy did the pumping for me. Larissa drove the rest of the night going from Vermont to Maine. It was rainy and she was insecure about what she was doing. A car pulled behind us so Larissa started hanging to the right so the car could go around us. Instead, because it was a cop, he pulled us over. She handled it much better than I would have otherwise expected. Maybe because I was there with her. He thought she might be a drunk. Gave her a warning card and let us go. Could have been a whole lot worse, but it was still annoying. He checked her out, but was really nice about the whole thing. Larissa was about to bad mouth Maine police but I was on their side which stopped her from going off. After all, don't you want cops to stop drunk drivers? The incident definitely woke us up. Of course not too long after that Larissa was falling asleep. Water spider webs at us.

June 11, Tuesday

Long day and late driving yesterday meant a late start for today. Neither Larissa nor I could figure out why we wanted to go to Maine other than it was at the opposite side of the country. We went to Portland and found a little trendy looking place. Giobbi – Italian, sort of. Ordered a crab sandwich. We sat on the deck and enjoyed the day. The dining room area smelled particularly fishy. There was another couple on the deck when we arrived. He was on the phone when we first arrived and he didn't seem too pleased. He reminded me of a Harvard man. They had a quiet baby. It was our waitress' first day back. She was tall and bubbling with enthusiasm. From there we were on our way to Cambridge. It took some doing but we found Harvard. Didn't really realize we had found it at first which caused some extra sight-seeing. Almost hit three girls. Walked around a bit to breathe in the Harvard air. Went to the bathroom in Emerson Hall just when I was beginning to think Harvard students must never need to pee. Went across the street to a shirt shop. Foreign girl learning USA ropes from Columbia dork. Bought sodas at Mr. Bartley's Burger Cottage. It was the ultra in cool. Bookstore was not what I had in mind. Parking was up. Had to say goodbye to cobblestone and archways. Salem was next in our plot. The witch museum that Larissa looked up in the tour book was supposed to be open until 7 p.m. and it was 5:30 and closed. I wasn't ready to get back in the car. We weren't the only tourists to come too late and be annoyed by the closure. A man, my guess was a native was polite as he passed us. He reminded me of someone. It's so hard to find people who are that polite anymore. We all travel in our own little worlds so much that we're oblivious to others. The park across the street was cool looking but I had to go to the bathroom and didn't really feel like doing much walking. Looking for dinner in Salem. Luckily found a little eatery called Derby's. It was Salem. Our waiter was all concerned over business and our care. He also had a sweet little Massachusetts accent that I could have stood to listen to for a whole lot longer. Larissa and I both ordered lobster, but neither of us had ever had it nor had I ever seen someone break into one of these things. I was lost and lord knows the lobster wasn't about to help me. It was pure comedy routine. We had the bibs and everything. Larissa hit my glasses. The couple that came in next to us were also tourists. The husband had a droning beaten out of life voice. His wife wasn't much better and I think they were east coasters. As we were leaving four guys were having a problem starting their car. Hood was up and they were having a good time fussing over it. Stopped at a grocery store before heading out of town. We were on our way to Connecticut and in hopes of an easier time at Yale. Disappointed that we missed the witch stuff but we didn't have the time to stop if we were going to get to the other things on our list.

Rest stop off of 64 exit in Connecticut
Tour bus at bus stop

June 12, Wednesday
Fisherman's Platter
Truck stop is always the first place. 76 Auto/Truck in Westbrook area. A man just had a birthday the day before and received a lighter that cost $140. I wouldn't have spent $10 for the thing. A group of young locals came in and took over a round table. Talked about cooking. One girl's sister doesn't even boil water. The man's sister doesn't cook. He felt that was a big deal because of his Hispanic origins and the expectancy of women to be in the kitchen. Everyone pretty much seemed to know the truckers. Two greeted each other across the salad bar. Yale was pretty easy to locate and find parking but the adjacent park was a little alarming. The buildings were very old time cool and Larissa liked them much better than Harvard. She didn't like Harvard's small cobblestone. Never saw anything that looked like a bookstore but saw a Cronies across the street which made a fine substitute. Just when we were about to leave we came across the center for British Art. Oh, we bought Pecan Myrtles that the lady proudly informed us were from Chicago which ironically was disappointing news to us. The Center was very cool. The second Floor displayed a lady in a black dress right after you got off of the elevator. I was taken. The dress was alive. Told Larissa I would wear it to the Oscars and she said everyone would laugh at me. As if I care. The Forge displays were all dot work. It was a little bit much. Fourth Floor Larissa gave up and took to resting her eyes. I roamed a lot. It was a lot of Rococo work which usually appeals to me. Two

guards were talking. One young, one old. Young had been somehow screwed by someone else that eventually was caught, but never confessed. Larissa was happy to leave. Not far from New York at all. The gas station man had to work the pump even though we pulled into self. He talked about the weather – very eager. We checked in at the Nanuet Inn and showered. Unfortunately Larissa didn't ask for two beds so we had to share the double. I relaxed while she showered. It was nice to finally have some sense of real privacy again. It took us a long time to get out of the room. We headed for downtown and somehow made a $7.50 mistake by passing on bridges we should not have had to take. Got off in Queens but eventually found our way back to the Empire State Building. Poor weather conditions resulted in a two mile visibility but we were there so had to go. The top level was closed so we only made it to the 86th Floor. It was still pretty cool. A couple under an umbrella, boats in the dock. A woman, her brother and her lover. From the Empire State Building we went to Houlihan's (steak, sweet peas, smashed potatoes) which was right there. They were five minutes out from stopping service but a waitress directed us to sit down anyway. Lone black man at the table next to us. Seemed like he could have been 'somebody' but we couldn't place who. The waitress gave him the "usual" treatment. Groups of three. Two girls, one guy also had the Let's Go book. Bull's won the game. Two dating and one singer. Girl and guy and guy over at the side. Carnival smells. Man at window picking his nose as if no one could see. We sat under the Beatles. Larissa didn't get her cheesecake, but we made it out alive. Hotel room around 2 a.m. And we were supposed to finish with NYC tomorrow. How to fit everything in? No way. Had to decide what was to stay and what adventures would be sacrificed. Statue of Liberty was a goner.

June 13, Thursday
Larissa greeted me this morning with a 'finally' rolling eyeballs routine. I woke up at 8 a.m. with her and the alarm. She went to the bathroom and came back to bed. And she was waiting for my eyes? I had been tossing and turning ever since. We decided to pass on taking showers. Larissa used the bathroom and the toilet gurgled. I used it and it wouldn't flush. Left around 11:30 and headed for downtown NYC. Found it this

time. Larissa was alarmed by how well I fit in. Drove by Dave's and then down to NYU and Greenwich Village. Ate at a cute little Italian eatery and then had Italian ices as we strolled past Washington Square Park to NYU. It all looked like a group of downtown buildings. Gruffy guy gave street transient some coins. Shakespeare's turned out to be a bookstore so headed back to the car. Larissa felt I would fit in here. The culture and surroundings suited me. But too soon we were off to Princeton. The junctions made it a bit confusing. It's a town built around a college. Wealthy neighborhoods. Larissa asked some guy what day it was. Bottom level sales clerk was a little too smiley. He was creeping me out. Walking back Larissa asked if they call it Ivy League because of all the ivy growing up the buildings. I attacked the wall. Larissa said I could definitely be a student here. From Princeton we went to Philadelphia. Took Larissa on vacation to get her to exercise. Lots of walking today. Went to the Society Hill Hotel Restaurant. The place had a live musician. It was good Philly Phenomenon. Larissa was willing to wander dark alleys and I tripped on the way to the Liberty Bell. We walked back up to the car, got lost in the postage stamp known as Delaware before making our way to Maryland and the House RA.

June 14, Friday
Stopped at the Buck Horn Restaurant (steak and eggs) where the guy setting up the salad buffet took his work and turned it into an art form. They had TV sets available for quarters at the booths. People behind Larissa tuned in but hardly paid any attention. They just wanted the added noise, I guess. The ATM machine wasn't doing its job. The waitress mumbled to herself. You could hardly say that she talked to us. Stopped at a Baltimore island and bought them out. The younger tough chick seemed to be more on the ball but she has her problems too. Saw a map t-shirt that was cool, but had enough from inside to go with it. From there it was to Washington. Parking was interesting. Larissa doesn't know how to parallel park. It was 12 noon and the sun was full in bloom. Man griped because we didn't talk to him. Larissa wouldn't climb the stairs of the Capitol. There was a presentation of the history of the army flag going on. I went alone. Cool view of the Washington Monument. Larissa would have to live through a

picture. Walked to the White House. Got two waters and a discounted price on tees. Took a picture of two ladies in front of the White House so they returned the favor. Thanks. Street vendor t-shirt deal meant cash in hand. I had a one. Larissa forgot to grab her money. Nationsbank was right there. Friday afternoon downtown, oh the line. Wasn't even sure if I could make a charge against my account for cash, but what do you know? Got to talking with the vendor briefly. Wish I could remember his name. Oh well. We got our shirts. I was willing to forgo the Planet Hollywood because our meter had run out, but Larissa figured we were already late so why not. It's because it's something she wanted. No to Northwestern, yes to Planet Hollywood. So screwed. No ticket. Larissa drove us away. She doesn't trust that I look while she's driving. She keeps telling me to look here and there but when I'm at the wheel she'll just do her note taking, obviously not taking in any scenery. Made our way through Virginia. Ate at Pizza Hut, then later we stopped for Frostys. Girl had a gentle voice. You could barely hear her and that's if you were paying attention. Saw the Blue Ridge Mountains live and up close. It was another long day that made me happy for the night and the journey home.

June 15, Saturday
Got some pancakes in Tennessee. We saw another Perkin's Family Restaurant and had to stop. We figured we had a long drive in front of us but wanted to beat it to Graceland. We would be gaining an hour, but still wouldn't make it to Graceland before four. We noticed Tennessee is dominated by Villes. Knoxville, Nashville and a whole slew I can't remember right now. We made it to Graceland and decided to do the mansion tour. When signing the register I was cut off by Texas assholes. Interesting conversations about marriage/weddings. The girl was a little bitch. Check out guy got all excited about NYU. Stopped late in Arkansas for dinner. A cockroach went by that really freaked out Larissa. Didn't bother me until number two came around the bend and made a bee line for our table. When we pointed it out to the waitress she kicked it to the side and stepped on it. We lost our appetites. The pulled BBQ pork sandwich tasted great but if the bugs roam so freely in the front of the restaurant what the hell does the back look

like. Had the creeps from that moment on. Wanted to get the hell out of there. The dead cockroach was still there next to our booth when we left.

June 16, Sunday
This was the sweatiest wake-up we had on the whole trip. Man did I feel gross. Had breakfast in Cow Creek. After last night's truck stop, visiting Cow Creek was a blessing. The food was great, but even better – the place was clean. It was also pretty quiet. An elderly couple came in just to get dessert. It was so cute. It reminded me of an old-fashioned date. Ordered another BBQ Pork Sandwich, but at least this time I wasn't squirming and felt like I could complete the whole meal. Their gift shop offered poo pets to fertilize your garden. Heard a man talking about his special idea of meatloaf presentation. On lettuce leaves. Wow! Stopped for gas in Oklahoma. The guy behind the counter was wearing a Hawaii T-shirt. A lady was in with her car. The mechanic was teasing her about being 2,000 miles late on her oil change. She had been at the Jungle Club the night before – as her daughter reported much to her embarrassment. The mechanic had some feminine qualities. Larissa took forever. I had been dreaming in the car and couldn't wait to hit the bathroom. It was a good thing I did when I did. Gas man was friendly with Larissa too. He and his wife usually go to somewhere in Pennsylvania for vacation. There's a lake close by. We made it all the way through Oklahoma to have dinner in Amarillo, Texas at the Big Texan. Not much there except lodging and food. The deal they offer for free steak is four and a half pounds of steak and all the sides must be eaten within one hour. Mine was just under one pound and it was more than enough. Rib eye – tasted like perfection. Those Texas people sure were friendly. Claustrophobia is a Texan in Rhode Island said the check-out lady. Our waitress asked if we were sisters. First time in a long time someone asked us that. Made me wonder how much weight I had gained. At least the waitress didn't ask if we were twins. We hate that because we don't actually look alike. Mom clued us in long ago that anyone asking if we're twins is only looking at the fat and not beyond it because our features aren't alike at all. Larissa started to drive me nuts as we made our way through New Mexico. She can really be such a baby. We

paused at a rest stop, but she didn't stay because of the lighting and a posted – Watch out for poisonous snakes – sign. I wanted to sleep under the stars but no. Sometimes she just has to have her way. I think she wanted to press on so we could make it to the Grand Canyon even though we agreed our time was up.

June 17, Monday
BBQ bacon burger, Pringles, El Rey Taco beef and cheese burrito, beef taquitos
Woke up at the Arizona border by New Mexico. Noticed the same California lady that was at the rest stop yesterday morning. She's making great time, especially since she is traveling alone. I drove all the way home. Larissa thought we'd do a switch off but I was really tired of her music and if she drove the tunes would be of her choosing. Drove just over 660 miles. Wasn't sure if I was ready to get back to my life at home but I knew I was definitely ready to get out of being cooped up in that car with Larissa. We had a music fight on the way in that killed conversation. That part was fine by me. Dad was at work and Mom was at a meeting when we arrived. Weird walking into a quiet, empty home. We dropped our stuff and then went back out to pick up El Rey Taco for dinner. We ate and then started pulling tags and prices off of the things we purchased on the road. Set them up on the dining room table to share with Mom and Dad and then Larissa and I sort of sat back looking at each other wondering just when Mom and Dad would arrive. That's when we decided to go check out Mom's calendar to find out where in the world our parents were. I stood still in shock. John Nelson died on the 14th after having a heart attack/car crash on the 7th. His funeral is Wednesday at 11 a.m. only Mom won't be going because her mammogram results showed evidence of a tumor in her left breast so she'll be having a lumpectomy. Tina Bennett had her baby and Annette is having a surprise birthday party the day of Matthew and Gladys's 25th Wedding Anniversary party. Life doesn't stop for vacation. When Mom and Dad returned home they expressed relief that we were home. Wished we called more often. Disturbing news not on the calendar… No calls were going through to Grandma and Grandpa at their summer

home. I asked if they'd tried sending a letter or contacted authorities. No, but good idea and not yet but considering it.

June 18, Tuesday
Beans, pasta salad (3), avocado, strawberries (1 lb), brownies, Pringles

Larissa and her – you owe, I owe, has reached a new height in her ability to irritate me. I had to pay for gas. Never mind my car needing gas and I couldn't find Dad's Mobil card. Had to return the rental though. Intentionally got on the I-5 to piss off Larissa but then her directions to Alamo weren't as explicit as they could have been. Came home the long way, but it was a silent annoying trip. Stopped by the grocery before coming home. Still haven't gotten over my craving for strawberries. Didn't really get much fruit on the road. Apparently fruit isn't a real push to some people out there. Of course it does have a short life span. Called Rachel to let her know I can be put back on the schedule and she let me know that she's looking for a new job. Sees the writing on the wall and would rather quit than be fired. Awesome. I've wanted to get a different job for a while, but there's a new sense of urgency to it now, which is so what I needed to hear. Welcome back. Made a batch of brownies. Mom did a pasta salad. Don't like it as much as mine. She doesn't add enough cheese or peppers. She also uses onions that are okay but not preferred. I still downed the stuff. Man did I inhale it. She doesn't chop her veggies enough. Had to go to bed early and mentally prepare for the long day ahead of me tomorrow. First day of summer school, a funeral and Mom's lumpectomy – what fun. I also need to get back to fasting. The road is rough on the waistline.

June 19, Wednesday
Fast, bits of rice

What a long ass day. Spanish professor is an older woman and definitely kooky. Reviewed chapter 10 briefly. Was late to Mr. Nelson's funeral because I HAD to go to school today. Could not afford to have the teacher drop me for being absent on the first day. The church was definitely packed. Saw Sandy and talked to Emily and Lisa and Mrs. Harris and others for quite a while. Huge hug from Emma who clearly knew what was going on with Mom. Had to go back to school to buy my textbook after the funeral. Didn't want to go back to school but I can't afford to slack off. Didn't eat. This was going to be day one. Need a fresh start. When I got home I became very disgusted. Larissa didn't go to work today in order to be able to spend the day with Mom and to go to the hospital with her. When I got home she hadn't moved her car, she was cleaning strawberries in the sink and you could tell she hadn't been up very long. That lazy bitch really pisses me off sometimes. I lost it. Grandma received my letter and called. They forgot to plug in the phone when they arrived. They're both fine. Just forgetful, thank goodness. When Mom and Dad came home from the hospital I talked about the funeral and everyone I caught up with and what's going on with them. It gave us something to discuss so I wouldn't be pouty face focusing on Mom. Eventually we had to get to it though. The tumor they removed was about the size of a golf ball and malignant. She'll have to go back for another surgery to take out the lymph nodes. There is a check-up scheduled for Friday for her to hear what kind of treatments she's in for, but it will most likely include both chemo and radiation, starting ASAP. She wasn't really hungry but I made her some rice and ended up having a few bites of it. But just a few. Gotta get back to losing weight and stay on track. Now more than ever.

www.ingramcontent.com/pod-product-compliance
Lightning Source LLC
Chambersburg PA
CBHW071654090426
42738CB00009B/1523